A COMPLETE GUIDE TO
CROCHET

EDITED BY
PAM DAWSON

CAVENDISH HOUSE

CONTENTS

crochet abbreviations

alt	alternate(ly)	**No.**	number
approx	approximate(ly)	**patt**	pattern
beg	begin(ning)	**rem**	remain(ing)
ch	chain(s)	**rep**	repeat
cm	centimetre(s)	**RS**	right side
cont	continu(e)(ing)	**ss**	slip stitch in crochet
dec	decrease	**sp**	space(s)
dc	double crochet	**st(s)**	stitch(es)
dtr	double treble	**tog**	together
foll	follow(ing)	**tr**	treble
grm	gramme(s)	**tr tr**	triple treble
gr(s)	group(s)	**WS**	wrong side
htr	half treble	**yd(s)**	yard(s)
in	inch(es)	**yrh**	yarn round hook
inc	increase	**yrn**	yarn round needle

Symbols
An asterisk, *, shown in a pattern row denotes that the stitches shown after this sign must be repeated from that point. Square brackets, [ ], denote instructions for larger sizes in the pattern. Round brackets, ( ), denote that this section of the pattern is to be worked for all sizes. Crochet hooks have been standardized into an International Size Range, (ISR), and these sizes will be used throughout these instructions.
To avoid confusion it is recommended that you decide whether to use metric or imperial measurements when beginning any pattern and adhere to the same method throughout these instructions.

Tension – this is the most important factor in successful crochet. Unless you obtain the tension given for each design, you will not obtain satisfactory results. Note that when converting inches to centimetres, tension samples will be given to the nearest exact equivalent, i.e. 10cm = 3.9in.

© Marshall Cavendish Limited 1974, 1975, 1976, 1981, 1982
This material was first published by Marshall Cavendish Limited in the publication *Fashion Maker*
First printing 1976
Second printing 1981
Third printing 1982

Printed in Yugoslavia

ISBN 0 85685 190 6

Photographers
Steve Bicknell; Roger Charity; Richard Dunkley; Jean Paul Froget; John Garret; Melvin Grey; Graham Henderson; Trevor Lawrence; Chris Lewis; Sandra Lousada; Peter Pugh-Cook; John Ryan; John Swannell; Jerry Tubby; Rupert Watts.

AN INTRODUCTION TO CROCHET

This publication gives a new and completely different approach to crochet, which will be of interest both to beginners and experts alike. It guides the reader clearly and concisely through the very early stages to the more complicated techniques and gives a new dimension on the ways in which crochet can be applied and extended.

Very little is known about the early history of crochet. For many centuries it was worked mostly by nuns, to the extent that it was often referred to as 'nuns' work'. During the mid-nineteenth century, the beautiful fabric formed by Irish crochet became most popular and throughout Queen Victoria's reign, crochet was applied to everything from antimacassars to camisole tops. However, some of the examples produced were unbelievably ugly and did nothing to enhance the natural beauty of this delicate craft.

After many years of mis-use, crochet declined in popularity and for almost fifty years it remained virtually unknown, other than in areas such as Ireland, where the craft was most fortunately kept alive.

During the 1950s, a tremendous revival of interest in all crafts began in America and this revival spread rapidly to Britain and the continent. One of the first crafts to re-appear was crochet and the demand was so phenomenal that designers and publishers were inundated with requests for patterns. For the first time, it was realized that crochet could be used to form a complete fabric and was not limited to merely being used as an applied trimming or insertion. Interest quickly gathered momentum and all aspects of the craft were eagerly researched to cope with the demand for fashion garments, as well as household linens.

Today, crochet is rightly appreciated as a unique way of interpreting fashion. As with knitting, you have complete control over the texture and colour of the fabric and the ultimate shape of the design, combining both the skills of a weaver and a dressmaker. The fabric can be tough and sturdy, or gossamer-light lace and the shape can be casual and practical, or softly romantic.

Almost any type of spun thread can be used in crochet, from the very finest cotton to chunky, machine-washable yarns. Apart from its fashion appeal, crochet remains one of the most popular of all crafts when it is applied to household items. Nothing else lends itself quite so successfully to the delicate lace fabric which can be used to produce heirloom bedspreads and tablecloths, or to edge such items as sheets and pillow cases.

With the aid of this book, all you really need to begin exploring the exciting possibilities which this craft has to offer is a crochet hook, a ball of yarn and a willing pair of hands. With surprisingly little effort even a complete beginner can make simple 'granny squares', which will soon build up into a complete garment. The more experienced crochet worker will be delighted to discover ways in which she can extend her knowledge to combine leather with crochet, or apply crochet to a net material for a most original and attractive fabric.

Pam Dawson

HISTORY OF CROCHET

Nobody can really pinpoint the day or year someone picked up a bone or stick and some yarn and started knotting chains of fabric into what is now known as crochet. If you were to ask a sample of the millions of people all over the world who carry out this simple yet creative craft you would not find many who could tell you much about its history. That is not as surprising as it sounds. Its origins are very obscure, but archaeological finds lead us to believe that Arabia may have been the original area where wool was first worked with just one needle or hook.

Ancient crochet specimens have been found in Egypt and it can be presumed that the craft is of an age parallel with knitting, its sister craft. It goes back at least as far as the days of Solomon (around 950 BC) and some biblical historians credit its use even earlier – 1200 BC – when the Israelites fled Egypt during the Exodus. They were said to have worked wool this way during their long trek across the Sinai desert.

The evidence for this early use is quite substantial. Recorded civilization dates from the time when the Sumerians settled in the plain of Shinar in the area later called Babylon – now Iraq. Babylon became the centre for woollen crafts, in the same way that Egypt was known as the home of fine linen weaving.

Babylon's pleasant, hospitable climate certainly made sheep-rearing a good prospect, but that was not the only reason that woollen crafts flourished there. Unlike the Egyptians, who appeared to have loved clarity of line in everything, the Babylonians were fond of complicated, almost fussy, clothes made of heavy woollen fabric and covered with the most elaborate decoration. It is almost certain that crochet work was used for this purpose. Later in Babylonian history there was a revolt against the luxury of over-ornate clothes and people resorted to the simple wool 'sack', often knitted or worked in crochet.

Crochet and other wool crafts had a very profound place in the philosophy of the time. Creating fabric without any artificial aid was seen as a declaration of their link with a god. It was an acknowledgment that they owed their skill and intellect to some greater being.

Crochet patterns in use in India are very similar to Muslim patterns found in North Africa – giving strength to the theory that crochet has been a continuously-used craft in the Middle East for thousands of years.

Although it never quite died out over the centuries crochet did suffer an eclipse when more mechanical fabric-making methods were developed. However, it began to flourish again during the Renaissance period. Ecclesiastical crochet, in common with other fabrics of the time, acquired a high standard of technique and beauty. Much crochet work during that period was imitative of the more expensive lace or embroidery such as needlepoint, Richelieu, Guipure, Honiton or filet.

It is no wonder that crochet earned the rather derogatory nickname of 'nuns' work'. Woollen crafts such as crochet or knitting were a common occupation for the nuns of the time and, unlike weaving which ordinary people carried out in their own homes, these skills remained almost exclusively within the confines of the convent.

Later on, crochet was thought to be suitable for the richer young ladies of the parish to learn. Nuns established it as one of the main crafts learned in the 'finishing courses' of the day.

The word 'crochet' is probably derived from the French word *croc* – meaning hook – but has only really been in popular use in Britain since the early 1800s, when the production of fine cotton thread from the newly set-up mills made it easy to carry out the craft.

Paradoxically it took a disaster to make the craft a really widespread and popular pastime. It was the Irish potato famines of the 1840s and '50s which revived an almost forgotten skill and made it into a major cottage industry. Crop failures forced millions of farming families to look for an alternative method of earning much-needed cash. Making crochet collars, frills and other adornments was a simple if time-consuming method. It was just as well that fine crochet work was much in demand by the well-to-do ladies of the time.

There had been a history of crochet in Ireland since the end of the eighteenth century when it was probably introduced from France. One young Irish woman, Honoria Nagle, is often given much of the credit for this. She was lucky enough to be sent to Paris to be educated, and became aware of the vast gulf between the classes. The squalor of the poor compared with the ludicrous extravagance of the court and society people made her determined to do something worthwhile in her homeland.

When she returned home, she recruited four other young women who were sympathetic to her aims. They, too, went to learn the craft from the Carmelite nuns in France, so that the five of them would be in a strong position to pass on the skill to the poor of Cork. Anyone could learn the basic skills. Whenever there was a spare hour or two you would find these hard-working people busy with the hook. It was not just women's work either. Boys tending sheep or goats on the hills were expected to chip in, too. Many used the extra money to save for their passage to America, taking their skills with them. There were many happy immigrants well settled in the prosperous mid-West who could thank the humble crochet hook for deliverance from the starvation which killed thousands in their homeland.

Irish crochet became a craft in its own right. Its workers incorporated beautiful designs taken from their rural backgrounds. Motifs included farmyard animals, roses, wheels and, of course, the legendary shamrock leaf. It became a widespread cottage industry and was also included in the syllabus of the Church-run education system.

The main crochet centres were Cork and its surrounding district in the south, and Monaghan in the north. County Cork became a principal centre of the industry and by the 1870s it is estimated that there were from 12,000 to 20,000 women in the area producing crochet, using continental patterns adapted from original lace designs from France, Italy and Greece.

Prince Albert's brainchild, the Great Exhibition of 1851, did a great deal in promoting the craft. It brought it to the attention of designers and manufacturers from all over the world. The Victorians almost smothered the art with their enthusiasm for it. Ladies became addicted to the crochet needle, and made coverings to decorate everything imaginable. Nothing escaped them. Antimacassars, bedspreads, table-cloths, coasters – all were churned out with great enthusiasm. One wonders now whether these objects were made as useful household items or merely to indulge their passion for crochet. Even piano legs were discreetly covered with crochet frills!

Unfortunately, this over-indulgence helped to put following generations off the craft and it ceased to be fashionable for several decades. Luckily it did not disappear completely. It has a remarkable survival record, and was revived in the 1950s along with the new appreciation of all the well-known handcrafts. The present reaction to mass-production has meant that crochet has become widely popular, and is probably used more creatively now than at any time in its long history.

Below: An early example of one of the many exquisite Irish crochet designs.

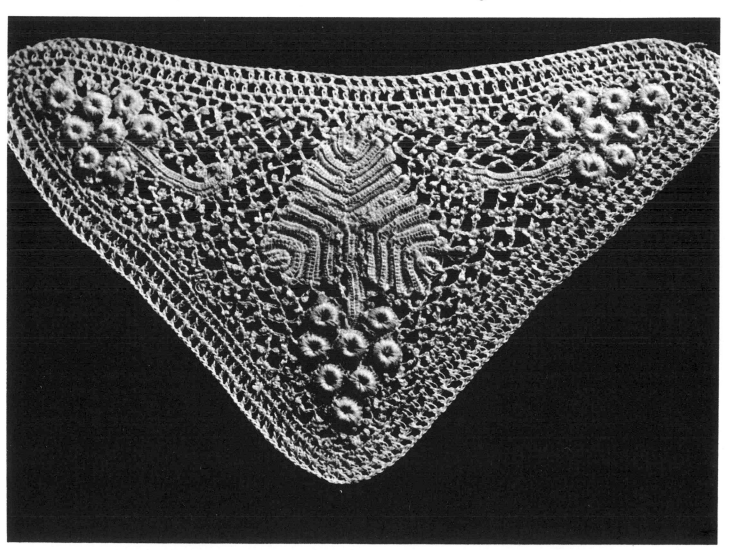

FIRST STEPS
BASIC STITCHES

The crochet hook

There are a variety of hook sizes to choose from and these range from very fine to very thick, and are graded into an International Size Range, such as 6.00 (ISR) and up to 10.00 (ISR). An appropriately sized hook should be selected for working each thickness of yarn. For example, use a size 10.00 hook for thick rug yarn, a size 7.00 hook for Aran type yarns, a size 5.00 hook for Double Knitting yarn and a 1.00 or .60 hook for finer cotton yarns. The beginner will find it much easier to work with a fairly large hook, such as a 5.00 size and a Double Knitting yarn.

Unlike knitting, all crochet is made up from one working loop on the hook at any time and this first working loop begins as a slip loop. To make a slip loop, hold the cut end of yarn in the left hand and wrap the yarn around the first and second fingers. Place the hook under the first finger and draw yarn through loop on the fingers, removing loop from left hand. Draw the yarn tightly on the hook to keep in place. This first slip loop does not count as a stitch, but is merely a working loop throughout any pattern and is the last loop fastened off at the end of the work. The left hand holds the yarn to feed towards the hook and there are several ways of holding this to control the flow of yarn to achieve an even fabric.

It is important to keep the thumb and first finger of the left hand as close to the hook as possible and move up the work as each new stitch is completed.

To work chain stitches

Hold the hook in the right hand between the thumb and first finger, letting the hook rest against the second finger, and place the hook under the yarn between the first and second finger of the left hand from front to back. Let the hook catch the yarn and draw through a loop on the hook, thus replacing the stitch. One chain has now been completed and the abbreviation for this is 'ch'. Repeat this action to make the required length of chains.

An alternative to this method of foundation chain is the double chain. To work this, make 2 chain in the normal way, insert hook into the 2nd chain from hook, * yarn round hook and draw through a loop, yarn round hook and draw through both loops on hook, *, continue to make a length of double chain by inserting the hook into the 2nd or left hand loop of the 2 loops which have just been dropped from the hook and repeat from * to *. This gives a firm foundation and is easy to work.

Left hand workers should reverse the instructions, reading left for right and right for left. To follow the illustrations, the book should be propped up before a mirror where the reversed image is quite clearly seen.

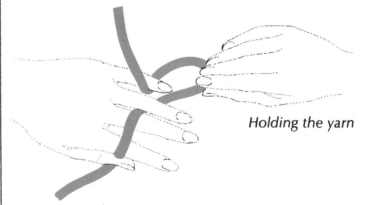

Holding the yarn

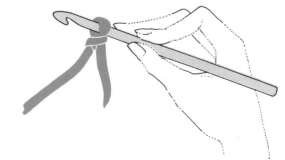

Position of hook to begin chain stitches

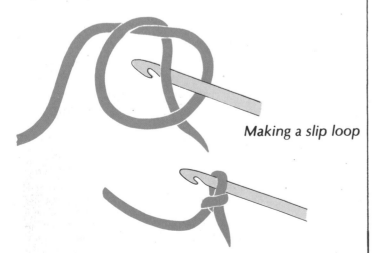

Making a slip loop

Basic stitches

Various stitches can now be worked into the foundation chain to form a crochet fabric. Each stitch gives a different texture and varies in depth, and every row gives a new chain line into which the next row is

4

Ridged double crochet

This is produced by working in dc, but the hook is inserted into the back loop only of each stitch of every row. The unworked front loop of each stitch gives a pronounced ridge effect.

Russian stitch

This is another stitch that is formed by working in double crochet, but the work is not turned at the end of each row. Instead the yarn must be fastened off and cut when each row has been completed and the cut ends darned in. There is a definite right and wrong side to this stitch.

Raised double trebles

These are worked on the surface of a basic double crochet fabric to give a vertical ridged effect. Make 21ch and work 1dc into 3rd ch from hook, then work 1dc into each ch to the end of the row. Turn work. Working 1ch to count as the first dc at the beginning of every row, work 3 more rows in dc. Turn work Start the pattern row with 1ch and 1dc into next dc, *yrh twice and insert hook into the horizontal loop of next dc in the third row below, yrh and complete the dtr in the normal way, 1dc into each of next 3dc, rep from * to the end of the row. Always working 3 rows of double crochet between the pattern rows, work subsequent pattern rows by inserting the hook under the vertical bar of the previous dtr and completing the dtr in the normal way.

Counterpane stitch

As the name implies counterpanes were made in this stitch. The fabric produced has a softness and elasticity suitable for the purpose. Work 11ch. Yrh, insert hook into 3rd ch from hook, yrh and draw a loop through this stitch and the first loop on the hook, yrh and draw through remaining 2 loops. Repeat this into each stitch throughout, always working 2ch to stand as the first stitch at the beginning of every row.

Trebles in relief

This is a more decorative stitch with a ridged effect. Make 12ch and work 1tr into 4th ch from hook, then work 1tr into each ch to the end of the row. Turn work. Start a new row with 3ch to count as the first tr and work across the row in tr by placing the hook between the first and second tr of the previous row horizontally, yrh and draw through a loop, yrh and complete the stitch. At the end of the row work 1tr into the 3rd of the 3 turning chain.

A selection of squares worked in the various stitches learnt so far may be made in Double Knitting yarn and a No. 5.00 (ISR) hook. Each will have a different texture and, made in a variety of colours, the squares will look most attractive. They can then be sewn together to make an attractive travelling rug.

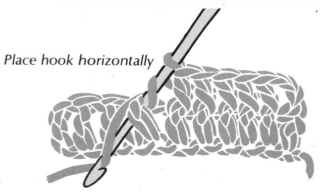

Place hook horizontally

7

First Projects

One of the most convenient ways of trying out new crochet stitches is to combine learning with making practical items. These two projects not only allow the beginner the opportunity to try out her new skills but also show the versatility of crochet when worked with unusual materials.

Mini cushions

These cushions, about 23cm (9in) square, are worked in half trebles but you could also use trebles and double crochet.

Materials

100grm (4oz) of tubular rayon macramé cord, raffia, or very narrow ribbon
One No. 7.00 (ISR) crochet hook
23cm (9in) square cushion pad made from calico and stuffed

Using No. 7.00 ISR hook make enough ch to make 23cm (9in), about 22ch, which includes one extra chain to count as turning ch.
1st row Into third ch from hook work 1htr, then 1htr into each ch to end. Turn. If you had 22ch to start with you should now have 21htr.
2nd row 2ch to count as first htr, miss first htr, 1htr into each htr to end, working the last htr under the turning ch of the previous row. Rep second row until work measures 46cm (18in) from beg. Fasten off.

To make up

Fold work in half WS tog and join 2 side edges with a ss. Insert cushion pad and join the remaining edge.

Rag rug

This rug, measuring 2.6m by 1.3m (8ft 8in by 4ft 4in) is another example of using materials other than crochet wools. If you have a lot of scrap cotton fabric in a ragbag, you can tear it up into strips about 2cm (¾in) wide. Wind up the strips into balls, separating the colours. Work

two or three rows with one colour then change to another to build up a pleasing pattern. Because the rug is worked in strips it is easy to handle while working. If you don't feel like tackling a rug, use slightly thinner strips of fabric – about 1.5cm (½in) – to make country-style table mats.

Materials

Lengths of cotton fabric in 4 colours. The total amount of material will depend on the length of rug required and the way in which stripes of colours are arranged, 5.5m (6yd) of 90cm (36in) wide fabric

will work out at about 76cm (30in) in length.
One No. 7.00 (ISR) crochet hook
Button thread

1st strip Using No. 7.00 (ISR) hook and any colour, make enough ch to make 33cm (13in) width, about 27ch should be right, which includes one ch for turning.
1st row Into third ch from hook work 1dc, then 1dc into each ch to end. Turn. If you had 27ch to start with you should now have 26dc.
2nd row 1ch to count as first dc, 1dc into each dc to end, working the last dc under the turning ch of the previous row. Turn. Rep second row for required length, changing colours as required and working over the ends each time a new strip is joined in, to secure them.
2nd strip Make enough ch (about 19 should be right including 1ch for turning) to make 23cm (9in) width.
3rd strip Make enough ch (about 35 should be right including 1ch for turning) to make 43cm (17in) width.
4th strip Work as given for first strip to make 33cm (13in) width.

To make up

Sew strips together with button thread.

SHAPING
Increasing and decreasing

Crochet patterns can be increased or decreased in two ways – either at the side edges or in the course of a row. More than one stitch may be increased or decreased at a time and this is usually worked at the beginning and ending of a row. To increase several stitches extra chains are added and to decrease several stitches at the beginning of a row, the required number are worked across in slip stitch and then remain unworked on subsequent rows, and at the end of a row, the required number of stitches are simply left unworked.

In most designs the shaping required to ensure either a well-fitting garment or make provision for essential openings, such as armholes and neckbands, is achieved by means of increasing or decreasing at a given point in the pattern. Because of the depth of most crochet stitches, unless this shaping is worked neatly and evenly, an unsightly gap can be left in the pattern which can spoil the appearance of the finished garment. The methods given here will overcome this problem and wherever you are instructed to increase or decrease in a pattern, without being given specific details, choose the appropriate method which will give the best results.

Increasing
To increase one stitch in the course of a row, simply work twice into the same stitch. When working in trebles for example, continue along the row in the normal way until you reach the position for the increase, put yarn over hook, insert hook into next stitch and draw through yarn giving three loops on the hook, yarn over hook and draw through two loops on hook, yarn over hook and draw through last two loops on hook, yarn over hook and insert hook into the same stitch again and draw through yarn giving three loops on the hook, yarn over hook and draw through two loops on hook, yarn over hook and draw through last two loops on hook. One loop is now left on the hook and one treble has been increased. This method applies to all the various stitches.

To increase one stitch at each end of a row, work twice into the first and last stitch of the previous row. When using thick yarns, however, a smoother edge is formed if the increase is worked into the second stitch at the beginning of the row and into the last but one stitch at the end of the row. This method applies to all the various stitches.

To increase several stitches at the beginning of a row, make a chain equivalent to one less than the number of extra stitches required plus the required number of turning chains. If six stitches are to be increased when working in trebles, for example, make five chains plus three turning chains, the next treble for the new row being worked into the fourth chain from the hook and noting that the three turning chains count as the first stitch.

To increase several trebles at the end of a row, the neatest way is to make provision for these extra stitches at the beginning of the previous row. To do this make three chain to count as the turning chain then make the exact number of chains required for the increased stitches, say six, work in slip stitch along these first six chains then complete the row by working one treble into each stitch of the previous row, noting that the three turning chains have already been worked to count as the first stitch.

To increase several stitches at the beginning and end of the same row, combine the two previous methods, noting that the increase row will end by working one treble into the turning chain and each of the six slip stitches of the previous row.

Decreasing
To decrease one stitch in the course of a row when working in double crochet, simply miss one stitch of the previous row at the given point. Because double crochet is a short stitch, this missed stitch will not leave a noticeable hole.
To decrease one stitch when working in half trebles, work along the row until the position for the decrease is reached, yarn over hook and insert hook into next stitch, yarn over hook and draw through loop, yarn over hook and insert hook into next stitch, yarn over hook and draw through loop (five loops on hook), yarn over hook and draw through all loops on hook. One half treble has now been decreased by making one stitch out of two.

To decrease one stitch when working in trebles, work along the row until the position for the decrease is reached yarn over hook and insert hook into next stitch, yarn over hook and draw through loop, yarn over hook and draw through two loops on hook, yarn over hook and insert hook into next stitch, yarn over hook and draw through loop, yarn over hook and draw through two loops on hook, yarn over hook and draw through remaining three loops on hook. One treble has now been decreased by making one stitch out of two.

To decrease one stitch when working in double trebles, work along the row until the position for the decrease is reached, yarn over hook twice and insert hook into next stitch, yarn over hook and draw through loop, yarn over hook and draw through two loops on hook, yarn over hook and draw through two loops on hook (two loops on hook), yarn over hook twice, insert hook into next stitch, yarn over hook and draw through loop, yarn over hook and draw through two loops on hook, yarn over hook and draw through two loops on hook (three loops on hook), yarn over hook and draw through all loops

on hook. One double treble has now been decreased by making one stitch out of two.

To decrease one stitch at each end of a row when working in double crochet, make two turning chains at the beginning of the row, miss the first two double crochet of the previous row noting that the turning chain forms the first stitch, work one double crochet into the next stitch, continue in double crochet along the row until one double crochet and the turning chain of the previous row remain, miss the last double crochet and work one double crochet into the turning chain.

To decrease one stitch at each end of a row when working in half trebles, make one turning chain at the beginning of the row instead of two, miss the first half treble of the previous row noting that the turning chain forms this stitch, work in half trebles along the row until one half treble and the turning chain of the previous row remain, work the last half treble and the turning chain together to make one stitch. At the end of the next row, work one half treble into the last half treble and miss the turning chain.

To decrease one stitch at each end of a row when working in trebles and double trebles, work as given for half trebles noting that only two and three turning chains respectively are worked at the beginning of the decrease row.

To decrease several stitches at the beginning of a row slip stitch over the required number of stitches, make the required number of turning chains for the stitch being used and continue along the row.

To decrease several stitches at the end of a row, continue along the row within the number of stitches to be decreased and turn the work, noting that the turning chain of the previous row must be counted as one of the stitches.

How to make a belt or cushion
To practice the methods of increasing and decreasing, attractive triangle shapes can be made with oddments of Double Knitting yarn and a No. 5.50 (ISR) crochet hook.

To make a belt, begin with three chain and work in double crochet, increasing one stitch at the beginning and end of every row until the required size is reached, then fasten off. Continue making triangles in this way for the required length of the belt, then sew them together as shown. Finish one end of the belt with a buckle.

To make a cushion you will need eight large triangles, four for each side. Begin with 70 chain for each triangle and work in half trebles, decreasing one stitch at each end of every row until two stitches remain, then work these two stitches together to form a point. Sew four triangles together for each side, points to centre, then sew outside edges together, inserting a zip fastener in centre of last edge. Insert a cushion pad to complete cushion.

A pretty pull-on hat

Size
To fit an average head

Tension
24 sts and 16 rows to 10cm (*3.9in*) patt worked on No.3.50 (ISR) crochet hook

Materials
3 × 25 grm balls of any Bri-Nylon Double Knitting
One No.3.50 (ISR) crochet hook
90cm (*1yd*) narrow ribbon

Hat

Using No.3.50 (ISR) hook make 5ch. Join with a ss to first ch to form circle.

1st round 3ch to count as first htr and 1ch sp, (work 1htr into circle, 1ch) 7 times. Join with a ss to 2nd of first 3ch. 8 sps.

2nd round 3ch to count as first htr and 1ch sp, work 1htr into first ch sp, 1ch, *work 1htr, 1ch, 1htr all into next ch sp – called inc 1 –, 1ch, rep from * to end. Join with a ss to 2nd of first 3ch. 16 sps.

3rd round 3ch, work 1htr into first ch sp, 1ch, work 1htr into sp between htr groups, 1ch, *inc 1 into next inc 1, 1ch, 1htr into sp between htr groups, 1ch, rep from * to end. Join with a ss to 2nd of first 3ch. 24 sps.

4th round 3ch, miss first 1ch sp, *work 1htr into next 1ch sp, 1ch, rep from * to end. Join with a ss to 2nd of first 3ch. The 4th round forms patt and is rep throughout.

5th round 3 ch, work 1 htr into first ch sp, 1ch, (1htr into next 1ch sp, 1ch) twice, *inc 1, 1ch, (1htr into next 1ch sp, 1ch) twice, rep from * to end. Join with a ss to 2nd of first 3ch. 32 sps.

6th round As 4th.

7th round 3ch, work 1htr into first ch sp, 1ch, (1htr into next 1ch sp, 1ch) 3 times, *inc 1, 1ch, (1htr into next 1ch sp, 1ch) 3 times, rep from * to end. Join with a ss to 2nd of first 3ch. 40 sps.

8th round As 4th.

Cont inc 8 sps in this way on next and every alt round until there are 64 sps. Mark end of last round with coloured thread to show beg of rounds. Work 4th patt round 16 times more, without inc and without joining rounds.

Shape brim

Next round *Patt 7 sps, inc 1, rep from * to end.

Next round *Patt 8 sps, inc 1, rep from * to end.

Rep 4th patt round 4 times more, without inc and without joining rounds, or until brim is required depth. Fasten off.

To make up

Do not press. Thread ribbon through lower edge of crown to tie at back.

DECORATIVE FABRIC STITCHES

This chapter is about decorative fabric stitches, telling you how to work them and how they might be used. They are all variations of the basic stitches already described. Included with them are examples of cluster and bobble stitches, which look most effective used with basic stitches such as trebles and double crochet as they form a raised surface and add texture to the work.

Aligned stitch

Using No. 5.00 (ISR) hook and Double Knitting, make 22ch.

1st row (Yrh and insert into 4th ch from hook, yrh and draw through a loop, yrh and draw through first 2 loops on hook) twice, yrh and draw through remaining 3 loops – one aligned st has now been formed –, rep this action into every ch to the end of the row. Turn.

2nd row 3ch to count as first st, miss first aligned st, * yrh and insert into next aligned st, (yrh and draw through a loop, yrh and draw through first 2 loops on hook), yrh and rep this action into the same st, yrh and draw through 3 remaining loops on hook, rep from * to the end of the row, working last aligned st into 3rd of the 3ch. Turn.

The last row is repeated throughout to form the pattern.

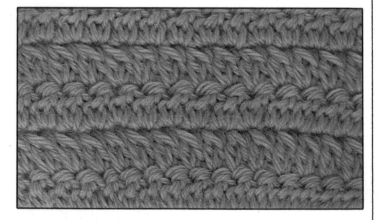

Crossed half trebles

Using No. 5.00 (ISR) hook and Double Knitting, make 21ch.

1st row Yrh and insert into 3rd ch from hook, yrh and draw through a loop, yrh and insert into next ch, yrh and draw through a loop, yrh and draw through all 5 loops on hook, 1ch, * yrh and insert into next ch, yrh and draw through a loop, yrh and insert into next ch, yrh and draw through a loop, yrh and draw through all 5 loops on hook, 1ch, rep from * to last ch, 1htr into last ch. Turn.

2nd row 3ch, yrh and insert into first 1ch space, yrh and draw through a loop, yrh and insert into next 1ch space, yrh and draw through a loop, yrh and draw through all 5 loops on hook, 1ch, * yrh and insert into 1ch space that was last worked into, yrh and draw through a loop, yrh and insert into next 1ch space, yrh and draw through a loop, yrh and draw through all 5 loops on hook, 1ch, rep from * to end, 1htr into 2nd of the 3ch. Turn.

The last row is repeated throughout to form the pattern.

Granite stitch

Using No. 5.00 (ISR) hook and Double Knitting, make 22ch.

1st row Into 3rd ch from hook work (1dc, 1ch and 1dc), miss next ch, * (1dc, 1ch and 1dc) into next ch, miss next ch, rep from * to last ch, 1dc into last ch. Turn.

2nd row 1ch, * (1dc, 1ch and 1dc) into 1ch space of next group, rep from * to end, 1dc into the turning ch. Turn.

The last row is repeated throughout to form the pattern.

Palm leaves

Using No. 5 00 (ISR) hook and Double Knitting, make 22ch.

1st row Into 4th ch from hook work 1dc, * 2ch, miss next 2ch, 1dc into next ch, rep from * to end. Turn.

2nd row 3ch to count as first tr, 1tr into first dc, * 3tr into next dc, rep from * to end, 2tr into first of the 3ch. Turn.

3rd row 3ch, 1dc into 2nd tr of the first 3tr group, * 2ch, 1dc into 2nd tr of next 3tr group, rep from * to end, working last dc into 3rd of the 3ch. Turn.

Repeat the 2nd and 3rd rows throughout to form the pattern.

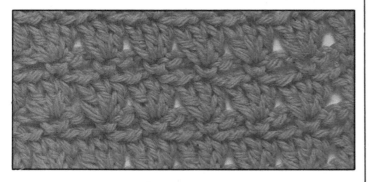

Cock's head trebles

Using No. 5.00 (ISR) hook and Double Knitting, make 22ch.

1st row Into 4th ch from hook work 1tr, * (yrh and insert into next ch, yrh and draw through a loop, yrh and draw through first 2 loops on hook) twice, yrh and draw through all 3 loops, 1ch, rep from * to end, omitting the 1ch at the end of the last rep.

2nd row 4ch, yrh and insert into first st, yrh and draw through a loop, yrh and draw through first 2 loops, miss next st, yrh and insert into next st, yrh and draw through a loop, yrh and draw through first 2 loops, yrh and draw through all 3 loops, * 1ch, yrh and insert into same st that last st was worked into, yrh and draw through a loop, yrh and draw through first 2 loops, miss next st, yrh and insert into next st, yrh and draw through a loop, yrh and draw through first 2 loops, yrh and draw through all 3 loops, rep from * to end, 1ch, 1tr into 3rd of the 3ch. Turn.

3rd row As 2nd, but note that the last st is worked into the 3rd of the 4ch. Turn.

The last row is repeated throughout to form the pattern.

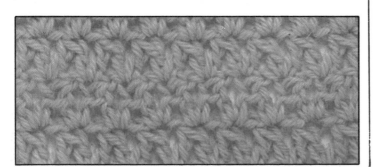

Forget-me-not stitch

Using No. 5.00 (ISR) hook and Double Knitting, make 25ch.

1st row Into 4th ch from hook work (1tr, 2ch and 1dc), * miss next 2ch, (2tr, 2ch and 1dc) into next ch, rep from * to end. Turn.

2nd row 3ch, (1tr, 2ch and 1dc) into first 2ch space, * (2tr, 2ch and 1dc) into next 2ch space, rep from * to end. Turn.

The last row is repeated throughout to form the pattern. This stitch looks very attractive when two colours are used on alternate rows.

To design a dirndl skirt

One of these attractive stitches that you have just learnt, together with your knowledge of tension checking are the main ingredients you will need to design a lovely dirndl skirt.

For example, if you are a hip size 91.5 centimetres (36 inches), you will need 2.5 centimetres (one inch) ease. This means that each piece of your skirt will measure 47 centimetres (18½ inches) across. If your tension is 4 sts to 2.5 centimetres (one inch), then you will require 18½ × 4 = 74 stitches for the basic pattern.

No shaping is required. You just work to the required length and gather the waist with rows of shirring elastic.

Wall hanging

Another use of the various stitches learnt so far is to make them into a wall hanging. This will look particularly attractive if you choose one colour and work each stitch in a different shade of this colour. A very stylish finishing touch would be to mount the hanging on a brass rail.

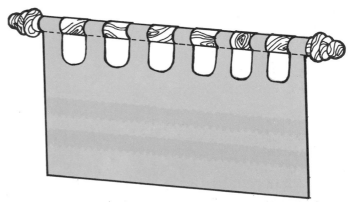

CLUSTER AND BOBBLE STITCHES

Cluster and bobble stitches

Edgings using either bobble or cluster stitch make ideal trimmings for the neckline or hemline of a dress and edgings for jackets, waistcoats and household linens. The same stitches can also be incorporated in making square or circular motifs for a bedspread or evening stole, or they can be used to replace stitches in a basic design and so add much more interest to the fabric.

Here three examples of cluster stitch are illustrated and explained in detail, but there are many other variations. For these samples a No. 4.50 (ISR) crochet hook and a Double Knitting yarn were used, but the hook size and type of yarn may vary depending on the final purpose of the work.

Cluster or pine stitch

Make 26ch.

1st row Into 3rd ch from hook work 1dc, 1dc into each ch to end. Turn.

2nd row 1ch to count as first dc, miss first dc, 1dc into each dc, ending with 1dc into the turning chain. Turn.

3rd row (cluster row) 4ch, miss first 2dc, ** yrh and insert into next dc, yrh and draw through a loop extending it for 1cm (⅜in), * yrh and insert it into same dc, yrh and draw through a loop extending it for 1cm (⅜in), rep from * 3 times, yrh and draw through all 11 loops on hook – called 1cl –, 1ch, miss next dc, rep from ** ending with 1tr into the turning chain. Turn.

4th and 5th rows Work in dc. Fasten off.

Using the cluster stitch practise making square motifs. Worked in one colour and a cotton yarn, they are ideal for a quilt or tablecloth, or worked in fine, multi-coloured yarns they make an attractive evening stole.

The instructions for the square motif are given using 4 colours which are referred to as A, B, C and D.

Square motif

With A, make 5ch. Join into circle with ss.

1st round 1ch to count as first dc, 15dc into circle, ending with ss into first ch. 16dc. Fasten off A and join in B.

2nd round 4ch to count as first tr and linking ch, * 1tr into next dc, 1ch, rep from * ending with ss into 3rd of the 4ch. Fasten off B and join in C.

3rd round Ss into next 1ch space, * 3ch, 1cl into same 1ch space, rep from * ending with 3ch, ss into top of first cl. Fasten off C and join in D.

4th round Ss into next 3ch space, 1ch, 2dc into same space, 3dc into each of next 2 spaces, * (1htr, 1tr, 2ch, 1tr, 1htr) into next space for corner, 3dc into each of next 3 spaces, rep from * twice more, 1 corner into next space, ss into first ch. Fasten off.

Raised clusters

By using the method of raising clusters on a basic fabric, many designs such as diagonals and zig-zags may be built up according to the position of the clusters. The instructions given below are for raised clusters on a double crochet fabric.

Make 25ch.

1st to 3rd rows Work in dc as given for basic cluster sample.

4th row 1ch to count as first dc, miss first dc, 1dc into each of next 3dc, * insert hook into next dc, yrh and draw through a loop, (yrh and insert into space on the 3rd row directly below this stitch position, yrh and draw through a loop, yrh and draw through first 2 loops on hook) 5 times, yrh and draw through all 6 loops on hook – called 1 raised cl – , 1dc into each of next 4dc, rep from * to end.

5th to 7th rows Work in dc.

8th row Repeat the raised cluster on every 5th stitch depending on the effect that you want to create.

You will see that diagonals or alternating clusters have been formed on our illustrations. Repeat rows 1 to 8 to achieve this effect.

Two more raised stitches are the bobble and the popcorn stitch. Here the instructions given are for an all-over bobble design and popcorn stitch that is worked into a braid.

Bobble stitch

Make 26ch.

1st row Into 3rd ch from hook work 1dc, 1dc into each ch to end. Turn.

2nd row 1ch to count as first dc, * 4ch, miss 2dc, leaving the last loop of each st on hook work 6tr tr into next dc, yrh and draw through all 7 loops on hook – called B1 – , 4ch, miss next 2dc, 1dc into next dc, rep from * ending with 1dc into turning chain. Turn.

3rd row 5ch to count as first tr and linking ch, 1dc into first B1, * 5ch, 1dc into next B1, rep from * ending with 2ch, 1tr into the turning chain. Turn.

4th row 5ch to count as first tr and linking ch, 1dc into next dc, * 4ch, B1 into next 5ch space, 4ch, 1dc into next dc, rep from * ending with 2ch, 1tr into 3rd of the turning chain. Turn.

5th row 1ch to count as first dc, * 5ch, 1dc into next Bl, rep from * ending with 5ch, 1dc into 3rd of the turning chain. Turn.

6th row 1ch to count as first dc, * 4ch, B1 into next 5ch space, 4ch, 1dc into next dc, rep from * ending with 1dc into the turning chain. Turn.

Repeat 3rd to 6th rows to form the pattern.

Bobble stitch

Popcorn stitch

Make 25ch.

1st row Into 4th ch from hook work 1tr, 1tr into each ch to end. Turn.

2nd row 3ch to count as first tr, miss first tr, 1tr into each tr, ending with 1tr into the turning chain.

3rd row 3ch to count as first tr, miss first tr, 1tr into next tr, * 1ch, 5tr into next tr, slip working st off the hook and pick up the ch st worked before the 5tr, pick up working loop and draw through the ch st – 1 popcorn st has now been worked – , 1tr into each of next 2tr, rep from * ending with 1tr into the turning chain. Turn.

4th and 5th rows Work in tr. Fasten off.

KNOW-HOW FOR PATTERNS

In the previous chapters, many stitches and ways of using them have been explained and a variety of materials have been used. This chapter is designed to give some useful hints on the treatment, pressing and making up of your work when finished and how these and various other interesting techniques can be applied to making useful and decorative bags.

Tension

Before commencing a piece of work that has a definite size requirement, for example, a jersey to fit a bust size 86.5cm (34in), it is important to make sure that the garment will measure the correct size when it is completed. A tension sample must be worked before you start. Follow the tension guide at the beginning of the pattern and, using the stated yarn and hook size, make a square. Place a rigid rule on the work and count how many stitches and rows there are to the centimetre (inch). If there are too many stitches, then your tension is too tight and you must practise with a larger hook until you gain the correct tension. Too few stitches mean that you are working too loosely and will have to use a smaller hook.

Pressing work

Part of the pleasing appearance of crochet is its textured surface and many people prefer not to press the work as they fear the effect of a warm iron and damp cloth will spoil this texture. Also with so many new and different kinds of yarn on the market, pressing could quite well be unnecessary. Always read the manufacturer's instructions on the yarn label to find if ironing is recommended and see the temperature advised.

As a general rule, most of the yarns containing a high percentage of natural fibres such as wool and cotton can be pressed under a damp cloth with a warm iron. Man-made yarns such as Nylon, Courtelle and Acrylics need a cool iron and dry cloth.

Blocking out

Most crochet, especially when it is very open in texture, should be blocked out on completion. Using a clean flat surface into which you can stick rustless dressmaking pins, pin the piece out to the correct measurements.

Cover with a damp cloth and leave until the cloth is absolutely dry.

Cotton crochet items such as delicate edgings or table cloths and tea cloths often look better for a light stiffening.

Use a starch solution (about two teaspoonfuls to a 600ml (1 pint) of hot water), or a gum arabic solution. Dab the solution over the article when it is blocked out.

Joining in new yarn

In crochet, it is better to avoid tying knots when joining in new yarn. Work until about 7.5cm (3in) of the yarn is left, lay it across the top of the previous row to the left, lay the beginning of the new yarn with it and work over both ends with the second ball of yarn.

If the join comes when chain is being worked, lay the

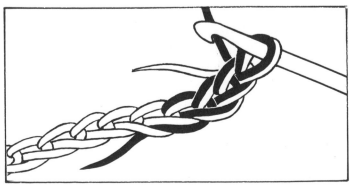

new thread alongside the first one, the ends pointing in opposite directions, and work with the double thickness until the first thread runs out.

Joining two pieces of crochet work

There are two methods of doing this — by sewing the pieces together or by using crochet stitches to join them.

Sewing Place the two pieces of work with right sides together and pin firmly. Oversew the edge using a matching yarn. When the seam is completed it may be necessary to press it.

Take care when joining stripes or patterns that the seams match exactly to ensure a professional finish.

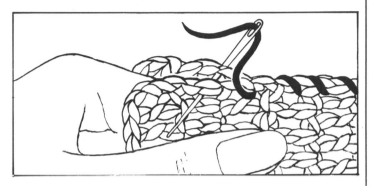

Crochet Joining work with crochet stitches can form part of the design and look very attractive. In the photograph you will see a section of a bag where the gusset has been joined to the main part with double crochet.

Methods of making a handbag

Generally there are two types of handbag, one with a gusset and one without. The gusset is a narrow piece of fabric between the two main sections to give the bag a three-dimensional effect.

Commercial handles for bags may be purchased from the needlework counters of most large stores. The

traditional wooden frames illustrated do not require a gusset. Simply work two pieces of crochet to the required size and join together either by sewing or crochet stitches, leaving a gap in the top edge for the handles to be inserted and hemmed into place.

If you have used crochet stitches to join your bag, then you could insert tassels through the joining stitches along the lower edge at whatever spacing you desired. Our sample illustration has been worked in different colours to clarify the various stages and the method of adding the tassels is shown clearly.

Other types of commercial handles available are the bamboo rings and various metal frames which have a screw-in bar and clasp fastening.

A firm handle may not be required and a gusset strip can be made to fit round the bag plus an extension which is left free for holding as in our illustration.

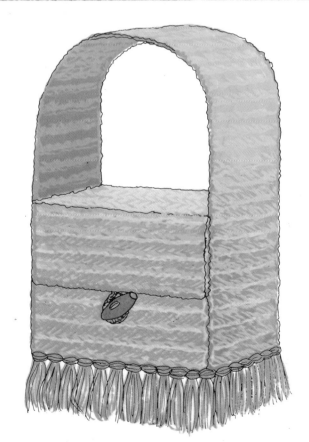

FIRST SIMPLE GARMENTS
Smart dress set

Sizes

To fit 81.5[86.5:91.5:96.5:101.5]cm (32[34:36:38:40]in) bust
86.5[91.5:96.5:101.5:106.5]cm (34[36:38:40:42]in) hips
Dress length to shoulder, 99[99:99.5:99.5:100.5]cm (39[39:39¼:39¼:39½] in)
Jacket length to shoulder, 59.5[59.5:59.5:61:61]cm (23½[23½:23½:24:24]in)
Sleeve seam 44.5cm (17½in)
The figures in brackets [ ] refer to the 86.5 (34), 91.5 (36), 96.5 (38) and 101.5cm (40in) bust sizes respectively

Tension

Dress and beret 19 sts and 24 rows to 10cm (3.9in) over patt worked on No.4.00 (ISR) crochet hook
Jacket 21 sts and 13 rows to 10cm (3.9in) over patt worked on No.4.00 (ISR) crochet hook

Materials

Dress 10[11:12:13:13] × 50grm balls Jaeger Donegal
Jacket 8[8:9:9:10] × 50grm balls of same
Beret 2 × 50grm balls of same
One No.4.00 (ISR) crochet hook
One 51cm (20in) zip for dress
3 buttons for jacket

Dress front

**Using No.4.00 (ISR) hook make 111[115:121:125:131]ch.
Base row (WS) Into 2nd ch from hook work 1dc, 1dc into each ch to end. Turn. 110[114:120:124:130] sts.
Commence patt.
1st row 1ch, 1dc into each st to end. Turn.
This row forms patt. Work 7 more rows patt.
Shape sides
Cont in patt, dec one st at each end of next and every foll 8th row until 88[92:98:102:108] sts rem. Work 7 rows without shaping. **
Shape waist darts
1st row Dec one st, 1dc into each of next 21[22:25:26:28] sts, dec one st, 1dc into each of next 38[40:40:42:44] sts, dec one st, 1dc into each st to last 2 sts, dec one st. Turn.
Work 7 rows without shaping.
9th row Dec one st by working 2dc tog, 1dc into each of next 20[21:24:25:27] sts, dec one st, 1dc into each of next 36[38:38:40:42] sts, dec one st, 1dc into each st to last 2 sts, dec one st. Turn.
Work 7 rows without shaping. Cont dec in this way on next and every foll 8th row until 68[72:78:82:88] sts rem. Cont without shaping until work measures

62cm (24½in) from beg, ending with a WS row.
Shape bust darts
1st row 1ch, 1dc into same st, 1dc into each of next 17[18:21:22:24] sts, 2dc into next st, 1dc into each of next 30[32:32:34:36] sts, 2dc into next st, 1dc into each st to last st, 2dc into last st. Turn.
Work 7 rows without shaping.
9th row 1ch, 1dc into same st, 1dc into each of next 18[19:22:23:25] sts, 2dc into next st, 1dc into each of next 32[34:34:36:38] sts, 2dc into next st, 1dc into each st to last st, 2dc into last st. Turn.
Work 7 rows without shaping. Cont inc in this way on next and foll 8th row. 84[88:94:98:104] sts. Cont without shaping until front measures 80[80:80:82.5:82.5]cm (31½[31½:31½:32½:32½]in) from beg, ending with a WS row.
Shape armholes
1st row Ss over first 5[5:6:7:8] sts, 1ch, patt to last 5[5:6:7:8] sts, turn.
Dec one st at each end of next and every foll alt row until 62[66:70:70:74] sts rem. Cont without shaping until armholes measure 14.5[14.5:15:15:15.5]cm (5¾[5¾:6:6:6¼]in) from beg, ending with a WS row.
Shape neck
Next row Patt 25[27:28:28:30] sts, turn.
Complete this side first. Keeping armhole edge straight, dec one st at neck edge on next 7 rows, ending at armhole edge.
Shape shoulder
1st row Ss over first 3[4:5:5:4] sts, 1ch, patt to end. Turn.
2nd row Patt to last 4[4:4:4:5] sts, turn.
3rd row Ss over first 4[4:4:4:5] sts, 1ch, patt to end. Turn.
4th row Patt 3[4:4:4:4] sts. Fasten off.
With RS of work facing, miss first 12[12:14:14:14] sts for centre front neck, rejoin yarn to next st, 1ch, 1dc into each st to end. Turn.
Dec one st at neck edge on next 7 rows, ending at neck edge.
Shape shoulder
1st row Patt to last 3[4:5:5:4] sts, turn.
2nd row Ss over first 4[4:4:4:5] sts, 1ch, patt to end. Turn.
3rd row Patt 7[8:8:8:9] sts. Turn.
4th row Ss over first 4[4:4:4:5] sts, 1ch, patt to end. Fasten off.

Dress back

Work as given for front from ** to **
Shape waist darts
1st row Dec one st, 1dc into each of next 21[22:25:26:28] sts, dec one st, 1dc into each of next 38[40:40:42:44] sts, dec

one st, 1dc into each st to last 2 sts, dec one st. Turn.
Work 3 rows without shaping.
5th row 1ch, 1dc into each of next 21[22:25:26:28] sts, dec one st, 1dc into each of next 36[38:38:40:42] sts, dec one st, 1dc into each st to end. Turn.
Work 3 rows without shaping.
9th row Dec one st, 1dc into each of next 20[21:24:25:27] sts, dec one st, 1dc into each of next 34[36:36:38:40] sts, dec one st, 1dc into each st to last 2 sts, dec one st. Turn.
Work 3 rows without shaping.
13th row 1ch, 1dc into each of next 20[21:24:25:27] sts, dec one st, 1dc into each of next 32[34:34:36:38] sts, dec one st, 1dc into each st to end. Turn. 76[80:86:90:96] sts.
Work one row without shaping.
Divide for back opening
Next row 1ch, 1dc into each of next 37[39:42:44:47] sts, turn.
Complete this side first.
1st row 1ch, 1dc into each st to end. Turn.
2nd row Dec one st, 1dc into each of next 19[20:23:24:26] sts, dec one st, 1dc into each st to end. Turn.
Work 3 rows without shaping.
6th row 1ch, 1dc into each of first 19[20:23:24:26] sts, dec one st, 1dc into each st to end. Turn.
Work 3 rows without shaping.
10th row Dec one st, 1dc into each of next 18[19:22:23:25] sts, dec one st, 1dc into each st to end. Turn.
Work 3 rows without shaping.
14th row 1ch, 1dc into each of first 18[19:22:23:25] sts, dec one st, 1dc into each st to end. Turn.
Work 3 rows without shaping.
18th row Dec one st, 1dc into each of next 17[18:21:22:24] sts, dec one st, 1dc into each st to end. Turn.
Work 3 rows without shaping.
22nd row 1ch, 1dc into each of first 17[18:21:22:24] sts, dec one st, 1dc into each st to end. Turn. 29[31:34:36:39] sts.
Cont without shaping until back measures 62cm (24½in) from beg, ending with a WS row.
Shape side edge and dart
1st row 1ch, 1dc into same st, 1dc into each of next 17[18:21:22:24] sts, 2dc into next st, 1dc into each st to end. Turn.
Work 3 rows without shaping.
5th row 1ch, 1dc into each of next 18[19:22:23:25] sts, 2dc into next st, 1dc into each st to end. Turn.
Work 3 rows without shaping.
9th row 1ch, 1dc into same st, 1dc into each of next 18[19:22:23:25] sts, 2dc into next st, 1dc into each st to end. Turn.
Cont inc at side edge in this way on every foll 8th row and for dart on every

4th row until there are 41[43:46:48:51] sts. Cont without shaping until back measures same as front to underarm, ending at side edge.

Shape armhole

1st row Ss over first 5[5:6:7:8] sts, 1ch, patt to end. Turn.
Dec one st at armhole edge on next and every alt row until 31[33:35:35:37] sts rem. Cont without shaping until armhole measures same as front to shoulder, ending at armhole edge.

Shape shoulder

1st row Ss over first 3[4:5:5:4] sts, 1ch, patt to end. Turn.

2nd row Patt to last 4[4:4:4:5] sts, turn.

3rd row Ss over first 4[4:4:4:5] sts, 1ch, patt 7[8:8:8:9] sts, turn.

4th row Patt 3[4:4:4:4] sts. Fasten off. With RS of work facing, rejoin yarn to rem sts at back opening and complete to match first side, reversing shaping.

To make up

Press each piece lightly under a damp cloth with a warm iron. Join shoulder and side seams.

Neck and back opening edging Using No.4.00 (ISR) hook and with RS of work facing, rejoin yarn to left back neck edge at opening edge. Work one row dc round neck, down right back opening and up left back opening edge. Do not turn, but work one row of crab st, working in dc from left to right instead of from right to left.

Armhole edging Using No.4.00 (ISR) hook and with RS of work facing, work as given for neck and back edging. Press seams lightly. Sew zip into back opening.

Jacket right front

**Using No.4.00 (ISR) hook make 44[47:50:53:56] ch.

Base row (WS) Into 2nd ch from hook work 1dc, *2ch, miss 2ch, 1dc into next ch, rep from * to end. Turn. 43[46:49:52:55] sts.
Commence patt.

1st row 2ch, 1tr into first dc, *miss 2ch, 3tr into next dc, rep from * ending with miss 2ch, 2tr into last dc. Turn.

2nd row 1ch, 1dc into first tr, *2ch, miss 2tr, 1dc into next tr, rep from * to end. Turn.
The last 2 rows form patt. Work 7 more rows patt, ending with a RS row.

Shape side edge

Keeping patt correct, dec one st at beg of next and at same edge on every foll 3rd row until 37[40:43:46:49] sts rem. Cont without shaping until front measures 25.5cm (10in) from beg, ending with a RS row. **

Shape side and front edges

1st row Inc in first st, patt to last 2 sts, dec one st. Turn.

2nd and 3rd rows Patt to end. Turn.

4th row Dec one st, patt to end. Turn.

5th and 6th rows Patt to end. Turn.
Rep last 6 rows twice more. 34[37:40:43:46] sts.

Shape armhole

Next row Ss over first 4[5:5:6:6] sts, 1ch, patt to last 2 sts, dec one st. Turn.
Cont dec at front edge as before, *at the same time* dec one st at armhole edge on next 4[5:7:7:8] rows. Keeping armhole edge straight, cont dec at front edge on every 3rd row until 19[20:21:23:25] sts rem. Cont without shaping until armhole measures 18[18:18:19:19]cm (7[7:7:7½:7½]in) from beg, ending at armhole edge.

Shape shoulder

1st row Ss over first 4[5:5:5:7] sts, 1ch, patt to end. Turn.

2nd row Patt to last 5[5:5:6:6] sts, turn.

3rd row Ss over first 5[5:5:6:6] sts, 1ch, patt to end. Fasten off.

Left front

Work as given for right front from ** to **, reversing shaping.

Shape front and side edges

1st row Dec one st, patt to last st, inc in last st. Turn.

2nd and 3rd rows Patt to end. Turn.

4th row Patt to last 2 sts, dec one st. Turn.

5th and 6th rows Patt to end. Turn. Rep last 6 rows twice more. Turn.

Shape armhole

Next row Dec one st, patt to last 4[5:5:6:6] sts, turn.
Complete armhole and front edge shaping as given for right front, reversing shaping. Cont without shaping until armhole measures 18[18:18:19:19]cm (7[7:7:7½:7½]in) from beg, ending at neck edge. Turn.

Shape shoulder

1st row Patt to last 4[5:5:5:7] sts, turn.

2nd row Ss over first 5[5:5:6:6] sts, 2ch, patt to end. Turn.

3rd row Patt 5[5:6:6:6] sts. Fasten off.

Back

Using No.4.00 (ISR) hook make 92[98:104:110:116] ch. Work base row as given for right front. 91[97:103:109:115] sts. Work 9 rows patt as given for right front.

Shape sides

Dec one st at each end of next and every foll 3rd row until 79[85:91:97:103] sts rem. Cont without shaping until work measures 25.5cm (10in) from beg, ending with a RS row. Inc one st at each end of next and every foll 6th row 3 times in all. 85[91:97:103:109] sts.
Work 5 rows without shaping.

Shape armholes

Next row Ss over first 4[5:5:6:6] sts, 1ch, patt to last 4[5:5:6:6] sts, turn.
Dec one st at each end of next 4[5:7:7:8] rows. 69[71:73:77:81] sts.
Cont working in patt without shaping until armholes measure same as front to shoulder, ending with a RS row.

Shape shoulders

1st row Ss over first 4[5:5:5:7] sts, 1ch, patt to last 4[5:5:5:7] sts, turn.

2nd row Ss over first 5[5:5:6:6] sts, 2ch, patt to last 5[5:5:6:6] sts, turn.

3rd row Ss over first 5[5:5:6:6] sts, 1ch, patt over next 5[5:6:6:6] sts, ss over next 31 sts, patt over next 5[5:6:6:6] sts. Fasten off.

Sleeves

Using No.4.00 (ISR) hook make 41[44:44:47:47] ch. Work base row as given for right front. 40[43:43:46:46] sts. Work 3 rows patt as given for right front. Keeping patt correct, inc one st at each end of next and every foll 3rd row until there are 50[53:55:62:64] sts, then inc one st at each end of every foll 4th row until there are 64[67:69:72:74] sts. Cont without shaping until sleeve measures 44.5cm (17½in) from beg, ending with a RS row.

Shape top

Next row Ss over first 4[5:5:6:6] sts, 1ch, patt to last 4[5:5:6:6] sts, turn.
Dec one st at each end of every row until

34[35:37:34:36] sts rem. Dec 2 sts at each end of next 4 rows. 18[19:21:18:20] sts. Fasten off.

To make up

Press each piece under a damp cloth with a warm iron. Join shoulder seams. Set in sleeves. Join side and sleeve seams.
Border Using No.4.00 (ISR) hook and with RS of work facing, rejoin yarn to right front at lower edge. Work one row dc up right front edge, working 3dc into each 2 row ends, cont across back neck, working into each st, then work down left front as given for right front. Turn.

Next row 1ch, 1dc into each st to end. Turn. Rep last row once more. Mark position for 3 buttonholes on right front, first to come 1.5cm (½in) below first row of front edge shaping and last to come 6.5cm (2½in) from lower edge with 3rd evenly spaced between.

Next row (buttonhole row) Work in dc to end, making 3 buttonholes when markers are reached by working 3ch and missing 3 sts. Work 3 rows dc, working 3dc into 3ch buttonhole loop on first row. Fasten off. Press seams and border lightly. Sew on buttons.

Beret

Using No.4.00 (ISR) hook make 6ch. Join with a ss to first ch to form circle.

1st round 1ch, work 11dc into circle. Join with a ss to first ch. 12 sts.

2nd round 1ch, 1dc into same st, 1dc into next st, *2dc into next st, 1dc into next st, rep from * to end. Join with a ss to first 1ch. 18 sts.

3rd round 1ch, 1dc into same st, 1dc into each of next 2 sts, *2dc into next st, 1dc into each of next 2 sts, rep from * to end. Join with a ss to first 1ch. 24 sts.

4th round 1ch, 1dc into same st, 1dc into each of next 3 sts, *2dc into next st, 1dc into each of next 3 sts, rep from * to end. Join with a ss to first 1ch. 30 sts.
Cont inc in this way on every round until there are 132 sts. Work 10 rounds without shaping.

Shape headband

Next round *Dec one st, 1dc into each of next 20 sts, rep from * to end. Join with a ss to first st.

Next round *Dec one st, 1dc into each of next 19 sts, rep from * to end. Join with a ss to first st.
Cont dec in this way on every round until 84 sts rem. Turn.

Next round 1ch, 1dc into each dc to end. Join with a ss to first 1ch. Turn.
Rep last round 3 times more. Fasten off.

To make up

Press lightly as given for dress.

A simple lightweight dress

**

Sizes

To fit 86.5 [91.5:96.5:101.5]cm (34[36:38:
40]in) bust
Length to shoulder, 91.5[92:92.5:93]cm
(36[36¼:36½:36¾]in)
Sleeve seam, 12.5cm (5in)
The figures in brackets [] refer to the
91.5 (36). 96.5 (38) and 101.5cm (40in)
sizes respectively

Tension

20 sts and 9 rows to 10cm (3.9in) over
tr worked on No.3.50 (ISR) crochet hook;
22 sts and 20 rows to 10cm (3.9in) over
dc worked on No.3.50 (ISR) crochet
hook

Materials

13[15:17:19] × 50 grm balls of Twilley's
Stalite in main shade, A
1 ball each of contrast colours, B and C
One No.3.50 (ISR) crochet hook
51cm (20in) zip fastener

Skirt

Using No.3.50 (ISR) hook and A, make 111
ch and beg at waist, working from top to
lower edge.

1st row (RS) Into 3rd ch from hook work 1dc, 1dc into each of next 18ch, 1htr into each of next 20ch, 1tr into each of next 70ch. Turn. 110 sts.

2nd row 3ch to count as first tr, 1tr into front loop only of next 69tr, 1htr into front loop only of next 20htr, 1dc into front loop only of next 19dc, 1dc into turning ch. Turn.

3rd row 1ch to count as first dc, 1dc into front loop only of next 19dc, 1htr into front loop only of next 20htr, 1tr into front loop only of next 69tr, 1tr into turning ch. Turn.

The 2nd and 3rd rows form patt and are rep throughout. Cont in patt until work measures 63.5[68.5:73.5:78.5]cm (25[27:29:31]in) from beg, measured across dc waist edge. Fasten off.

Hem

Using No.3.50 (ISR) hook, B and with RS of work facing, rejoin yarn to lower edge of skirt.

Next row 2ch to count as first dc, (1tr, 1ch, 1tr, 1dc) into first row end, *1ch, 1dc into next row end, 1ch, (1dc, 1tr, 1ch, 1tr, 1dc) into next row end, rep from * to end. Break off B. Join in C. Do not turn.

Next row Rejoin yarn at beg of row, 2ch, (1tr, 1ch, 1tr, 1dc) into first ch sp between tr, *1ch, 1dc into next dc, 3ch, 1dc into same dc, 1ch, (1dc, 1tr, 1ch, 1tr, 1dc) into next 1ch sp between tr, rep from * to end. Fasten off.

Bodice

Using No.3.50 (ISR) hook, A and with RS of work facing, rejoin yarn and work 150[162:174:186]dc across waist edge. Work 3 rows dc, working into front loop only of each dc throughout.

Shape darts

Next row 1ch, work 1dc into each of next 40[43:46:49]dc, (2dc into next dc) twice, 1dc into each of next 19[22:25:28]dc, (2dc into next dc) twice, 1dc into each of next 22dc, (2dc into next dc) twice, 1dc into each of next 19[22:25:28]dc, (2dc into next dc) twice, 1dc into each of next 41[44:47:50]dc. Turn. 158[170:182:194]dc.

Work 3 rows without shaping.

Next row 1ch, work 1dc into each of next 41[44:47:50]dc, (2dc into next dc) twice, 1dc into each of next 21[24:27:30]dc, (2dc into next dc) twice, 1dc into each of next 24dc, (2dc into next dc) twice, 1dc into each of next 21[24:27:30]dc, (2dc into next dc) twice, 1dc into each of next 42[45:48:51]dc. Turn. 166[178:190:202]dc.

Work 3 rows without shaping. Cont inc 8 sts in this way on next and every foll

4th row until there are 198[210:230:242]sts. Cont without shaping until work measures 20.5cm (8in) from waist, or required length to underarm, ending with a WS row.

Divide for armholes

Next row Patt across 45[48:52:55] sts, turn.

Complete left back first. Dec one st at beg of next and at same edge on every row until 35[38:42:45] sts rem. Cont without shaping until armhole measures 14[14.5:15:15.5]cm (5½[5¾:6:6¼]in) from beg, ending at armhole edge.

Shape neck

Next row Patt across 20[22:24:26] sts, turn.

Dec one st at beg of next and at same edge on every row until 16[18:20:22] sts rem. Cont without shaping until armhole measures 18[18.5:19:19.5]cm (7[7¼:7½:7¾]in) from beg, ending at neck edge.

Shape shoulder

Next row Patt across 8[9:10:11] sts, turn and fasten off.

With RS of work facing, miss first 8[8:10:10] sts for underarm, rejoin yarn to next st and patt across 92[98:106:112] sts for front, turn.

Dec one st at each end of next 10 rows. 72[78:86:92] sts. Cont without shaping until armholes measure 9[9.5:10:10.5]cm (3½[3¾:4:4¼]in) from beg, ending with a WS row.

Shape neck

Next row Patt across 26[28:30:32] sts, turn.

Complete this side first. Dec one st at beg of next and at same edge on every row until 16[18:20:22] sts rem. Cont without shaping until armhole measures same as back to shoulder, ending at neck edge.

Shape shoulder

Next row Patt across 8[9:10:11] sts, turn and fasten off.

With RS of work facing, miss first 20[22:26:28] sts for centre neck, rejoin yarn to rem sts and patt to end. Complete to match first side, reversing shaping.

With RS of work facing, miss first 8[8:10:10] sts for underarm, rejoin yarn to rem sts and patt to end. Complete right back to match left back, reversing shaping.

Sleeves

Using No.3.50 (ISR) hook and A, make 22 ch and work from side edge to side edge.

1st row (RS) Into 4th ch from hook work 1tr, 1tr into each ch to end. Turn. 20tr.

2nd row 3ch to count as first tr, *1tr into front loop only of next tr, rep from * ending with 1tr into turning ch. Turn.

Shape top

Next row 3ch, 1htr into 3rd of these 3 ch, *1tr into front loop only of next tr, rep from * ending with 1tr into turning ch. Turn. 22 sts.

Next row 3ch to count as first tr, 1tr into front loop only of next 19tr, 1htr into front loop only of next htr, 1htr into turning ch. Turn.

Next row 3ch to count as first tr, 1htr into 3rd of these 3 ch, 1htr into front loop only of next 2htr, 1tr into front loop only of each tr to end. Turn. 24 sts.

Next row 3ch to count as first tr, 1tr into front loop only of next 19tr, 1htr into front loop only of next 3htr, 1 htr into turning ch. Turn.

Cont inc in this way, rep last 2 rows 4[5:6:7] times more. 32[34:36:38] sts.

Next row 5ch, 1dc into 3rd of these 5ch, 1dc into each of next 2ch, 1htr into front loop only of each of next 14[16:18:20] htr, 1tr into front loop only of each tr to end. Turn. 36[38:40:42] sts.

Next row 3ch, 1tr into front loop only of next 19tr, 1htr into front loop only of next 14[16:18:20] htr, 1dc into front loop only of next 3dc, 1dc into turning ch. Turn.

Rep last 2 rows 2[3:4:5] times more. 44[50:56:62] sts. Work 12 rows patt as now set without shaping, ending at top edge.

Next row Ss over first 4dc and into next dc, 1ch to count as first dc, patt to end. Turn. 40[46:52:58] sts.

Next row Patt to end. Turn.

Rep last 2 rows 2[3:4:5] times more. 32[34:36:38] sts.

Next row Ss over first 2htr and into next htr, 2ch to count as first htr, patt to end. Turn. 30[32:34:36] sts.

Next row Patt to end. Turn.

Rep last 2 rows until 20tr rem. Work 1 row tr. Fasten off.

Cuff

Using No.3.50 (ISR) hook, B and with RS of work facing, work along lower edge of sleeve as given for hem. Fasten off.

Neckband

Join shoulder seams. Using No.3.50 (ISR) hook, B and with RS of work facing, work evenly round neck edge as given for hem. Fasten off.

To make up

Press each piece under a damp cloth with a warm iron. Join sleeve seams. Set in sleeves, easing in fullness at top. Join centre back seam leaving opening for zip fastener to come to top of neckband. Sew in zip. Press seams.

Using the remaining yarn, make a twisted cord or plaited belt.

CROCHET IN ROUNDS
CIRCULAR MOTIFS

Crochet may very easily and effectively be made into a circle or square instead of working to and fro in rows. Each piece is worked from the same side which means that there is a definite right and wrong side to the work.

Circular shapes are an important technique in crochet. Sun hats, berets, bags and doilys are amongst the many articles formed from this method.

Attractive shapes may be joined together to give a patchwork fabric that is useful for shawls, rugs, waistcoats and evening skirts.

Again try experimenting in various yarns to see the many effects that may be achieved.

To work a circle in crochet

Using No. 5.00 (ISR) hook and Double Knitting, make 6ch. Join together to form a ring with a ss into the first ch.

1st round 3ch to count as the first tr, then work 15tr into the ring. Join with a ss to the 3rd of the first 3ch. 16tr.

2nd round 3ch, 2tr into each tr of the previous round, 1tr into the base of the first 3ch. Join with a ss to the 3rd of the first 3ch. 32tr.

3rd round 3ch, (1tr into next stitch, 2tr into next stitch) 15 times, 1tr into next stitch, 1tr into base of the first 3ch. Join with a ss into the 3rd of the first 3ch. 48tr.

4th round 3ch, (1tr into each of next 2 stitches, 2tr into next stitch) 15 times, 1tr into each of next 2 stitches,

1tr into base of the first 3ch. Join with a ss to the 3rd of the first 3ch. 64tr.

Continue in this way, working 1 extra tr on each round between increases, until the circle is the required size.

To practise this method of making a circle and produce useful items for the home at the same time, make two circles to any desired size and use them to cover a cushion pad or, using three thicknesses of Dishcloth Cotton and a No. 10.00 (ISR) hook, make a bath mat. A fringed edging would add the final touch to both these items.

Another way to make a circular motif

Make 6ch. Join with ss to first ch to form a circle.

1st round 2ch to count as first dc, work 7dc into circle. Do not join but cont working in rounds, working next 2dc into second of first 2ch.

2nd round Work 2dc into each dc to end. 16dc.

3rd round Work 1dc into each dc to end.

4th round Work 2dc into each dc to end. 32dc.

5th round Work 1dc into each dc to end.

6th round 2dc into first dc, 1dc into next dc, *2dc into next dc, 1dc into next dc, rep from * to end. 48dc.

7th round Work 1 round without shaping.

8th round 2dc into first dc, 1dc into each of next 2dc, *2dc into next dc, 1dc into each of next 2dc, rep from * to end. 64dc.

Cont inc 16dc on every other round until the motif is the required size.

To do this, the space between each 2dc into 1dc increases by one stitch every increasing round so, round 10, work 2dc into next dc, 1dc into next 3dc; round 12, work 2dc into next dc, 1dc into next 4dc. Cont increasing 16dc on every alternate round in this way until circle is required size. Ss into first st of previous round and fasten off.

String place mat (see page 24)
Size
A place mat 30cm (12in) diameter

Materials
1 ball of gardening twine (available from hardware and gardening stores)
No. 4.00 (ISR) crochet hook

Mat
Work as given for circular motif until 14 rounds have been worked, that is a total of 112dc, but do not fasten off.

Scallop edging
Next round 3ch to count as first dc and 1ch sp, miss first 2dc, 1dc into each of next 3dc, *1ch, miss 1dc, 1dc into each of next 3dc, rep from * to last 2dc, 1dc into each of last 2dc. Join with ss to second of first 3ch.
Next round Into each 1ch sp work (1dc, 3tr, 1dc). Join with ss to first dc. Fasten off.

Working circles to make a clown
The clown is made up of circles in various sizes. Oddments of any Double Knitting in red, yellow, orange and black and a No. 4.00 (ISR) hook are used.
For the main part make a total of 95 circles by working the first and second rounds of the circle motif. The black cuffs and ankle frills have the third round added, while the neck frill has the fourth round worked and the skirt has an additional fifth round.
Also make 2 small black circles for each hand and foot, join each pair of circles and stuff with cotton wool. Make the head in a similar way, but work 3 rounds of the circle motif and include a circle of stiff card with the stuffing.
Use elastic threaded through the centre of each circle and join them together in this way: each arm consists of 17 small circles and a cuff which is inserted 1 circle before the hand, the body has 11 circles plus the skirt, and the legs have 25 circles each plus a frill which again is inserted 1 circle before the foot.

Raffia belt
Size
To fit 58[63:68]cm (23[25:27]in) waist. Each motif measures 5.5cm (2¼in) diameter. The figures in [] refer to the 63cm (25in) and 68cm (27in) sizes respectively.

Materials
Total of 3[3:4] hanks of raffia in one colour or oddments.
No. 3.00 (ISR) crochet hook

Belt motifs
With No. 3.00 (ISR) hook and any colour work first 3 rounds as given for circular motif. Join next colour and work 2 more rounds as given for circular motif. Fasten off. Make 9 [10:11] more motifs in same way.

To make up
Join motifs tog where edges touch to form one row. Make 3 separate ch 122[127:132]cm (48[50:52]in) long. Working on wrong side, stitch one ch across back of top edge of motifs, one across centre and one across lower edge, to tie at centre front. Trim each end of ch with wooden beads to neaten ends if required.

WORKING WITH SQUARES

To work a square in crochet
Either make this square entirely in one colour or use a different colour for each round.
Using a No. 5.00 (ISR) hook and Double Knitting, make 6ch. Join together to form a ring with a ss into the first ch.

1st round 6ch, work (1tr and 3ch) 7 times into the ring. Join with a ss to the 3rd of the first 6ch.

2nd round Ss into the first 3ch space so that the next group of tr will be worked into a space and not into a stitch, work 3ch to count as the first tr, 3tr into this same space, (2ch and 4tr into the next space) 7 times, 2ch. Join with a ss to the 3rd of the first 3ch.

3rd round Ss into each of next 4 stitches to ensure that the next group of tr will be worked into a 2ch space, 3ch, 5tr into this same space, 1ch, (6tr and 3ch into next space, 6tr and 1ch into next space) 3 times, 6tr into next space, 3ch. Join with a ss to the 3rd of the first 3ch.

4th round Ss into each of next 6 stitches to ensure that the hook is over the next 1ch space, 4ch, (1dc into space between the 3rd and 4th tr of next 6tr group, 3ch, 2tr, 3ch, 2tr all into next 3ch space, 3ch, 1dc into space between 3rd and 4th tr of next 6tr group, 3ch, 1dc into next 1ch space, 3ch) 3 times, 1dc into space between 3rd and 4th tr of next 6tr group, 3ch, 2tr,

3ch, 2tr all into next 3ch space, 3ch, 1dc into space between 3rd and 4th tr of next 6tr group, 3ch. Join with a ss to 2nd of the first 4ch. Fasten off.

Granny squares using 2 or more colours
(Breaking off yarn at end of each round.) Make commencing ch and work first round as given for motif in one colour. Break off yarn and fasten off.

2nd round Join next colour to any 2ch sp with ss, 3ch to count as first tr, work 2tr into same ch sp, *1ch, work (3tr, 2ch, 3tr) into next 2ch sp to form corner, rep from * twice more, 1ch, 3tr into same 2ch sp as beginning of round, 2ch. Join with ss to third of first 3ch. Break off yarn and fasten off.

3rd round Join next colour to any 2ch sp with ss, 3ch to count as first tr, work 2tr into same ch sp, *1ch, 3tr into 1ch sp, 1ch, work (3tr, 2ch, 3tr) into 2ch sp, rep from * twice more, 1ch, 3tr into 1ch sp, 1ch, 3tr into same 2ch sp as beginning of round, 2ch. Join with ss to third of first 3ch. Break off yarn and fasten off.

4th round Join next colour to any 2ch sp with ss, 3ch to count as first tr work 2tr into same ch sp, *(1ch, 3tr into next 1ch sp) twice, 1ch, work (3tr, 2ch, 3tr) into 2ch sp, rep from * twice more, (1ch, 3tr into next 1ch sp) twice, 1ch, 3tr into same 2ch sp as beginning of round, 2ch. Join with ss to third of first 3ch. Break off yarn and fasten off. Darn in ends of yarn where colours were joined.

To make a half-square

Using one or more colours Each row must be started with a fresh strand of yarn from the same side at which the row was first begun.

Make 5ch. Join with ss to first ch to form circle.

1st row Using same colour, 4ch to count as first tr and 1ch sp, work (3tr, 2ch, 3tr) into circle, 1ch, 1tr into circle. Break off yarn and fasten off.

2nd row Join next colour to third of first 4ch with ss, 4ch, 3tr into first 1ch sp, 1ch, work (3tr, 2ch, 3tr) into 2ch sp, 1ch, 3tr into last 1ch sp, 1ch, 1tr into top of last tr in previous row. Break off yarn and fasten off.

3rd row Join next colour to third of first 4ch with ss, 4ch, 3tr into first 1ch sp, 1ch, 3tr into next 1ch sp, 1ch, work (3tr, 2ch, 3tr) into 2ch sp, (1ch, 3tr into next 1ch sp) twice, 1ch, 1tr into top of last tr in previous row. Break off yarn and fasten off.

4th row Join next colour to third of first 4ch with ss, 4ch, 3tr into first 1ch sp, 1ch, (3tr into next 1ch sp, 1ch) twice, work (3tr, 2ch, 3tr) into 2ch sp, (1ch, 3tr into next 1ch sp) 3 times, 1ch, 1tr into last tr. Break off yarn and fasten off.

Cushion

A cushion 40cm (16in) square

Materials

250grm (8¾oz) of Double Knitting in one colour; 50grm (1¾oz) in each of 7 contrasting colours, A, B, C, D, E, F and G. One No. 4.00 (ISR) crochet hook Cushion pad 40cm (16in) square 20cm (8in) zip fastener

Large square

Using No. 4.00 (ISR) crochet hook and any colour, work first 4 rounds as for square, changing colour for each round.

5th round Join in any colour with ss to corner 2ch sp, 3ch to count as first tr, 2tr into same sp, *(1ch, 3tr into next 1ch sp) 3 times, 1ch, (3tr, 2ch, 3tr) into corner 2ch sp, rep from * twice more, (1ch, 3tr into next 1ch sp) 3 times, 1ch, 3tr into same sp as beg of round, 2ch. Join with ss to third of first 3ch. Break off yarn and fasten off.

Cont in this way changing the colour as shown and working one more group of 3tr and 1ch on each side on every round until work measures 40cm (16in) across. Fasten off. Darn in all ends. Make another square.

To make up

With RS of squares tog, join 3 edges. Turn RS out. Insert cushion pad. Join rem

seam, leaving sp to insert zip in centre.

Edging Using No. 4.00 (ISR) hook and any colour, rejoin yarn with ss to any corner sp through both thicknesses. Into each ch sp round all edges work (1ss, 4tr, 1ss)

working through both thicknesses, except across zip fastener opening, where you only work through one thickness. Join with ss to first ss. Fasten off. Sew in zip.

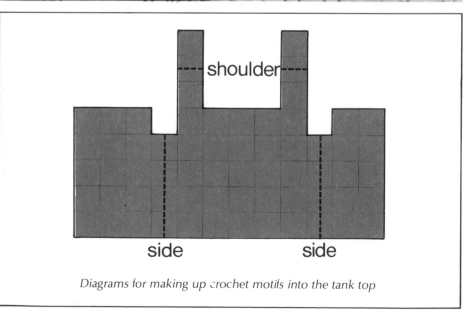

Diagrams for making up crochet motifs into the tank top

28

Crochet top

Sizes

86.5[91.5/96.5:99/101.5]cm (34[36/38: 39/40]in) bust
Length to shoulder, 49.5[53.5:57]cm (19½[21:22½]in)
The figures in brackets [] refer to the 91.5cm (36in), 96.5cm (38in) and 101.5cm (40in) sizes respectively

Tension

One square motif for first size measures 7.5cm × 7.5cm (3in × 3in) worked on No. 2.50 (ISR) hook; for second size measures 8cm × 8cm (3¼in × 3¼in) worked on No. 3.00 (ISR) hook; for third size measure 9cm × 9cm (3½in × 3½in) worked on No. 3.50 (ISR) hook

Materials

Wendy Double Knitting Nylonised 7[8:8] balls in main shade, A
contrast colour, B 6[8:8] balls of
One No. 2.50 [3.00:3.50] (ISR) crochet hook

Working the motifs

1st square motif (make 10)
Using No.2.50[3.00:3.50] (ISR) hook and B, make 4ch. Join with a ss into first ch to form a circle.
1st round 3ch to count as first tr, 2tr into circle, *1ch, 3tr into circle, rep from * twice more, 1ch. Join with a ss into 3rd of 3ch.
2nd round Ss into next ch sp, 3ch to count as first tr, 2tr into same sp, 1ch, 3tr into same sp, *1ch, into next ch sp work 3tr, 1ch and 3tr, rep from * twice more, 1ch. Join with a ss into 3rd of 3ch. Break off B.
3rd round Join in A. Ss into next ch sp, 3ch to count as first tr, 3tr into same sp, 1ch, 4tr into same sp, 1dc into next ch sp, *into next ch sp work 4tr, 1ch and 4tr, 1dc into next ch sp, rep from * twice more. Join with a ss into 3rd of 3ch.
4th round Ss into next ch sp, 3ch to count as first tr, 2tr into same sp, 1ch, 3tr into same sp, into next ch sp of 2 rounds below work 3dtr, 1ch and 3dtr, *into next ch sp of previous round work 3tr, 1ch and 3tr, into next ch sp of 2 rounds below work 3dtr, 1ch and 3dtr, rep from * twice more. Join with a ss into 3rd of 3ch. Fasten off.
2nd square motif (make 10)
As 1st square motif in colour sequence of 2 rounds A and 2 rounds B.
3rd square motif (make 11)
As 1st square motif in colour sequence of 1 round B, 2 rounds A and 1 round B.
4th square motif (make 10)
As 1st square motif in colour sequence of 1 round B, 1 round A, 1 round B and 1 round A.

5th square motif (make 11)
As 1st square motif in colour sequence of 1 round A, 2 rounds B and 1 round A.
6th square motif (make 12)
As 1st square motif in colour sequence of 1 round A, 1 round B, 1 round A and 1 round B.
64 square motifs should be worked in all to complete the top.

To make up

Press each square under a damp cloth with a warm iron. Using A, join squares as shown in diagram making a patchwork with the different colour combinations.

Edging Using No.2.50[3.00:3.50] (ISR) hook and A, work 1 row dc round each armhole, neck and shoulder edges and lower edge.

A bright bag
from Granny squares

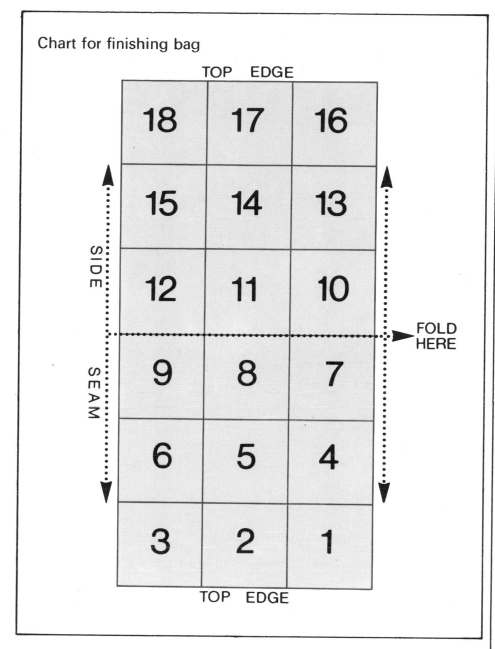

Chart for finishing bag

TOP EDGE

18	17	16
15	14	13
12	11	10
9	8	7
6	5	4
3	2	1

SIDE SEAM

◀ FOLD HERE

TOP EDGE

after last petal, 3ch. Join with a ss to 2nd of first 2ch.

5th round Using C, 1ch, *4ch, into 4ch sp work (3tr, 3ch, 3tr) to form corner, 4ch, 1dc into htr, 1dc into 3ch sp, 1dc into htr, rep from * twice more, 4ch, work corner, 4ch, 1dc into htr, 1dc into 3ch sp. Join with a ss to first ch. Break off C. Join in D.

6th round Using D, 1ch, *5ch, 1tr into each of next 3tr, 5ch, insert hook into 3rd ch from hook and work 1dc to form picot – called 5ch picot –, 2ch, 1tr into each of next 3tr, 5ch, ss into next dc, 4ch, insert hook into 3rd ch from hook and work 1dc to form picot – called 4ch picot –, 1ch, miss 1dc, ss into next dc, rep from * twice more, 5ch, 1tr into each of next 3tr, 5ch picot, 2ch, 1tr into each of next 3tr, 5ch, ss into next dc, 4ch picot, 1ch. Join with a ss to first ch. Fasten off.

Second motif

Using colours as required, work as given for 1st motif until 5th round has been completed.

6th round (joining round) Using any colour, 1ch, *5ch, 1tr into each of next 3tr, 2ch, with RS of 1st motif facing RS of 2nd motif work 1dc into 5ch picot at corner of 1st motif, 2ch, 1tr into each of next 3tr of 2nd motif, ss into first of 5ch after last tr on 1st motif, 4ch, ss into next dc of 2nd motif, 1ch, 1dc into 4ch picot of 1st motif, 1ch, miss 1dc on 2nd motif, ss into next dc on 2nd motif, 4ch, ss into last ch before next 3tr on 1st motif, 1tr into each of next 3tr on 2nd motif, 2ch, 1dc into 5ch picot at corner of 1st motif, 2ch, complete round as given for 1st motif. Work 16 more motifs in same way, using colours as required and joining each motif where edges touch, as shown in diagram.

To make up

Darn in all ends. Press on WS under a dry cloth with a cool iron.

Top edges Using No.5.00 (ISR) hook, A and with RS of work facing, rejoin yarn to corner picot at end of motif, 3ch to count as first tr, work 14 more tr evenly across first motif, work (15tr across next motif) twice. Turn. 45tr. Work 2 more rows tr. Fasten off. Work along other end in same way.

With RS facing fold motifs in half and join side seams as shown in diagram. Seam lining in same way. Turn bag RS out and insert loose lining. Fold top edge over handle to WS and sl st down. Work other handle in same way. Sl st top of lining to WS of top edge, easing in fullness. Sew lining to side edges of opening.

Size

45.5cm (18in) wide by 45.5cm (18in) deep

Tension

Each motif measures 15cm (6in) by 15cm (6in) worked on No.5.00 (ISR) crochet hook

Materials

3 × 50 grm balls of Mahony Blarney Claude in main shade, A
1 ball each of 5 contrast colours, B, C, D, E and F
One No.5.00 (ISR) crochet hook
2 round wooden handles
Lining material 45.5cm (18in) wide by 91.5cm (36in) long

First motif

Using No.5.00 (ISR) hook and A, make 6ch. Join with a ss to first ch to form circle.

1st round Using A, 2ch to count as first dc, work 15dc into circle. Join with a ss to 2nd of first 2ch.

2nd round Using A, 5ch to count as first htr and 3ch, *miss 1dc, 1htr into next dc, 3ch, rep from * 6 times more. Join with a ss to 2nd of first 5ch. Break off A. Join in B.

3rd round Using B, work (1dc, 1htr, 1tr, 1htr, 1dc, 1ch) into each ch sp to end. Join with a ss to first dc. 8 petals. Break off B. Join in C.

4th round Using C, 2ch to count as first htr, *3ch, 1dc into tr of next petal, 4ch, 1dc into tr of next petal, 3ch, 1htr into 1ch sp before next petal, 3ch, 1htr into same ch sp, rep from * twice more, 3ch, 1dc in tr of next petal, 4ch, 1dc in tr of next petal, 3ch, 1htr into last 1ch sp

SQUARE AND WHEEL MOTIFS

The simple stitches you have learnt can be used for all sorts of motifs, including these two completely different lacy ones. The motifs can be worked in fine or thick yarns, depending on purpose or personal choice.

Square lace motif

Make 6ch. Join with ss to first ch to form circle.

1st round 2ch to count as first dc, work 15dc into circle. Join with ss to second of first 2ch.

2nd round 4ch to count as first htr and 2ch, *miss 1dc, 1htr into next dc, 2ch, rep from * 6 times more. Join with ss to second of first 4ch.

3rd round Work (1dc, 1htr, 1tr, 1htr, 1dc, 1ch) into each ch sp to end. Join with ss to first dc. 8 petals.

4th round 2ch to count as first htr, *3dc, 1dc into tr of next petal, 4ch, 1dc into tr of next petal, 3ch, 1htr into 1ch sp before next petal, 2ch, 1htr into same ch sp, rep from * twice more, 3ch, 1dc into tr of next petal, 4ch, 1dc into tr of next petal, 3ch, 1htr into last 1ch sp after last petal, 2ch. Join with ss to second of first 2ch.

5th round 1ch, *4ch, into 4ch sp work (3tr, 3ch, 3tr) to form corner, 4ch, 1dc into htr, 1dc into 2ch sp, 1dc into htr, rep from * twice more, 4ch, into 4ch sp work (3tr, 3ch, 3tr), 4ch, 1dc into htr, 1dc into 2ch sp. Join with ss to first ch.

6th round 1ch, *5ch, 1tr into each of next 3tr, 5ch, insert hook into third ch from hook to form a little loop (see diagram) and work 1dc to form picot – called 5ch picot – 2ch, 1tr into each of next 3tr, 5ch, ss into next dc, 4ch, insert hook into third ch from hook and work 1dc to form picot – called 4ch picot –

Forming a picot loop

1ch, miss 1dc, ss into next dc, rep from * twice more, 5ch, 1tr into each of next 3tr, 5ch picot, 2ch, 1tr into each of next 3tr, 5ch, ss into next dc, 4ch picot, 1ch. Join with ss to first ch. Fasten off.

Catherine wheel motif

Make 8ch. Join with ss to first ch to form circle.

1st round 1ch to count as first dc, work 15dc into circle. Join with ss to first ch. 16 sts. Do not break off yarn.

First spoke

1st row Make 14ch, work 1dc into third ch from hook, 1dc into next ch, work 10dc around, and not into, the ch, 1dc into each of last 3ch, ss into next dc along the circle, turn.

2nd row Work 1dc into each of first 3dc, (4ch, miss 1dc, 1dc into next dc) 5 times, 1dc into each of next 2dc, 1dc into second of first 2ch. Turn.

3rd row 1ch to count as first dc, 1dc into each of next 3dc, (4dc into 4ch loop, 1dc into next dc) 5 times, 1dc into each of last 2dc, ss into next dc along the circle, turn.

Second spoke

1st row Make 13ch, ss into centre st of third loop along first spoke, turn, work 1dc into each of next 3ch, work 10dc around the ch, 1dc into each of last 3ch, ss into next dc along circle, turn and complete as for first spoke but on next row end with 1dc into each of last 3dc instead of last 2dc and turning ch.

Work 6 more spokes in the same way and when working the last one, join the centre of the 3rd loop to the tip of the first spoke. Fasten off. 8 spokes.

Last round Rejoin yarn with ss to top of any spoke, 1ch to count as first dc, work 1dc into each st round outside edge of motif. Join with ss to first ch. Fasten off.

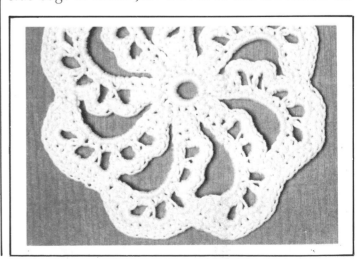

Cafe curtain

Size

Curtain 140cm (55in) wide by 140cm (55in) long, excluding tabs, each motif measures 13cm (5in) diameter

Materials

11 × 84m (77yd) balls of 4 ply cotton in main shade, A, 10 balls of contrast colour, B, 9 balls of contrast colour, C and 7 balls each of contrast colours, D and E. 1 ball makes 2 motifs
One No. 3.00 (ISR) crochet hook
Length of wooden curtain rail

Curtain

Make 22 catherine wheel motifs in A, 20 in B, 18 in C, 14 in D and 13 in E.

To make up

Join motifs tog as shown in diagram on opposite page.

Tabs Using No. 3.00 (ISR) hook, appropriate colour and with RS of first top motif facing, rejoin yarn with ss to fifth dc along edge, 3ch to count as first tr, work 1tr into each of next 5dc, turn. 6 sts. Cont working rows of tr across these 6 sts until tab is long enough to go over top of curtain rail and down to top of motif. Fasten off. Work 10 more tabs in same way. St tabs in place to back of each motif.

Place mat and coaster

Size

For place mat 28cm ($11\frac{1}{4}$in) wide by 23cm (9in) deep and coaster 11cm ($4\frac{1}{2}$in) square. Each motif measures 5.5cm ($2\frac{1}{4}$in) square

Materials

40grm of No. 20 cotton (1 ball makes approximately 23 motifs)
One No. 1.50 (ISR) crochet hook.

Mat

Work as given for square lace motif, joining 5 motifs to form one row, 4 rows in all, total 20 motifs.

Coaster

Work as given for square lace motif, joining 2 motifs to form one row, 2 rows in all, total 4 motifs.

Below: Crochet place mat and coaster

To join square lace motifs

Work first 5 rounds as given for motif.
6th round (joining round) 1ch, *5ch, 1tr into each of next 3tr, 2ch, with RS of completed motif A facing RS of motif B which is to be joined work 1dc into 5ch picot at corner of motif A, 2ch, 1tr into each of next 3tr of motif B, ss into first of 5ch after last tr on motif A, 4ch, ss into next dc of motif B, 1ch, 1dc into 4ch picot of motif A, 1ch, miss 1dc on motif B, ss next dc on motif B, 4ch, ss into last ch into before next 3tr on motif A, 1tr into each of next 3tr on motif B, 2ch, 1dc into 4ch picot at corner of motif A, 2ch. One side has been joined. Complete round motif B as given for square lace motif A. Fasten off. Where the squares have to be joined on two sides continue in the same way.

Above: Diagram to show how Catherine wheel motifs are joined for a café curtain

Above: Catherine wheel motifs used as edging for a circular tablecloth

35

USING COLOUR
PATCHWORK EFFECTS

This chapter explains how to work crochet, using various colours to form a patchwork effect, all in one process. Several samples are shown and explained in detail to help you follow the methods involved in this technique. As with patchwork crochet using separate shapes (see later) it is best to use the same weight of yarn throughout the work to make sure you keep an even tension and so give a good fabric. Multi-coloured fabrics can be worked in straight lines, or circles and other shapes in the same way as plain coloured crochet. The most popular stitch to give a good fabric is the double crochet.

Sample 1

Two colours of double knitting yarn, A and B, have been used to work this basic patchwork design which is formed from checked squares. The techniques covered in this sample are the method of joining in a new colour and the method of carrying the colour not in use in with the work. To help you work this first sample, we are giving both written instructions and a chart.

Using No.4.50 (ISR) hook and A, make a length of chain with multiples of 5+1 stitches.

Note Practise the method of joining in a new colour which is given in the 1st row as it is important that the new colour is joined into the stitch preceding the stitches to be worked in the new colour. Further

instructions for joining in new colours will not be given in detail, but this method should be used throughout. The colour not in use is held along the line of work and this is kept in place by the crochet stitch being worked over the yarn. This avoids ugly loops appearing on the work and also ensures that the work is completely reversible.

1st row Using colour A, into 3rd ch from hook work 1dc, 1dc into each of next 2ch, insert hook into next ch, yrh and draw through a loop, yrh with colour B and draw through both loops on hook, using colour B, work 1dc into each of next 5ch, using colour A, work 1dc into each of next 5ch, cont in this way working 5 sts alternately in A and B to end of row. Turn.

2nd row Using same colour as last 5dc of previous row and working over colour not in use as before, work 1ch to count as first dc, 1dc into each of next 4dc, change colour, 1dc into each of next 5dc, cont in this way to end of row, working last dc into turning ch. Turn.

3rd to 5th rows As 2nd.

6th to 10th rows As 2nd, working a square of colour A over colour B and a square of colour B over colour A. The 1st to 10th rows form the colour sequence for this sample. When you have completed this sample, you will see how the instructions compare with the squared diagram and you will be able to make up your own designs using this technique.

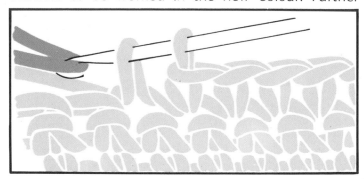

Joining in a new color in the middle of a row

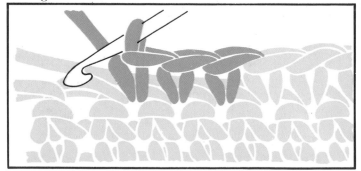

Working over the color which is not in use

Sample 2

Here we have used the same techniques as explained in sample 1, but a much more varied effect has been achieved by using three colours and random shapes. As there is no definite pattern of shapes, oddments of colour can quite easily be used. A further technique is employed here, where the yarn not in use is left on the wrong side of the work ready for taking into the work again on the next row. This method is used when a coloured yarn is being used in one block only. Remember that should a colour of yarn which is already in use be required further along the row, then this yarn must be carried along the row until required. Using No.4.50 (ISR) hook and 3 colours of double knitting yarn, make 24ch. Work in double crochet and follow the chart to make our sample.

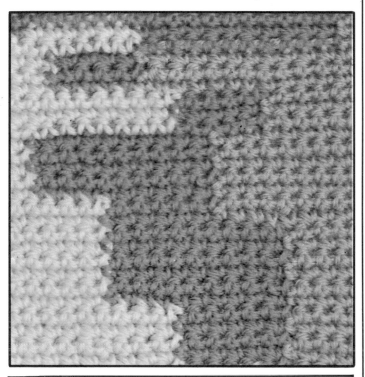

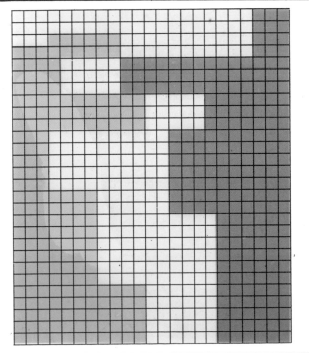

Sample 3

This is a lovely patchwork fabric made up of traditional church window shapes worked in many different colours. The effect of these colours and shapes is very fashionable when they are made into garments such as long skirts, waistcoats or tank tops. Household items such as cushion covers and rugs also look very attractive when they are worked in this way.

As so many colours are used it is a good idea to work a single church window shape to estimate how much yarn is required for each individual shape. Then, when you are deciding on your colours, wind each colour of yarn into balls of the correct length.

Using No.4.50 (ISR) hook and double knitting yarn, make a chain with multiples of 8+1 stitches and follow our diagram, changing colour for each shape. There is no need to work over the colour not in use. This should be left behind the work until the next row where it is required. When a shape in one colour is finished, leave the end of yarn hanging free and darn in all ends on the wrong side of the work when it is completed.

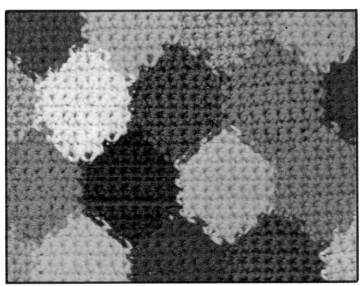

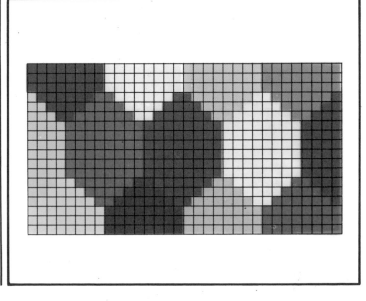

COLOUR DESIGNS

Here we continue our chapters on the use of different coloured yarns within a single piece of crochet work, by showing how lines of colour can be incorporated into a design. This sort of design would be ideal for border patterns on a plain piece of work such as a scarf, skirt or bedcover. In some of the samples shown here the lines of colour are raised from the background by applying a technique known as blistering and this is described in detail.

Sample 1

This is a double sided fabric, worked in two colours of double knitting yarn, A and B. Using No.4.50 (ISR) hook and A, make 21ch.

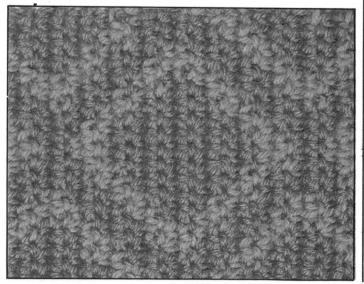

1st row Into 3rd ch from hook work 1dc, 1dc into next ch, join in B as explained in previous chapter, using B and working over A (see previous chapter), work 1dc into each of next 2ch, using A and working over B work 1dc into each of next 10ch, using B and working over A work 1dc into each of next 2ch, using A and working over B work 1dc into each of next 3ch. Turn. Continue in this way, working in pattern from the chart.

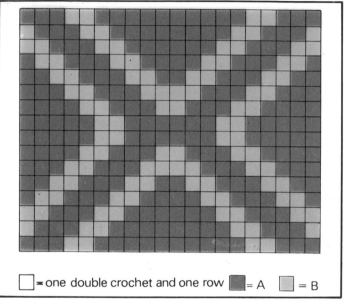

☐ = one double crochet and one row ■ = A ☐ = B

Sample 2

Here two colours of double knitting yarn, A and B, have been used to give a raised, or blistered, effect to the work. When working individual narrow lines of colour which follow through a design, it is not always necessary to carry the yarn not in use in with the work. Just leave this yarn behind the work ready to be worked into the crochet on the next row. There is a definite right and wrong side to the work when this technique is used. Using No.3.50 (ISR) hook and A, make 21ch.

1st row Into 3rd ch from hook work 1dc, 1dc into each of next 5ch, join in B as explained in previous chapter, leaving A hanging on WS of work, using B work 1dc into each of next 6ch joining in A on the last st, pull A taut to form a blister, using A work 1dc into each of next 7ch. Turn.

2nd row Using A work 1ch to count as first dc, miss first st, 1dc into each of next 6dc joining in B on the last st and placing A towards you whilst you work, 1dc into each of next 6dc using B and joining in A on the last st worked, leave B on WS of work (towards you) and pull A taut to form a blister, using A work 1dc into each of next 7dc. Turn.

3rd row Using A work 1ch to count as first dc, miss first st, 1dc into each of next 6dc joining in B on the last st, leave A on WS of work (away from you), work 1dc into each of next 6dc using B and joining in A on the last st, leave B on WS of work and pull A taut to form a blister, using A work 1dc into each of next 7dc. Turn.

The 2nd and 3rd rows are repeated throughout.

Sample 3

In this sample the two techniques of working over the yarn not in use or leaving it free at the back of the work are mixed. The background colour, A, is carried throughout, whilst the other colours in the design, B, C and D are left free at the back of the work when not in use. Using No. 3.50 (ISR) hook and A, make 17ch.

1st row Join in colour B see previous chapter, using B work 1dc into 3rd ch from hook, 1dc into each of next 2ch working over A, using A work 1dc into each of next 2ch, using C work 1dc into each of next

2ch, using A work 1dc into each of next 2ch, using D work 1dc into each of next 4ch, using A work 1dc into next ch. Turn.

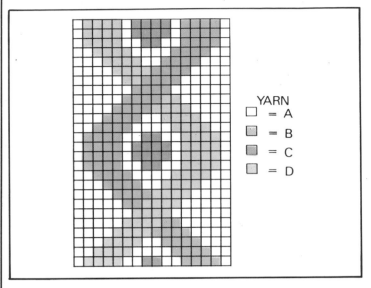

YARN
☐ = A
▨ = B
▩ = C
▦ = D

2nd row Using A work 1ch to count as first dc, miss first st, 1dc into next dc, using D work 1dc into each of next 4dc, using A work 1dc into each of next 4dc, using B work 1dc into each of next 4dc, using A work 1dc into each of next 2dc. Turn.

Continue working in this way from the chart, noting that yarn C forms a small area of colour so that the yarn may be cut after each motif is finished to avoid unnecessary yarns hanging behind the work.

Sample 4

Our belt has been worked in 3 colours of double knitting yarn, using a No.3.50 (ISR) hook. Follow the chart given for sample 3, omitting colour C and form a blistered or raised effect on the crossover lines by applying the technique used in sample 2 and keeping A taut whilst it is not in use. A large bead has been added as decoration in the centre of each diamond.

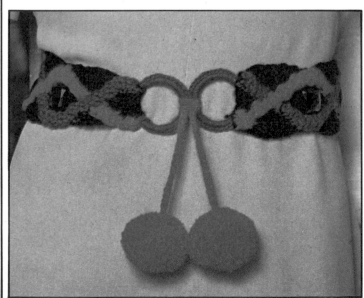

A hat of many colours

Size
To fit an average head

Tension
12htr and 9 rows to 5cm (*2in*) over patt worked on No.3.50 (ISR) crochet hook

Materials
1× one oz ball Lister Lavenda 4 ply in each of 5 colours, A, B, C, D and E
One No.3.50 (ISR) crochet hook

Note
When using two different coloured yarns in the same round, always work over the colour not in use and when changing colour, draw the new colour through all the loops on the hook of the last st in the old colour

Hat
Using No.3.50 (ISR) hook and A, make 6ch. Join with a ss into first ch to form circle.

1st round Using A, 2ch to count as first htr, 7htr into circle. Join with a ss into 2nd of 2ch. 8htr. Break off A.

2nd round Using B, 2ch to count as first htr, 1htr into st at base of ch, *2htr into next htr, rep from * to end. Join with a ss into 2nd of 2ch. 16htr.

3rd round Using 4 sts each of B and C all round, work 2ch to count as first htr, 2htr into next htr, *1htr into next htr, 2htr into next htr, rep from * to end. Join with a ss into 2nd of 2ch. 24htr.

Break off B and C.

4th round Using D, 2ch, 1htr into next htr, 2htr into next htr, *1htr into each of next 2htr, 2htr into next htr, rep from * to end. Join with a ss into 2nd of 2ch. 32htr.

5th round Using 5 sts each of D and E all round, work 2ch, 1htr into each of next 2 htr, 2htr into next htr, *1htr into each of next 3 htr, 2htr into next htr, rep from * to end. Join with a ss into 2nd of 2ch. 40 htr. Break off E.

6th round Using D, 2ch, 1htr into each of next 3 htr, 2htr into next htr, *1htr into each of next 4 htr, 2htr into next htr, rep

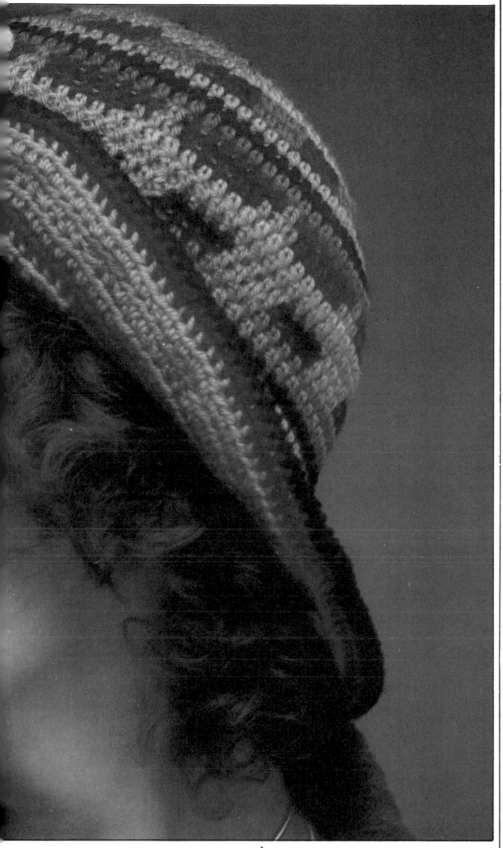

each of next 7 htr, 2htr into next htr, rep from * to end. Join with a ss into 2nd of 2ch. 72htr. Break off A.

10th round Using E, 2ch, 1htr into each of next 7 htr, 2htr into next htr, *1htr into each of next 8 htr, 2htr into next htr, rep from * to end. Join with a ss into 2nd of 2ch. 80htr. Break off E.

11th round Using 4 sts each of B and D all round, 2ch, 1htr into each of next 8 htr, 2htr into next htr, *1htr into each of next 9 htr, 2htr into next htr, rep from * to end. Join with a ss into 2nd of 2ch. 88htr.

12th round Using 4 sts each of B and D and working into same colours in previous round, 2ch, 1htr into each htr to end. Join with a ss into 2nd of 2ch. Break off B and D.

13th round Using E, as 12th. Break off E.

14th round Using C, as 12th. Break off C.

15th round Using B, as 12th. Break off B.

16th round Using one st of A and 7 sts of D all round, as 12th.

17th round Using 3 sts of A and 5 sts of D all round, as 12th. Break off A and D.

18th round Using E, as 12th. Break off E.

19th round Using A, as 12th.

20th round Using 4 sts of A and 4 sts of C all round, as 12th.

21st round As 20th. Break off A and C.

22nd round Using B, as 12th. Break off B.

23rd round Using A, as 12th.

24th round Using C, as 12th.

25th round Using 3 sts of B and 5 sts of E all round, as 12th. Break off B and E.

26th round Using D, as 12th.

27th round As 26th.

Shape brim

28th round Using E, 2ch, 2htr into next htr, *1htr into next htr, 2htr into next htr, rep from * to end. Join with a ss into 2nd of 2ch. 132htr. Break off E.

29th round Using B, as 12th. Break off B.

30th round Using C, as 12th. Break off C.

31st round Using 8 sts of A and 4 sts of E all round, as 12th. Break off A and E.

32nd round Using D, 2ch, 1htr into each of next 4 htr, 2htr into next htr, *1htr into each of next 5 htr, 2htr into next htr, rep from * to end. Join with a ss into 2nd of 2ch. 154htr. Break off D.

33rd round Using A, as 12th.

34th round Using 4 sts of A and 3 sts of B all round, as 12th. Break off A and B.

35th round Using E, 2ch, 1htr into each of next 5 htr, 2htr into next htr, *1htr into each of next 6 htr, 2htr into next htr, rep from * to end. Join with a ss into 2nd of 2ch. 176htr. Break off E.

36th round Using D, as 12th. Break off D.

37th round Using C and working from left to right (i.e. in a backwards direction), work 1dc into each htr to end. Join with a ss into first dc. Fasten off.

from * to end. Join with a ss into 2nd of 2ch. 48htr. Break off D.

7th round Using C, 2ch, 1htr into each of next 4 htr, 2htr into next htr, *1htr into each of next 5 htr, 2htr into next htr, rep from * to end. Join with a ss into 2nd of 2ch. 56htr. Break off C.

8th round Using A, 2ch, 1htr into each of next 5 htr, 2htr into next htr, *1htr into each of next 6 htr, 2htr into next htr, rep from * to end. Join with a ss into 2nd of 2ch. 64htr.

9th round Using A, 2ch, 1htr into each of next 6 htr, 2htr into next htr, *1htr into

PATCHWORK CROCHET

Patchwork crochet

Traditionally we think of patchwork as a means of using oddments of fabric to obtain a quilt or garment. Today there is a great revival of interest in the art, and fabrics are carefully selected and co-ordinated to create colourful and exciting designs.

The same designs may be worked in crochet, again using oddments of yarn to use up scraps, or choosing a selection of colours to produce a desired effect. A pleasing choice of colours is a vital point in patchwork for this can make or mar a design. Closely related colours are usually a satisfactory choice, so that if you choose red, then you may use all the various shades of red from deep ruby to oranges and yellows. Our samples have been worked in blues and greens to illustrate the same idea.

Patchwork crochet has many purposes both for garments and in the home. Typical examples of household items are quilts, cushion covers, rugs, wall hangings and room dividers. The most suitable garments are ones which require little or no shaping, such as straight skirts, jerkins and belts.

In order to achieve a high standard of work, it is necessary to use the same weight of yarn throughout, although to add interest they may be of different textures. As the yarn should be of one weight, then the same size crochet hook may be used for each. Firm, even stitches, such as double crochet or half trebles, should be used for the crochet in order to make a precise shape.

The shapes described in this chapter are all geometrical and include the square, rectangle, diamond, triangle and hexagonal. They are all worked in a double knitting yarn using a No.4.00 (ISR) crochet hook.

To join the separate shapes you should place the right sides together and oversew with a firm stitch in the same yarn. The seam may be pressed on the wrong side under a damp cloth with a warm iron. Where there is more than one colour used in the same shape, such as samples 5 and 6, these are joined into the work as required.

Sample 1

To work the diamond shape Make 3ch.
1st row Into 3rd ch from hook work 1dc. Turn. 2 sts.
2nd row 1ch to count as first st, 1dc into st at base of ch, 1dc into turning ch. Turn. One st increased.
3rd row 1ch to count as first st, 1dc into st at base of ch, 1dc into next st, 1dc into turning ch. Turn. One st increased.
Cont in this way, inc one st at beg of every row, until

there are 20 sts.
Next row 1ch to count as first st, miss next st, 1dc into next st, 1dc into each st to end, finishing with 1dc into turning ch. Turn. One st decreased.
Cont in this way, dec one st at beg of every row, until 2 sts rem. Fasten off.

Sample 2

To work the church window shape Work as given for sample 1, but when the required size or width is reached (20 sts, for example), work 14 rows without shaping. Then work the decrease shaping as before.

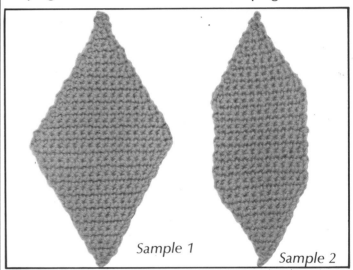

Sample 1

Sample 2

Sample 3

To work the triangle Make 3ch.
1st row Into 3rd ch from hook work 1htr. Turn. 2 sts.
2nd row 2ch to count as first htr, 1htr into st at base of ch, 2htr into 2nd of 2ch. Turn. 2 sts increased.
3rd row 2ch to count as first htr, 1htr into st at base of ch, 1htr into each of next 2 sts, 2htr into 2nd of 2ch. Turn. 2 sts increased.
Cont in this way, inc one st at each end of every row, until there are 24 sts or the triangle is the required size. Fasten off.

Sample 4

To work the hexagon Make 5ch. Join with a ss into first ch to form a circle.
1st round 4ch, *1tr into circle, 1ch, rep from * 10 times more. Join with a ss into 3rd of 4ch.
2nd round 3ch to count as first tr, 2tr into next 1ch sp, 1tr into next tr, 1ch, *1tr into next tr, 2tr into next 1ch sp, 1tr into next tr, 1ch, rep from * 4 times more. Join with a ss into 3rd of 3ch.
3rd round 3ch to count as first tr, 1tr into st at base of ch, 1tr into each of next 2tr, 2tr into next tr, 2ch, *2tr

into next tr, 1tr into each of next 2tr, 2tr into next tr, 2ch, rep from * 4 times more. Join with a ss into 3rd of 3ch. Fasten off.

This completes the sample illustrated, but a smaller or larger shape could be achieved by working in the same way, inc one st at each end of every block of tr and one ch between blocks on every round, until the shape is the desired size.

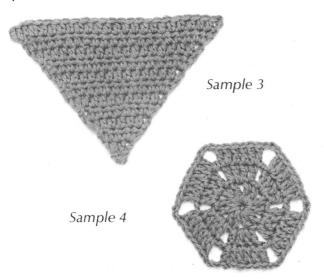

Sample 3

Sample 4

Sample 5

Four colours, A, B, C and D, are used for this sample which illustrates a square. See the effect of the colours when four squares are joined together. Using A, make 17ch.

1st row Into 3rd ch from hook work 1dc, 1dc into each ch to end. Turn. 16 sts.

2nd row 1ch to count as first dc, 1dc into each dc to end, finishing with 1dc into turning ch. Turn.

Rep last row twice more. Break off A. Join in B.

Note Care should be taken when joining in a new colour. It is better to work 2 turning chains instead of 1 and then pull up the old colour tightly. Work 4 rows in dc with each of B, C and D. Fasten off. Sew in the cut ends. Place squares to give the desired pattern and sew together.

Sample 6

Here four triangular shapes, as given in sample 3, have been worked with four colours in each and then joined together.

Work 2 triangles with 4 rows each in A, B, C and D, and then 2 more triangles using the colour sequence of D, C, B and A. Position with alternate colours meeting and then sew together. Neaten the cut ends by threading back into the work on the wrong side.

Sample 7

This sample is made up of brick shapes. There are 16 in all, 4 in each colour.

To work the brick shape Make 11ch.

1st row Into 3rd ch from hook work 1dc, 1dc into each ch to end. Turn. 10 sts.

2nd row 1ch to count as first dc, 1dc into each dc to end, finishing with 1dc into turning ch. Turn.

Rep last row 3 times more. Fasten off.

Work the required number of bricks in each colour and position carefully in rows of one colour before sewing into place. When finished, sew in all the cut ends on the wrong side of the work.

A patchwork jacket

Sizes

To fit 86.5[91.5:96.5:101.5]cm (34[36:38: 40]in) bust/chest
Length to shoulder, 68.5[68.5:76:76]cm (27[27:30:30]in)
Sleeve seam, 46[46:51:51]cm (18[18:20: 20]in)
The figures in brackets [] refer to the 91.5 (36), 96.5 (38) and 101.5cm (40in) sizes respectively

Tension

18 sts and 9 rows to 10cm (3.9in) over tr worked on No.3.50 (ISR) crochet hook

Materials

11[12:12:13] × 50grm balls of Mahony Killowen Double Knitting in main shade, A
2[2:2:2] balls each of contrast colours, B and C
1[1:1:2] balls of contrast colour, D
1[2:2:3] balls of contrast colour, E
One No.3.50 (ISR) crochet hook
66[66:71:71]cm (26[26:28:28]in) open ended zip fastener

Back

Using No.3.50 (ISR) hook and A, make 82 [88:94:96]ch.
1st row Into 4th ch from hook work 1tr, 1tr into each ch to end. Turn. 80[86:92: 94]tr.
2nd row 3ch to count as first tr, miss first tr, 1tr into each tr to end. Turn.
Rep 2nd row 40[40:49:49] times more.
Shape raglan armholes
Next row Ss across first 6[6:7:7]tr, 1tr into each tr to last 6[6:7:7]tr, turn.
Next row 3ch to count as first tr, yrh, insert hook into next tr, yrh and draw through loop, yrh and draw through 2 loops on hook, yrh and insert hook into next tr, yrh and draw through loop, yrh and draw through 2 loops on hook, yrh and draw through 3 loops on hook – called dec 1 –, 1tr into each tr to last 3tr, dec 1, 1tr into last tr. Turn.
Rep last row 19[19:21:21] times more. Fasten off.

Sleeves

Using No.3.50 (ISR) hook and A, make 40 [40:49:49]ch. Work 1st row as given for back. 38[38:47:47]tr.
1st and 2nd sizes only
Work 2 rows tr.
4th row 3ch, 2tr into next tr – called inc 1 –, 1tr into each tr to last 2tr, inc 1, 1tr into last tr. Turn.
Work 2 rows tr without shaping. Cont inc in this way on next and every foll 3rd row until 34 rows have been worked from beg, then inc in same way on every foll 2nd row 5 times in all. 70[70]tr.

3rd and 4th sizes only

Work 4 rows tr. Inc as given for 1st and 2nd sizes on next and every foll 4th row until 21 rows have been worked from beg, then inc in same way on every foll 3rd row until there are 77[77]tr.
All sizes
Shape raglans
Next row Ss across first 6[6:7:7]tr, 3ch, 1tr into each tr to last 6[6:7:7]tr, turn.
Dec one st at each end of every row until 30[30:31:31]tr rem.
Next row 3ch, dec 1, 1tr into each of next 9tr, dec 1, 1tr into each of next 2[2:3:3]tr, dec 1, 1tr into each of next 9tr, dec 1, 1tr into last tr. Turn.
Next row 3ch, dec 1, 1tr into each of next 7tr, dec 1, 1tr into each of next 2[2:3:3]tr, dec 1, 1tr into each of next 7tr, dec 1, 1tr into last tr. Turn.
Cont dec in this way on next 4 rows. 6[6:7:7]tr. Fasten off.

Left and right fronts

Work motifs for fronts, noting that colours may be varied as required and should be twisted at back of work when changing colours.
1st motif
Using A, make 16[16:18:18] ch.
1st row Into 4th ch from hook work 1tr, 1tr into each ch to end. Turn. 14[14:16:16] tr.
2nd row 3ch to count as first tr, miss 1tr, 1tr into each tr to end. Turn.
Rep 2nd row 5[5:6:6] times more.
Fasten off and darn in ends. Work 1 more motif in same way using A, then 2 motifs each in B, C, D and E. 10 motifs, 5 for each front.
2nd motif
Using A, work first 2 rows as given for 1st motif. Break off A. Join in E. Complete as given for 1st motif. Work 1 more motif in same way, then 2 more using D and C and 2 more using E and B. 6 motifs, 3 for each front.
3rd motif
Using B, make 7[7:8:8] ch, join in D and make 9[9:10:10] ch.
1st row Using D, into 4th ch from hook work 1tr, 1tr into each of next 5[5:6:6] ch working last 2 loops of last tr with B – called 1trNc –, using B, work 1tr into each ch to end. Turn. 7[7:8:8] tr each in D and B.
2nd row Using B, 3ch to count as first tr, 1tr into each of next 6[6:7:7] tr, putting B to front of work and D to back under hook to work 1trNc with D on last tr, using D, work 1tr into each tr to end. Turn.
3rd row Using D, 3ch, work 1tr into each of next 6[6:7:7] tr, keeping yarn at back of work and working 1trNc with B on last

tr, using B, work 1tr into each tr to end. Turn.

Rep 2nd and 3rd rows twice more, then 2nd row 0[0:1:1] times more. Fasten off and darn in ends. Work 1 more motif in same way, then 2 motifs using A and D and 2 using C and E. 6 motifs, 3 for each front.

4th motif
Using B and C, work first 3 rows as given for 3rd motif.

4th row Using B, 3ch, 1tr into each tr to end. Turn.

5th row Using B, 3ch, 1tr into each of next 6[6:7:7] tr, keeping yarn at back of work join in C and work 1trNc on last tr, using C, 1tr into each tr to end. Turn.

6th row Using C, 3ch, 1tr into each of next 6[6:7:7] tr, putting C to front of work and B back under hook to work 1trNc with B on last tr, using B, 1tr into each tr to end. Turn.

7th row As 5th.

Rep 6th row 0[0:1:1] times more. Fasten off and darn in ends. Work 1 more motif.

5th motif
Using B, work first 3 rows as given for 1st motif, joining in E and working 1trNc on last tr. Break off B.

4th row Using E, 3ch, work 1tr into each of next 6[6:7:7] tr, join in C and work 1trNc on last tr, using C, 1tr into each tr to end. Turn.

5th row Using C, 3ch, work 1tr into each of next 6[6:7:7] tr, 1trNc with C on last tr using E, 1tr into each tr to end. Turn.

Rep 4th and 5th rows once more, then 4th row 0[0:1:1] times more. Fasten off and darn in ends. Work 1 more motif in same way, then 2 more using C, E and D and 2 more using A, B and E. 6 motifs, 3 for each front.

6th motif
Using E, make 7[7:8:8] ch, join in D and make 9[9:10:10] ch.

1st row Using D, into 4th ch from hook work 1tr, 1tr into each of next 4[4:5:5] ch, keeping yarn at back of work join in C and work 1trNc on last tr, using C, 1tr into each of next 2ch, keeping yarn at back of work join in E and work 1trNc on last tr, using E, 1tr into each of next 6[6:7:7] ch. Turn.

2nd row Using E, 3ch, 1tr into each of next 4[4:5:5] tr, putting E to front of work and C to back under hook and working 1trNc with C on last tr, using C, 1tr into each of next 4tr, putting C to front of work and D to back under hook and working 1trNc with D on last tr, using D, 1tr into each tr to end. Turn.

3rd row Changing colours as for 1st row, using D, 3ch, 1tr into each of next 3[3:4:4] tr, using C, 1tr into each of next 6tr, using E, 1tr into each tr to end. Turn.

4th row Changing colours as for 2nd row, using E, 3ch, 1tr into each of next 2[2:3:3] tr, using C, 1tr into each of next 8tr, using D, 1tr into each tr to end. Turn.

5th row Changing colours as for 1st row, using D, 3ch, 1tr into next tr, using C, 1tr into each of next 10tr, using E, 1tr into each tr to end. Turn.

6th row Changing colours as for 2nd row, using E, 3ch, 1tr into each of next 0[0:1:1] tr, using C, 1tr into each of next 12tr, using D, 1tr into each tr to end. Turn.

7th row Using C, 3ch, 1tr into each tr to end. Turn.

Rep 7th row 0[0:1:1] times more. Fasten off and darn in ends. Work 1 more motif in same way, then 2 using B, A and C, 2 using E, C and B, 2 using A, D and B, 2 using B, C and E and 2 using D, A and E. 12 motifs making 6 diamond shapes, 3 for each front.

Quarter raglan motif
Using D, make 10[10:12:12] ch. Work 1st row as given for 1st motif. 8[8:9:9] tr.

2nd row 3ch, dec 1, 1tr into each tr to end. Turn.

3rd row 3ch, 1tr into each tr to last 3tr, dec 1, 1tr into last tr. Turn.

Rep 2nd and 3rd rows twice more, then 2nd row 0[0:1:1] times more. Fasten off. Make another quarter motif in same way.

Three-quarter raglan motif
Using C, make 16[16:18:18] ch. Work 1st row as given for 1st motif. 14[14:16:16] tr.

2nd row 3ch, 1tr into next tr, dec 1, 1tr into each tr to end. Turn.

3rd row 3ch, 1tr into each tr to last 4tr, dec 1, 1tr into each of last 2 tr. Turn.

Rep 2nd and 3rd rows twice more, then 2nd row 0[0:1:1] times more. 8[8:9:9] tr. Fasten off.

Neck motif
Using E, make 16[16:18:18] ch.

1st row Into 4th ch from hook work 1tr, 1tr into each ch to last 4ch, dec 2 working over next 3ch as given for dec 1, 1tr into last ch. Turn.

2nd row 3ch, dec 2, 1tr into each tr to end. Turn.

3rd row 3ch, 1tr into each tr to last 4tr, dec 2, 1tr into last tr. Turn.

Rep 2nd and 3rd rows once more, then 2nd row once more. Fasten off.

To make up

Press each piece under a damp cloth with a warm iron. Sew motifs tog with cast off edge to cast on edge, with exception of 6th motif which must be sewn cast on edges tog to form diamond shape. Join 3 motifs, arranging as required or as shown in diagram, to form one row. Join 5 more rows in same way, then join these 6 rows tog to form one front to underarm. Join 2 motifs working from front edge for 7th row then join quarter raglan motif for armhole edge. Join one motif for front edge with three-quarter raglan motif for armhole edge for 8th row, then join neck motif to raglan edge of armhole, leaving 9tr at neck edge free for 9th row. Join other front in same way, reversing motifs.

Collar Using No.3.50 (ISR) hook, A and with RS of work facing, work 86[86:90:90] dc round neck edge. Work 1 row tr, dec one st at each side of sleeve, (4 dec). Cont dec in same way, work 1 row dc and 1 row tr. Work 2[2:3:3] rows dc without shaping. Fasten off.

Lower edge Using No.3.50 (ISR) hook, A and with RS of front facing, work 2[2:3:3] rows tr along lower edge for hem. Fasten off. Work other front in same way.

Front edges Using No.3.50 (ISR) hook, A and with RS of work facing, work 3 rows dc along each front edge. Fasten off. Join raglan, side and sleeve seams. Turn up hem at lower edge and sl st down. Turn up 2[2:3:3] rows tr at cuffs and sl st down. Sew in zip. Press seams.

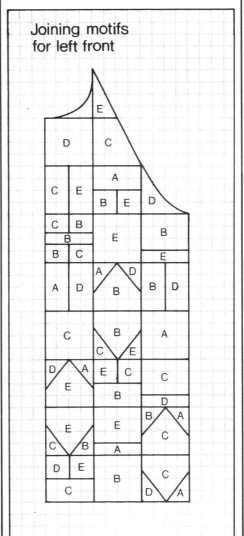

Joining motifs for left front

FREE SHAPING

This chapter illustrates a creative and individual application for crochet, the main feature of which is a breakaway from the accepted traditional methods of working in straight lines to and fro.

Here the method of making free and unusual lines and shapes, which are then worked around to form a flat fabric, is exploited. To achieve this type of work, increased and decreased stitches must be introduced at certain points on the work, so our samples are explained in detail to help you understand the technique and encourage you to try out your own ideas.

You will see that colour is very important here as the fabric is formed by using different colours of yarn for each new row, or section of a design so creating a patchwork effect.

Begin by making a square or rectangular shape which could be used as a cushion cover, or enlarged to

make a rug. Later on fashion garments can be attempted or, more simply, a border design on a plain skirt.

Sample 1

The basic shapes here are two circles. By using the same method of work and varying the number of stitches between increases and decreases, you could use several circles in a row, three to form a triangle or four to form a square. The sample has been worked in five colours of double knitting yarn, A, B, C, D and E.

To work the basic circles (make 2) Using No.3.50 (ISR) hook and A, make 3ch. Join with a ss into first ch to form a circle.

1st round 1ch to count as first dc, 7dc into circle. Join with a ss into first ch.

2nd round 1ch, 1dc into st at base of ch, *2dc into next dc, rep from * to end. Join with a ss into first ch. 16dc.

3rd round 1ch, 1dc into st at base of ch, 1dc into next dc, *2dc into next dc, 1dc into next dc, rep from * to end. Join with a ss into first ch. 24dc.

4th round 1ch, 1dc into st at base of ch, 1dc into each of next 2dc, *2dc into next dc, 1dc into each of next 2dc, rep from * to end. Join with a ss into first ch. 32dc.

5th round 1ch, 1dc into st at base of ch, 1dc into each of next 3dc, *2dc into next dc, 1dc into each of next 3dc, rep from * to end. Join with a ss into first ch. 40dc. Break off A, but leave working st on a safety pin.

Join in B to either circle. **Replace working st on to hook, 1ch, 1dc into st at base of ch, 1dc into each of next 4dc, *2dc into next dc, 1dc into each of next 4dc, rep from * to end of round. Join with a ss into first ch. ** Turn work.

1st row 1ch to count as first dc, miss first dc, 1dc into each of next 5dc. Turn work.

2nd—6th rows As 1st.

Join in 2nd circle Place circle to be joined behind the present work with RS tog and rep from ** to ** as given for 1st circle, working through double fabric for first 7 sts. Break off yarn, thread cut end through working st and pull up tightly.

Join in C With RS of work facing, join C to first increased dc of left hand circle (as shown in diagram) and work in an anti-clockwise direction around the circle, 1ch, 1dc into st at base of ch, 1dc into each of next 5 sts, (2dc into next dc, 1dc into each of next 5 sts) 5 times, cont along row ends of straight strip in B by working 2dc tog, 1dc into each of next 4 sts, work 2dc tog, then cont round right hand circle by working (1dc into each of next 5dc, 2dc into next dc) 6 times, 1dc into each of next 5dc and finally cont along 2nd side of straight strip in B by working 2dc tog, 1dc into each of next 4 sts, work 2dc tog, 1dc into each of next 5 sts. Join with a ss into first ch. Break off yarn, thread cut end through working st and pull up tightly.

Join in D With RS of work facing, join in D by inserting hook into first ch of last round and cont in an anti-clockwise direction around entire shape by working 1ch, 1dc into st at base of ch, (1dc into each of next 6 sts, 2dc into next st) 5 times, 1dc into each of next 5 sts, work 2dc tog, 1dc into each of next 3 sts, work 2dc tog, 1dc into each of next 5 sts, (2dc into next st, 1dc into each of next 6 sts) 5 times, 2dc into next st, 1dc into each of next 5 sts, work 2dc tog, 1dc into each of next 3 sts, work 2dc tog, 1dc into each of next 5 sts. Join with a ss into first ch. Break off yarn, thread cut end through working st and pull up tightly.

Join in E With RS of work facing, join in E by inserting hook into first ch of last round and cont round shape by working 1ch, 1dc into st at base of ch, (1dc into each of next 7 sts, 2dc into next st) 5 times, 1dc into each of next 4 sts, work 3 sts tog using tr instead of dc, 1tr into each of next 2 sts, work 3tr tog, 1dc into each of next 4 sts, (2dc into next st, 1dc into each of next 7 sts) 5 times, 2dc into next st, 1dc into each of next 4 sts, work 3tr tog, 1tr into each of next 2 sts, work 3tr tog, 1dc into each of next 4 sts. Join with a ss into first ch. Break off yarn, thread through working st and pull up tightly.

Join in B With RS of work facing, join in B by inserting hook into first ch of last round and cont round shape by working 1ch, 1dc into st at base of ch, (1dc into each of next 8 sts, 2dc into next st) 5 times, 1dc into each of next 2 sts, work 3tr tog, 1tr into each of next 3 sts, work 3tr tog, 1dc into each of next 2 sts, (2dc into next st, 1dc into each of next 8 sts) 5 times, 2dc into next st, 1dc into each of next 2 sts, work 3tr tog, 1tr into each of next 3 sts, work 3tr tog, 1dc into each of next 2 sts. Join with a ss into first ch. Break off yarn, thread through working st and pull up tightly.

Join in A Cont as before by working 1ch, 1dc into st at base of ch, (1dc into each of next 9 sts, 2dc into next st) 5 times, work 3tr tog, 1tr into each of next 4 sts, work 3tr tog, 2dc into next st, (1dc into each of next 9 sts, 2dc into next st) 5 times, work 3tr tog, 1tr into each of next 4 sts, work 3tr tog. Join with a ss into first ch.

Final round Using A, 1ch, 1dc into st at base of ch, (1dc into each of next 10 sts, 2dc into next st) 4 times, 1dc into each of next 29 sts, (2dc into next st, 1dc into each of next 10 sts) 4 times, 1dc into each of next 8 sts. Join with a ss into first ch. Fasten off.

Sample 2

Five colours of double knitting yarn, A, B, C, D and E have been used for this sample. Using No.3.50 (ISR) hook and A, make a chain with multiples of 6+1 stitches.

1st row Into 3rd ch from hook work 1dc, 1dc into each ch to end. Turn.

2nd row 1ch to count as first dc, miss first st, 1dc into each of next 5ch, *10ch, into 3rd ch from hook work 1dc, 1dc into each of next 7ch, 1dc into each of next 6dc, rep from * to end. Turn.

3rd row Join in B, 1ch, miss first st, 1dc into each of next 4dc, *work 2dc tog, 1dc into each of next 7dc, 3dc into tip of chain length, 1dc into each of next 7 sts, work 2dc tog, 1dc into each of next 4 sts, rep from * ending with 1dc into turning ch. Turn.

4th row Join in C, 1ch, miss first st, 1dc into each of next 3 sts, *work 2dc tog, 1dc into each of next 7 sts, (2dc into next st) twice, 1dc into each of next 7 sts, work 2dc tog, 1dc into each of next 3 sts, rep from * ending with 1dc into turning ch. Turn.

5th row Join in D, 1ch, miss first st, 1dc into each of next 2dc, *work 2dc tog, 1dc into each of next 7 sts, (2dc into next st) 3 times, 1dc into each of next 7 sts, work 2dc tog, 1dc into each of next 2 sts, rep from * ending with 1dc into turning ch. Turn.

6th row Join in E, 1ch, miss first st, 1dc into next dc, work 2dc tog, 1dc into each of next 7 sts, *(2dc into next st, 1dc into next st) twice, 2dc into next st, 1dc into each of next 7 sts, work 2dc tog, miss next st, work 2dc tog, insert hook into last dc but one just worked, yrh and draw a loop through st on hook, (insert hook into next dc on right, yrh and draw through a loop, insert hook into next dc on left, yrh and draw through a loop, yrh and draw through all loops on hook) 7 times to join shapes tog, rep from * omitting joining on last rep and working in dc to end. Fasten off.

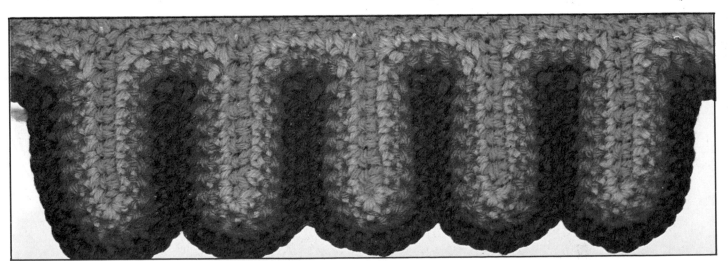

Counterpane in colour

Size

To fit average single bed, 91.5cm (36in) wide

Tension

Motifs 1, 2 and 3 measure 21.5cm (8½in) square

Materials

Wendy Double Knitting Nylonised
8 × 1oz balls Aquamarine, A
5 balls Turquoise, B
6 balls Clematis, C
8 balls Lincoln Green, D
9 balls Emerald, E
9 balls Black, F
6 balls Blue Velvet, G
5 balls Lichen Random, H
5 balls Purple Zodiac Random, I
One No. 5.50 (ISR) crochet hook

Counterpane

The counterpane is made of 8 square motifs using variations of 9 colours which are sewn tog and then borders and more motifs are worked on to the basic shape.

Square motif (1)

Using No. 5.00 (ISR) hook and A, work 4ch. Join with a ss into first ch to form a circle.

1st round 3ch, 11tr into circle. Join with a ss into 3rd of the 3ch.

2nd round Ss into first sp between tr, 3ch, 1tr into same sp, *2tr into next sp between tr, rep from * all round. Join with a ss into 3rd of the 3ch. Break off A and join in B.

3rd round Ss into first sp between tr, 3ch, 2tr into same sp, miss next sp, * 3tr into next sp, miss next sp, rep from * all round. Join with a ss into 3rd of the 3ch. Break off B and join in G.

4th round Ss into first sp between grs of 3tr, (3ch, 2tr, 1ch – to form corner sp, 3tr) into same sp, miss next 2 sp between tr, 1tr into each of next 4 sp, miss next 2 sp, *(3tr, 1ch, 3tr) into next sp, miss next 2 sp, 1tr into each of next 4 sp, miss next 2 sp, rep from * all round. Join with a ss into 3rd of the 3ch. Break off G and join in E.

5th round Ss into corner sp, (3ch, 2tr, 1ch, 3tr) into same sp, *miss next 2 sp between tr, 1tr into each of next 5 sp, miss next 2 sp, (3tr, 1ch, 3tr) into corner sp, rep from * all round. Join with a ss into 3rd of the 3ch. Break off E and join in A.

6th round Ss into corner sp, (3ch, 2tr, 1ch, 3tr) into same sp, *miss next 2 sp between tr, 1tr into each of next 6 sp, miss next 2 sp, (3tr, 1ch, 3tr) into corner sp, rep from * all round. Join with a ss

into 3rd of the 3ch.
Break off A and join in G.

7th round Ss into corner sp, (3ch, 2tr, 1ch, 3tr) into same sp, *(miss next 2 sp between tr, 3tr into next sp – thus forming 1sh) 3 times, (3tr, 1ch, 3tr) into corner sp, rep from * all round. Join with a ss into 3rd of the 3ch. Fasten off G and join in C.

8th round Ss into corner sp, (3ch, 2tr, 1ch, 3tr) into same sp, *(miss next sh, 3tr into sp between next 2 shs) 4 times, miss next sh, (3tr, 1ch, 3tr) into corner sp, rep from * all round. Join with a ss into 3rd of the 3ch. Break off C. Make another motif in the same way.

Square motif (2)

Make 3 motifs in the same way as above, but work in colour sequence as foll:

1st and 2nd rounds Work with H.
3rd round Work with A.
4th round Work with D.
5th round Work with E.
6th round Work with B.
7th round Work with H.
8th round Work with C.

Square motif (3)

Make 3 motifs using colour sequence as foll:

1st and 2nd rounds Work with B.
3rd round Work with I.
4th round Work with B.
5th round Work with F.
6th round Work with G.
7th round Work with D.
8th round Work with C.

Using C, join these 8 motifs tog as shown in diagram.

Next round Join E to corner sp marked (a) on diagram, (3ch, 2tr, 1ch, 3tr) into corner, *work a 4tr sh into each sp between shs to (b) on diagram, 2tr into (b), (4tr sh into each sp to next corner, (3tr, 1ch, 3tr) into corner) twice, rep from *all round motifs. Join with a ss into 3rd of the 3ch. Break off E and join in D.

Next round Ss into corner sp, (3ch, 2tr, 1ch, 3tr) into same sp, *4tr sh into each sp between shs to within one sp of point (b), 1tr into next sp, miss 2tr at (b), 1tr into next sp, (4tr sh into each sp to corner, (3tr, 1ch, 3tr) into corner) twice, rep from * all round. Join with a ss into 3rd of the 3ch. Break off D.

Semi-circular motif (4)

Using No. 5.50 (ISR) hook and A, work 4ch. Join with a ss into first ch to form a circle.

1st row 3ch, 6tr into circle. Turn.
2nd row Ss into first sp, 3ch, 1tr into same sp, 2tr into each sp to end. Turn. Break off A and join in B.

3rd row As 2nd row.
Break off B and join in E.

4th row Ss into first sp, 3ch, 1tr into same sp, miss next sp, *3tr sh into next sp, miss next sp, rep from * to last sp, 2tr into last sp. Turn. Break off E and join in H.

5th row 3ch, 3tr sh into each sp between shs, 1tr into 3rd of the 3ch. Turn.

6th row Ss into first sp, 3ch, 1tr into same sp, *4tr sh into next sp between shs, rep from * to last sp, 2tr into last sp. Turn. Break off H and join in E.

7th row 3ch, 4tr sh into first sp between shs, *5tr sh into next sp, rep from * to last sp, 4tr into last sp, 1tr into 3rd of the 3ch. Turn. Break off E.

Make 3 more motifs in the same way and join to the main section as shown in the diagram. Cont working a border round the main shape as foll:

1st round With RS of work facing join A to point (*) on diagram and work 4tr shs into each sp between shs to point (b), dec at (b) by working 1tr into sp at either side of previous dec, cont in shs to next corner, 4tr into corner, *3tr sh into 3rd tr of previous 5tr sh, 3tr sh into next sp between shs, rep from * all round semi-circular motif and cont round shape dec at each point (b), working (3tr, 1ch, 3tr) into each corner and working round motifs as shown above. Break off A and join in G.

2nd round As 1st round, but work 3tr shs into each sp between shs round motif 4. Break off G and join in F.

3rd round As 2nd round. Break off F and join in G.

4th round Work all round 1tr into each tr and 1tr into each sp, 1tr into each of 3 sp at point (b), (3tr, 1ch, 3tr) into each corner, missing 3tr between and after each corner sp. Break off G and join in F.

5th round Work all round 1tr into each tr, (3tr, 1ch, 3tr) into each corner, and at point (b) dec over 3tr by working 1tr into each of the 3tr and leaving the last lp of each on hook, yrh and draw through all 4 lps on hook. Break off F and join in D.

6th round As 4th round, but dec over 5tr at each point (b). Break off D and join in F.

7th round As 5th round, but dec over 5tr at each point (b). Break off F and join in C.

8th round As 7th round, but work 2tr into every 10th tr round motif 4. Break off C and join in D.

9th round As 7th round. Break off D and join in F.

10th round As 7th round, but at each point (b) dec over 2tr, 1dtr into next tr, dec over next 2tr. Break off F and join in G.

11th round As 7th round, but dec over

50

2tr only at each point (b).
Break off G and join in H.

12th round As 7th round, but do not dec at point (b) and work 5tr shs into each corner sp. Break off H and join in B.

13th round As 12th round, but work 5tr into 3rd tr of previous 5tr sh at corners. Break off B and join in E.

14th round As 12th round.

Motif (5)

Work as given for semi-circular motif (4) until 2nd row has been completed. Break off A and join in B.

3rd row 3ch, miss first sp, 1tr into next sp, 2tr into each sp to last 2sp, 1tr into each of last 2sp. Turn. Break off B and join in E.

4th row 3ch, 1tr into first sp, *miss next sp, 3tr into next sp, miss next sp, 2tr into next sp, rep from * to end. Turn.

Break off E and join in H.

5th row 3ch, *2tr into next sp, 3tr into next sp, rep from * to end, 1tr into 3rd of the 3ch. Turn.

6th row 3ch, 1tr into first sp, *3tr into next sp, 2tr into next sp, rep from * to end. Turn. Break off H and join in E.

7th row 3ch, 3tr into each sp to end, 1tr into 3rd of the 3ch. Turn. Break off E and join in H.

8th row 3ch, 2tr into first sp, *3tr into next sp, rep from * to last sp, 2tr into last sp, 1tr into 3rd of the 3ch. Turn. Break off H and join in E.

9th row 4ch, 1dtr between 1st and 2nd tr (4dtr into next sp) twice, *4tr into next sp, rep from * to last 2 sp, 4dtr into each of next 2 sp, 1dtr between last 2tr, 1dtr into 4th of the 4ch. Turn.

10th row 4ch, 2dtr into first sp, 5dtr into next sp, *5tr into next sp, rep from * to last 2 sp, 5dtr into next sp, 2dtr into last sp, 1dtr into 4th of the 4ch. Turn. Break off E and join in H.

11th row 4ch, 5dtr into first sp, *5tr into next sp, rep from * to last sp, 5dtr into last sp, 1dtr into 4th of the 4ch. Break off H.

Make one more motif in the same way and join to the main section as shown in the diagram. Cont with the border as foll

15th round Join in A and work 1tr into each tr all round and (3tr, 1ch, 3tr) into 3rd tr of every 5tr sh. Break off A and join in D.

16th round *3tr sh into next sp, miss next 2 sp, rep from * all round, but work (3tr, 1ch, 3tr) into each corner. Break off D and join in A.

17th round Work 3tr shs into each sp and over motif (5), 4tr shs over the curves and (3tr, 1ch, 3tr) into each corner. Break off A and join in F.

18th round As 17th round. Break off F and join in C.

19th round As 17th round. Break off C and join in I.

20th round As 17th round. Break off I. Complete the counterpane by working the foll extensions:

1st row Join I to point marked (c) on diagram, 3ch and 3tr into same sp, 4tr sh into each sp between shs to point marked (d) on diagram. Turn. Break off I and join in B.

2nd row Ss into first sp between shs, 3ch and 3tr into same sp, 4tr sh into each sp to end. Turn. Break off B and join in E.

3rd row As 2nd row. Break off E and join in H.

4th row As 2nd row. Break off H and join in D.

5th row As 2nd row. Break off D and join in A.

6th row As 2nd row. Break off A.

Work a similar extension at the opposite end of the cover, then work around the cover as foll:

Join E to any sp between shs, 3ch and 3tr into same sp, 4tr sh into each sp between shs all round, ss into 3rd of the 3ch. Break off E. Finish off all ends.

To make up

Tassels (make 6)

Cut 51cm (20in) lengths of every colour. Using 40 strands tog, tie them in the middle, fold in half and tie again 5cm (2in) from the top. Attach the tassels as shown in the diagram.

Fringe

Cut lengths of every colour as given for tassels. Using 8 strands draw centre of threads through each sp between shs round edge and knot.

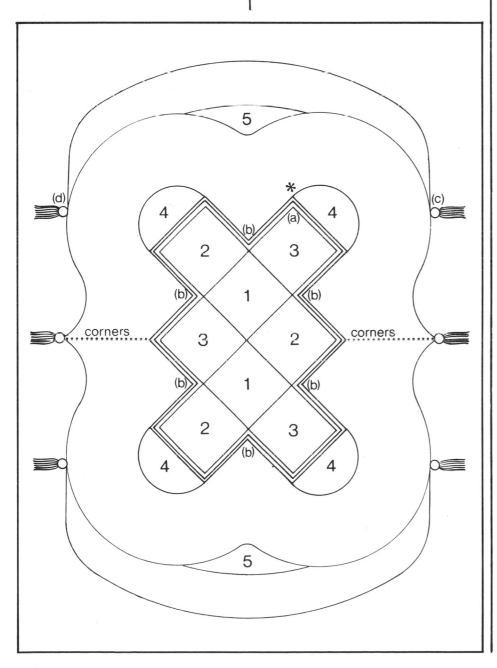

LACE CROCHET
FILET CROCHET

Filet crochet

Filet is the French name for 'net' and you will recognise this type of crochet by its simple lacy qualities. It is made up of two simple stitches, already learnt, the chain and treble. The trebles are worked in groups so forming a solid block and the space between each block is enclosed by a length of chain which corresponds in number to the group of trebles over which it is worked.

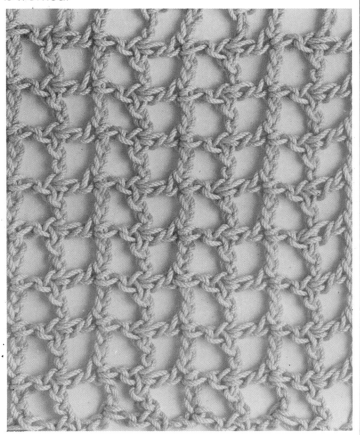

Filet net forms the basis of the work and this is composed very simply with single trebles and usually two chain separating them. However, when random spaces are filled in with trebles, a block is formed and from the basic net many different designs can be made.

An easy way of designing your own pattern is to use squared paper. Presume that each square across represents a stitch and each square up equals a row, then block in squares accordingly to create your own individual design.

Instructions are given for working the basic net and one of the many variations on this theme. Most yarns are suitable for filet crochet, although cotton or finer yarns are more popular as they add to the lightness and airiness of the work.

Basic filet crochet

Using No. 2.50 (ISR) hook and a cotton yarn, make 32ch.

1st row Into 8th ch from hook work ltr, *2ch, miss next 2ch, ltr into next ch, rep from * to end. Turn.

2nd row 5ch to count as first tr plus linking ch, miss first 2ch space, ltr into next tr, *2ch, miss next 2ch space, ltr into next tr, finishing with 1 tr into 3rd of the turning chain. Turn.

The last row is repeated throughout.

Filet crochet using blocks and spaces

Using No. 2.50 (ISR) hook and a cotton yarn, make 32ch.

1st row Work as given for 1st row of basic filet crochet.

2nd row 5ch to count as first tr plus linking ch, miss first 2ch space, ltr into next tr, *2ch, miss next 2ch space, (ltr into next tr, 2tr into next 2ch space) twice, ltr into next tr, rep from * once more, 2ch, miss next 2ch space, ltr into next tr, 2ch, ltr into 3rd of the turning chain. Turn.

3rd row 5ch, miss first 2ch space, ltr into next tr, *2ch, miss next 2ch space, ltr into each of next 7tr, rep from * once more, 2ch, miss next 2ch space, ltr into next tr, 2ch, 1tr into 3rd of the turning chain. Turn.

4th row 5ch, miss first space, ltr into next tr, 2ch, miss next space, ltr into next tr, (2ch, miss next 2tr, ltr into next tr) twice, 2tr into next space, (ltr into next tr, 2ch, miss next 2tr) twice, ltr into next tr, 2ch, miss next space, ltr into next tr, 2ch, ltr into 3rd of the turning chain. Turn.

5th row 5ch, miss first space, ltr into next tr, (2ch, miss next space, ltr into next tr) twice, 2ch, miss next space, ltr into each of next 4tr, (2ch, miss next space, ltr into next tr) 3 times, 2ch, 1tr into 3rd of the turning chain. Turn.

6th row 3ch, (2tr into next space, ltr into next tr) twice, (2ch, miss next space, ltr into next tr) 5 times, 2tr into next space, ltr into next tr, 2tr into last space, ltr into 3rd of the turning chain. Turn.

7th row 3ch, miss first tr, ltr into each of next 6tr, (2ch, miss next space, ltr into next tr) 5 times, ltr into each of next 5tr, ltr into 3rd of the turning chain. Fasten off.
If you have managed to work this sample successfully, then it's time to make up your own design using the method described above.
Very fine cotton used for this work produces a beautiful filet crochet lace. Worked into strips this can be used for a lace insertion or edging or make the strips a bit deeper and cover the cuffs of your favourite blouse. Follow the instructions below to make two simple lace edgings.

Lace edging 1
Make a chain the length that you require, making sure that you have a repeat of 3 stitches plus 2 extra.
1st row Into 4th ch from hook work ltr, ltr into every ch to end. Turn.
2nd row 5ch to count as first tr plus 2 linking ch, miss first 3tr, ltr into next tr, *2ch, miss 2 tr, ltr into next tr, rep from * finishing with 1 tr into 3rd of the turning chain. Turn.
3rd row 3ch, *2tr into next space, ltr into next tr, rep from * to end. Fasten off.

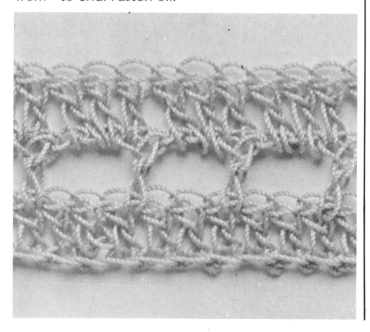

Lace edging 2
Make a chain the length that you require, making sure that you have a repeat of 6 stitches plus 5 extra.
1st row Into 8th ch from hook work ltr, ltr into each of next 3ch, * 2ch, miss next 2ch, 1tr into each of next 4ch, rep from * to end. Turn.
2nd row 5ch, miss first 3tr, *ltr into next tr, 2tr into next space, ltr into next tr, 2ch, miss 2tr, rep from * finishing with 1tr into next tr, 2tr into last sp and last tr into 3rd of the turning chain. Turn.
3rd row As 2nd. Fasten off.

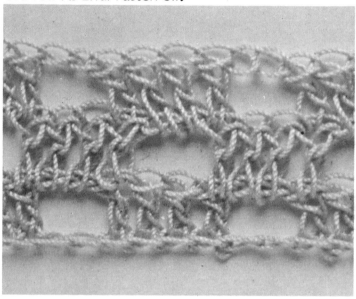

Using the same technique, and still working in very fine yarns, other items made this way are cushion covers, table cloths and other fine household items. Similar strips to those described above, if they are worked in thicker yarns make attractive braids and belts.

Belt with plastic strip threaded between trebles.

FILET LACE TRIMMINGS

This chapter continues our previous work on filet lace crochet which is comprised of blocks and spaces, with different and more advanced techniques. We shall particularly deal with the use of finer yarns for the more traditional types of work done in this form. A filet lace, or crochet lace as it is sometimes called, in its finest form is a popular trimming for underclothes, nightdresses and household linens. Today it is also fashionable for decorating roller blinds, Tiffany lamp shades and tablecloths – although probably for all of these you will need to use a slightly thicker yarn.

There is a fine cotton yarn available in a wide range of colours and thicknesses, varying from No.3 which is the thickest to No.100, the finest. The normal range of crochet hooks to use with fine cotton would vary in size from No.0.60 (ISR) hook to No.2.00 (ISR) hook.

Traditionally filet lace crochet is produced in white or ecru, but modern designs sometimes demand coloured yarns. It is particularly important if you are making underclothes or a nightdress to have the correct shade of lace. If this is unobtainable, dye your yarn with a water dye. The ball of cotton should first be rewound into a skein and then, for dyeing, follow the manufacturer's instructions.

When the lace trimming has been completed, it should be washed and pressed before it is applied to a garment. This will avoid any shrinkage at a later stage. Use neat hemming or chosen embroidery stitches to sew the lace on to the garment.

There are two methods of working the lace trimming – in narrow strips, beginning with the number of stitches required for the depth of the lace and working until the required length has been completed or working the number of stitches to give the required length of work and then working in rows to give the correct depth.

Our photograph shows a sample of filet lace crochet where blocks and spaces have been increased and decreased. You will also see a chart of this design. Earlier, we gave a simple way of charting a design, but now we shall teach you the professional way of charting.

In our chart here one space across represents either a block of trebles or a space and one space up represents a row. To help you follow the chart, the techniques of increasing and decreasing are explained in detail below and then there are instructions of how to work our sample.

To increase a block at the beginning of a row. Work 5ch. Into 4th ch from hook work 1tr, 1tr into next ch,

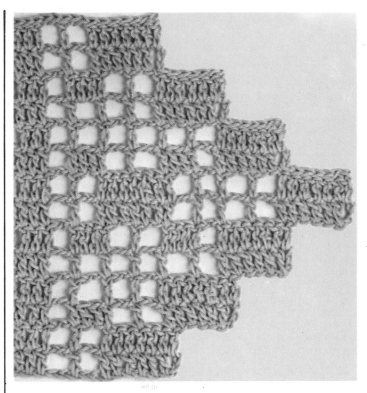

Use this chart to work the sample

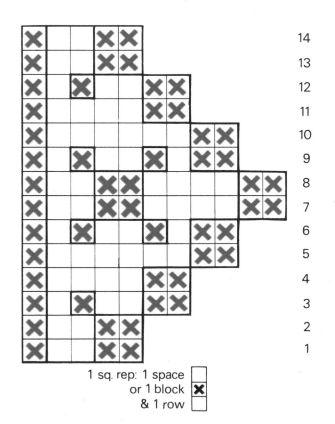

1 sq. rep: 1 space
or 1 block
& 1 row

1tr into next st (i.e. the last st of the previous row), continue across the row in pattern. To increase two blocks as in our chart, work 8ch. Into 4th ch from hook work 1tr, 1tr into each of next 4ch, 1tr into next st.

To increase a space at the beginning of a row Work 7ch which will represent a 2ch space at the end of the last row, 3ch to count as the first tr of the new row and another 2ch between the first tr and the next st, then work 1tr into last st of the previous row.

To decrease a block or space at the beginning of a row Miss the first st, ss loosely into each of the next 3 sts, then work 3ch to count as the first tr and continue in pattern.

To increase a block at the end of a row Provision has to be made for this increase by working 7ch at the beginning of the previous row, miss the first ch, ss into each of next 3ch, there are 3ch remaining which count as the first tr of the new row, then complete the row in pattern. At the end of the following row work 1tr into each of the 3ss, thus increasing one block.

To increase a space at the end of a row Work as given for increasing a block at the end of a row, but when the increasing is reached work 2ch, miss next 2 sts, 1tr into the last st.

To decrease a block or space at the end of a row Work to within the last block or space, then turn the work and proceed in pattern.

To work the sample
Make 18ch.

1st row Into 4th ch from hook work 1tr, 1tr into each of next 5 sts, (2ch, miss next 2ch, 1tr into next ch) twice, 1tr into each of next 3ch. Turn.

2nd row 3ch to count as first tr, 1tr into each of next 3tr, (2ch, 1tr into next tr) twice, 1tr into each of next 5tr, 1tr into 3rd of the 3ch. Turn.

3rd row Increase 2 blocks by working 8ch, 1tr into 4th ch from hook, 1tr into each of next 5 sts, (2ch, miss next 2 sts, 1tr into next st) twice, 1tr into each of next 3 sts, 2ch, miss next 2 sts, 1tr into each of next 3 sts, 1tr into 3rd of the 3ch. Turn.

Continue by working in pattern from the chart, increasing 2 blocks at the beginning of the 5th and 7th rows and decreasing 2 blocks at the beginning of the 9th, 11th and 13th rows. The 13 rows may be repeated to whatever length you require.

Here are the instructions and chart for a simple edging which would make an ideal tasselled trimming for a roller blind. You will notice that this sample is worked by using the required number of stitches for the width and working until the lace is the required length.

Trimming with tassels
Make 17ch.

1st row Into 8th ch from hook work 1tr, 1tr into each of next 3ch, (2ch, miss 2ch, 1tr into next ch) twice. Turn.

2nd row 5ch, 1tr into 2nd tr, 1tr into each of next 3 sts, 2ch, miss next 2 sts, 1tr into next st. Turn, thus decreasing one space.

3rd row 7ch thus increasing one space, 1tr into first tr, 1tr into each of next 3 sts, 2ch, miss next 2 sts, 1tr into next tr, 2ch, 1tr into 3rd of the 5ch. Turn.

The 2nd and 3rd rows are repeated throughout. Thread two tassels through each increased space.

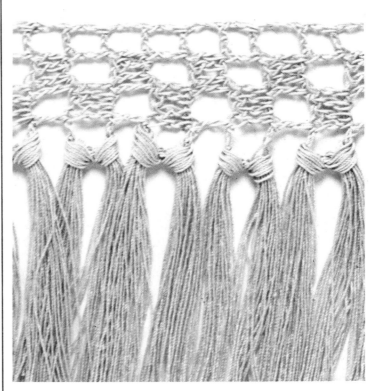

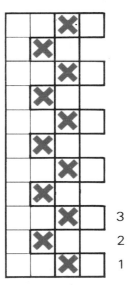

3
2
1

1 sq. rep: 1 space □
or 1 block ☒
& 1 row □

DESIGNING AND WORKING CORNERS

The technique of designing and working corners in filet crochet may present problems, but here we shall explain these two processes in detail. If you follow our charts and instructions, you should no longer have any difficulty in producing a beautiful mitred corner suitable for use on a fitted divan cover or details on clothing such as square necklines.

In the last chapter we told you how to create your own designs in filet crochet by using squared paper, remembering that each square across represents either a block or a space and each square up represents a row. Our basic filet grid in the samples here is formed by working single trebles with two chain between each, but you can make the grid to your own design.

When designing a corner, first draw a diagram and then a line through the corner at an angle of 45 degrees from the outer edge of the design. On one side of the corner sketch in your pattern as you would like it to appear, stopping at the corner line, then mirror your design exactly over this line.

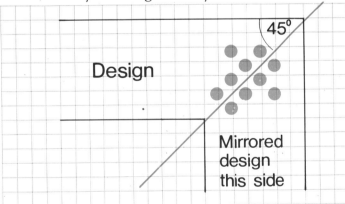

To work sample 1

In our photograph of a mitred corner two colours have been used to clarify the working process. You

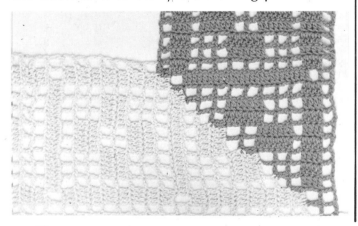

will also see a chart of the design which it will be necessary for you to follow in places. Make 41ch.

1st row Into 8th ch from hook work 1tr, 2ch, miss next 2ch, 1tr into each of next 25ch – thus forming 8 blocks –, (2ch, miss next 2ch, 1tr into next ch) twice. Turn.

2nd to 9th row Work in patt from the chart.

10th row Dec one square by missing first st, ss into each of next 3 sts, 5ch, miss 2tr, 1tr into each of next 25 sts, 2ch, miss 2tr, 1tr into next tr, 2ch, 1tr into 3rd of the 5ch. Turn.

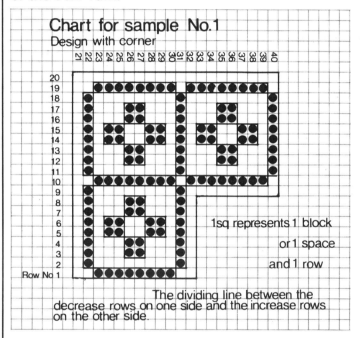

11th row 5ch, miss 2ch, 1tr into each of next 4 sts, (2ch, miss 2tr, 1tr into next tr) 8 times, turn thus decreasing one square.

12th row Dec one square by missing first st, ss into each of next 3 sts, 5ch, miss 2ch, 1tr into next tr, 2ch, miss 2ch, 1tr into each of next 7 sts, (2ch, miss 2ch, 1tr into next tr) 3 times, 1tr into each of next 3tr, 2ch, 1tr into 3rd of the 5ch. Turn.

13th row 5ch, miss 2ch, 1tr into each of next 4tr, (2ch, miss 2ch, 1tr into next tr) 3 times, 1tr into each of next 6tr, 2ch, miss 2ch, 1tr into next tr, turn thus decreasing one square.

14th row Dec one square by missing first st, ss into each of next 3 sts, 5ch, miss 2tr, 1tr into next tr, 2ch, miss 2tr, 1tr into each of next 7sts, 2ch, miss 2ch, 1tr into each of next 4tr, 2ch, 1tr into 3rd of the 5ch. Turn.

15th row 5ch, miss 2ch, 1tr into each of next 4tr, 2ch, miss 2ch, 1tr into each of next 7tr, 2ch, miss 2ch, 1tr into next tr, turn thus decreasing one space.

16th row Dec one square by missing first st, ss into each of next 3 sts, 5ch, miss 2tr, 1tr into next tr, 2ch, miss 2tr, 1tr into next tr, 2ch, miss 2ch, 1tr into each of next 4tr, 2ch, 1tr into 3rd of the 5ch. Turn.

17th row 5ch, miss 2ch, 1tr into each of next 4tr, (2ch, miss 2ch, 1tr into next tr) twice, turn thus decreasing one space.

18th row Dec one square by missing first st, ss into each of next 3 sts, 5ch, miss 2ch, 1tr into each of next 4tr, 2ch, 1tr into 3rd of the 5ch. Turn.

19th row 5ch, miss 2ch, 1tr into next tr, 2ch, miss 2tr, 1tr into next tr, turn thus decreasing one space.

20th row Decrease one space by missing first st, ss into each of next 3 sts, 5ch, 1tr into 3rd of the 5ch of previous row. Turn the work and ss into each of the sts across the top of last space worked.

21st row 5ch, ss into corner of last space on left of the previous row. Do not turn.

22nd row 3ch, 1tr into each of next 2ch, (i.e. down side of space), ss into corner of last space on left of the previous row, turn, miss first st, ss into each of next 3 sts, 2ch, miss 2ch, 1tr into 3rd of the 5ch. Turn.

23rd row 5ch, miss 2ch, 1tr into each of next 4tr, 2ch, ss into corner of last space of the row on the left. Do not turn.

24th row 5ch, ss into corner of last space of the row on the left, turn, miss first st, ss into each of next 3 sts, 2ch, miss 2ch, 1tr into each of next 4tr, 2ch, 1tr into 3rd of the 5ch. Turn.

25th row 5ch, miss 2ch, 1tr into each of next 4tr, 2ch, miss 2ch, 1tr into each of next 6 sts, ss into corner of last space of the row on the left. Do not turn.

26th row 5ch, ss into corner of last space of the row on the left, turn, miss first st, ss into each of next 3 sts, 1tr into each of next 6tr, 2ch, miss 2ch, 1tr into each of next 4tr, 2ch, 1tr into 3rd of the 5ch. Turn.

27th row 5ch, miss 2ch, 1tr into each of next 4tr, 2ch, miss 2ch, 1tr into next tr, (2ch, miss 2tr, 1tr into next tr) twice, 1tr into each of next 5 sts, ss into corner of last space of the row on the left. Do not turn.

28th row 5ch, ss into corner of last space of the row on the left, turn, miss first st, ss into each of next 3 sts, 1tr into each of next 6tr, (2ch, miss 2ch, 1tr into next tr) 3 times, 1tr into each of next 3tr, 2ch, 1tr into 3rd of the 5ch. Turn.

29th row 5ch, miss 2ch, 1tr into each of next 4tr, (2ch, miss 2 sts, 1tr into next st) 6 times, 2ch, ss into corner of last space of the row on the left. Do not turn.

30th row 3ch, 1tr into each of next 2 sts, ss into corner of last space of the row on the left, turn, miss first st, ss into each of next 3 sts, 1tr into each of next 21 sts, 2ch, miss 2tr, 1tr into next tr, 2ch, 1tr into 3rd of the 5ch. Turn.

31st row 5ch, miss 2ch, 1tr into each of next 4 sts, (2ch, miss 2tr, 1tr into next tr) 8 times, 1tr into each of next 2 sts, ss into corner of last space of the row on the left. Do not turn.

32nd row 5ch, miss 2 sts (i.e. the side of last space in 10th row), 1tr into next st, turn, miss first st, ss into each

of next 3 sts, 1tr into each of next 4tr, (2ch, miss 2ch, 1tr into next tr) 3 times, 1tr into each of next 6 sts, (2ch, miss 2ch, 1tr into next tr) 3 times, 1tr into each of next 3tr, 2ch, 1tr into 3rd of the 5ch. Turn.

33rd to 39th row Work in patt from the chart.

To work sample 2
Above we give details of how to work sample 1, but it is possible to work entirely from a chart. Practise working sample 2 from the chart. This illustrates the same technique, but it is worked in a very fine yarn and in one colour to give the true effect of the technique.

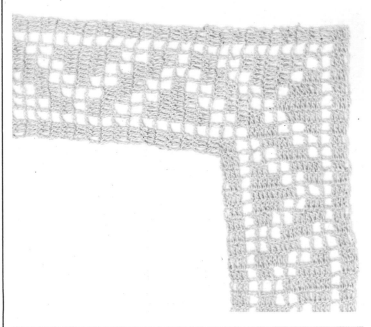

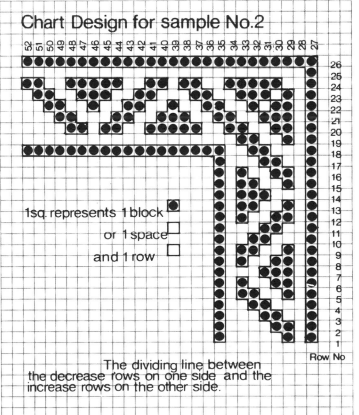

Chart Design for sample No.2

1sq. represents 1 block ●
or 1 space ▫
and 1 row ▫

The dividing line between the decrease rows on one side and the increase rows on the other side.

A butterfly top

Sizes
To fit 81.5[86.5:91.5]cm (32[34:36]in) bust
Side seam, 35.5[35.5:37]cm (14[14:14½]in)
The figures in brackets [ ] refer to the 86.5 (34) and 91.5cm (36in) sizes respectively

Tension
8 sp and 12 rows to 10cm (3.9in) over patt worked on No.3.00 (ISR) crochet hook

Materials
3 × 20grm balls Wendy Minuit Lurex
One No.3.00 (ISR) crochet hook
3 press studs
2 glass beads for eyes

Back
Using No.3.00 (ISR) hook make 83[89:95]ch.
Base row Into 8th ch from hook work 1tr, *2ch, miss 2ch, 1tr into next ch, rep from * to end. Turn.

1st row 5tr to count as first tr and 2ch, 1tr into next tr, * 2ch, 1tr into next tr, rep from * to end, working last tr into 3rd of 7ch. Turn. 26[28:30]sp. Rep last row 4[4:6] times more, noting that on subsequent rows last tr will be worked into 3rd of 5 turning ch.

Shape sides
1st row 3ch to count as first tr, 1tr into first tr, patt to end, working 2tr into 3rd of 5ch. Turn.
2nd row 3ch, 1tr into first tr, 1tr into next tr, patt to end, working 2tr into 3rd of 3ch. Turn.
3rd row 3ch, 1tr into first tr, 1tr into each of next 2tr, patt to last 2tr, 1tr into each of next 2tr, 2tr into 3rd of 3ch. Turn.
4th row 5ch, miss 2tr, 1tr into next tr, patt to last 3tr, 2ch, miss 2tr, 1tr into 3rd of 3ch. Turn. 2 sp inc.
Rep last 4 rows twice more. 32[34:36] sp. Cont without shaping until 31[31:33] rows in all have been worked.
Next row 3ch, *2tr into next sp, 1tr into next tr, rep from * to end. Fasten off.

Front
Work as given for back until 2[2:4] rows

have been completed. Commence butterfly patt.
1st row Patt 7[8:9] sp, 1ch, 1tr into next sp, 1tr into next tr, patt 10 sp, (1tr into next sp, 1ch, 1tr into next tr, patt to end. Turn.
2nd row Patt 7[8:9] sp, 1tr into next 1ch sp, 1tr into each of next 2tr (1 block of 4tr has been worked), patt 4 sp, 1ch, 1tr into next sp, 1tr into next tr, 1tr into next sp, 1ch, 1tr into next tr, patt 4 sp, 1tr into next tr, 1tr into next 1ch sp, 1tr into next tr, patt to end. Turn.
3rd row Patt 6[7:8] sp, 2tr into next sp, 1tr into each of next 4tr, patt 4 sp, 1tr into next 1ch sp, 1tr into each of next 3tr, 1tr into next 1ch sp, 1tr into next tr, patt 4sp, 1tr into each of next 3tr, 2tr into sp, 1tr into next tr, patt to end. Turn.
Cont working butterfly in this way from chart, *at the same time* shaping sides as given for back, until 28 rows of patt have been completed.
Note The chart represents a filet crochet grid of blocks, spaces, half blocks and half spaces. Spaces are formed by working single trebles with 2ch between them and blocks are spaces which have been filled in by working 2tr into the appropriate 2ch sp. Here spaces have been subdivided into half block/half space by working 1tr and 1ch into a 2ch sp.

Patt one more row in sp. Work last row as given for back. Fasten off.

Straps (make 2).
Using No.3.00 (ISR) hook make 8ch.
1st row Into 4th ch from hook work 1tr, 1tr into each ch to end. Turn. 6tr.
2nd row 3ch to count as first tr, 1tr into each tr to end. Turn.
Rep 2nd row until strap measures 35.5cm (14in) from beg, or required length. Fasten off.

To make up
Do not press. Join right side seam. Join left side seam to within 7.5cm (3in) of lower edge.
Edging Using No.3.00 (ISR) hook and with WS of work facing, rejoin yarn to first ch at lower edge, 3ch, *2tr into first sp, 1tr into next tr, rep from * all round lower edge. Turn.
Next row 3ch, *1tr into next tr, rep from * to end.
Cont working in tr up side of opening working 1tr into each tr and 2tr into each sp, turn and work down other side in same way. Fasten off.
Turn edging to WS on front edge of side opening and sl st into position to form overflap. Sew press studs along opening. Sew straps in position. Sew on beads for eyes.

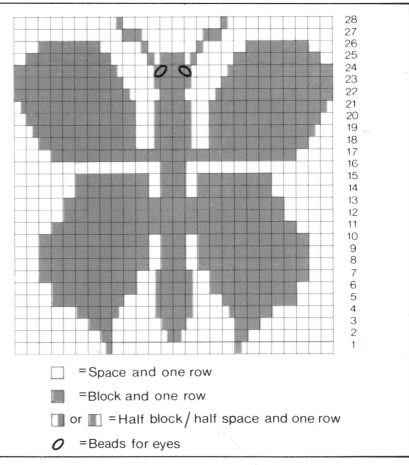

☐ = Space and one row

■ = Block and one row

◧ or ◨ = Half block / half space and one row

O = Beads for eyes

Filet crochet smock

Sizes

To fit 81.5[86.5:91.5]cm (32[34:36]in) bust
Length to shoulder, 71[72.5:73.5]cm
(28[28½:29]in)
Sleeve seam, 48.5cm (19in)
The figures in brackets [ ] refer to the
86.5 (34) and 91.5cm (36in) sizes
respectively

Tension

24 sts and 12 rows to 10cm (3.9in) over
tr worked on No.3.00 (ISR) crochet hook

Materials

11[12:12] × 50grm balls Patons Purple
Heather 4 ply
One No.2.50 (ISR) crochet hook
One No.3.00 (ISR) crochet hook
11 small buttons

Back

Using No.2.50 (ISR) hook make
200[212:224]ch for lower edge.
1st row (WS) Into 3rd ch from hook work
1dc, 1dc into each ch to end. Turn.
199[211:223] sts.
Change to No.3.00 (ISR) hook. Commence
patt.
2nd row 5ch to count as first tr and 2ch,
miss first 3 sts, 1tr into next st, *2ch,
miss 2 sts, 1tr into next st, rep from * to
end. Turn.
3rd row 5ch, miss first tr, 1tr into next
tr, *2ch, 1tr into next tr, rep from * ending
with last tr into 3rd of 5ch. Turn.
The last row forms the main patt. Cont
in patt until work measures 5cm (2in)
from beg, ending with a WS row. Cont in
patt, placing rose motifs as foll:
Next row 5ch, miss first tr, (1tr into next
tr, 2ch) 1[2:3] times, work across next
85 sts as given for 1st row of rose motif
from chart, (2ch, 1tr into next tr) 5[7:9]
times, 2ch, work across next 85 sts as
given for 1st row of rose motif from
chart, (2ch, 1tr into next tr) 1[2:3] times,
2ch, 1tr into 3rd of 5ch. Turn.
Next row 5ch, miss first tr, (1tr into next
tr, 2ch) 1[2:3] times, work across next
85 sts as given for 2nd row of rose motif
from chart, (2ch, 1tr into next tr) 5[7:9]
times, 2ch, work across next 85 sts as
given for 2nd row of rose motif from
chart, (2ch, 1tr into next tr) 1[2:3] times,
2ch, 1tr into 3rd of 5ch. Turn.
Cont working in this way until 30 rows
of rose motif from chart have been
completed. Cont in main patt as before
until work measures 51cm (20in) from
beg, ending with a RS row.
Shape yoke
Next row 3ch, (1tr into next 2ch sp, 1tr
into each of next 2tr) 13[14:15] times,
1tr into next 2ch sp, 1tr into next tr,

1tr into next 2ch sp, 1tr into each of
next 3tr, 1tr into each of next three 2ch
sps, 1tr into each of next 3tr, 1tr into next
2ch sp, 1tr into each of next 3tr, 1tr into
next 2ch sp, (1tr into next 2ch sp, 1tr
into each of next 2tr) 13[14:15] times,
1tr into last ch sp, 1tr into 3rd of 5ch.
Turn. 98[104:110] sts.
Next row 3ch, miss first st, 1tr into each
st, ending with last tr into 3rd of 3ch.
Turn.
Rep last row once more. **
Shape armholes
1st row Ss over first 3 sts and into next
st, 3ch, (yrh, insert into next st, yrh and
draw through a loop, yrh and draw
through first 2 loops on hook) 3 times,
yrh and draw through all 4 loops on
hook – called dec 2 –, 1tr into each st to
last 7 sts, dec 2, 1tr into next st, turn.
88[94:100] sts.
2nd row 3ch, miss first st, dec 2, 1tr into
each st to last 4 sts, dec 2, 1tr into 3rd of
3ch. Turn.
3rd row 3ch, miss first st, (yrh, insert into
next st, yrh and draw through a loop, yrh
and draw through first 2 loops on hook)
twice, yrh and draw through all 3 loops
on hook – called dec 1 –, 1tr into each st
to last 3 sts, dec 1, 1tr into 3rd of 3ch.
Turn.
Rep last row 5[6:7] times more. 72[76:80]
sts. Cont in tr without shaping until
armholes measure 18[19:20.5]cm
(7[7½:8]in) from beg, ending with a WS
row.
Shape shoulders
Next row Ss over first 4[5:5] sts, 1dc into
each of next 5 sts, 1htr into each of next
5 sts, 1tr into each st to last 14[15:15] sts,
1htr into each of next 5 sts, 1dc into each
of next 5 sts. Fasten off.

Front

Work as given for back to **.
Shape armholes and divide for opening
1st row Ss over first 3 sts and into next st,
3ch, dec 2, 1tr into each of next
40[43:46] sts, turn. Cont on these
42[45:48] sts for first side as foll:
2nd row 3ch, miss first st, 1tr into each st
to last 4 sts, dec 2, 1tr into 3rd of 3ch.
Turn.
3rd row 3ch, miss first st, dec 1, 1tr into
each st to end. Turn.
4th row 3ch, miss first st, 1tr into each st
to last 3 sts, dec 1, 1tr into 3rd of 3ch.
Turn.
Rep 3rd and 4th rows 2[2:3] times more.
34[37:38] sts.
2nd size only
Rep 3rd row once more. 36 sts.
All sizes
Cont in tr without shaping until armhole
measures 11.5[12.5:14]cm (4½[5:5½]in)

from beg, ending at armhole edge.
Shape neck
1st row 3ch, miss first st, 1tr into each st
to last 9[10:11] sts, dec 2, 1tr into next st,
turn.
2nd row 3ch, miss first st, dec 2, 1tr into
each st to end. Turn.
3rd row 3ch, miss first st, 1tr into each st
to last 4 sts, dec 2, 1tr into 3rd of 3ch.
Turn.
Rep 2nd and 3rd rows once more.
19[20:21] sts. Cont without shaping until
front matches back to shoulder, ending
at armhole edge.
Shape shoulder
Next row Ss over first 4[5:5] sts, 1dc into
each of next 5 sts, 1htr into each of next
5 sts, 1tr into each of next 5[5:6] sts.
Fasten off.
With RS of work facing, return to beg of
opening and leave centre 4 sts
unworked, rejoin yarn to next st, 3ch, 1tr
into each st to last 7 sts, dec 2, 1tr into
next st, turn. Complete to match first
side, reversing shapings.

Left sleeve

1st piece Using No.2.50 (ISR) hook make
23[25:27]ch.
1st row (WS) Into 3rd ch from hook work
1dc, 1dc into each ch to end. 22[24:26]
sts.
2nd row 1ch to count as first dc, miss
first st, 1dc into each st to end. Turn.
Rep last row until cuff measures 5cm
(2in) from beg, ending with a WS row.
Change to No.3.00 (ISR) hook.
Next row 5ch, miss first st, 1tr into next
st, *2ch, 1tr into next st, rep from * to
end. 64[70:76] sts.
Cont in main patt as given for back until
1st piece measures 10cm (4in) from beg,
ending with a WS row. Fasten off.
2nd piece Using No.2.50 (ISR) hook make
14ch.
1st row (WS) Into 3rd ch from hook work
1dc, 1dc into each ch to end. 13 sts.
2nd row 1ch to count as first dc, miss
first st, 1dc into each st to end. Turn.
Rep last row until cuff measures 5cm
(2in), ending with a WS row. Change to
No.3.00 (ISR) hook.
Next row 5ch, miss first st, 1tr into next
st, *2ch, 1tr into next st. Turn. 37 sts.
Cont in main patt as given for back until
2nd piece matches 1st piece, ending with
a WS row.
Next row Work in main patt across 37 sts
of 2nd piece, 2ch, then with RS of work
facing, patt across 64[70:76] sts of 1st
piece. 103[109:115] sts. Turn.
** Cont in main patt until sleeve
measures 54.5cm (18in) from beg
measured at centre, ending with a RS
row.

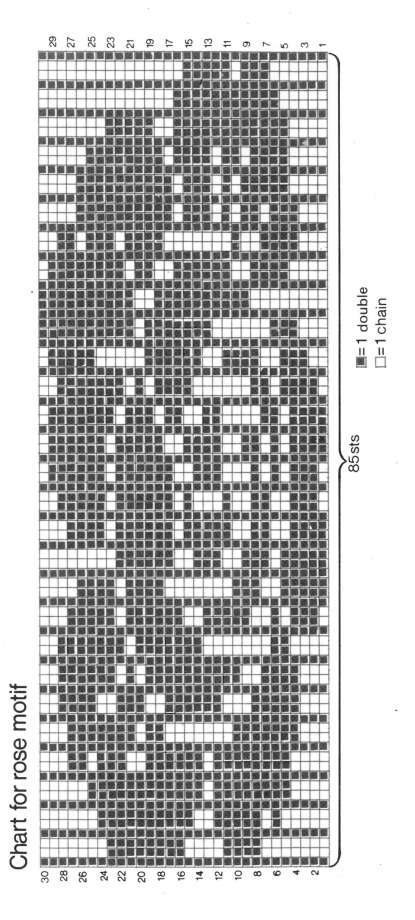

Chart for rose motif

■ = 1 double
□ = 1 chain

85 sts

Column numbers (top): 29 27 25 23 21 19 17 15 13 11 9 7 5 3 1

Column numbers (bottom): 30 28 26 24 22 20 18 16 14 12 10 8 6 4 2

Shape top

1st row Ss over first 3 sts and into next st, 3ch, dec 1, 1tr into each st to last 6 sts, dec 1, 1tr into next st, turn.

2nd row 3ch, miss first st, dec 1, 1tr into each st to last 3 sts, dec 1, 1tr into 3rd of 3ch. Turn.

Rep last row 9[9:11] times more. 40[44:44] sts.

Next row 3ch, miss first st, dec 2, 1tr into each st to last 4 sts, dec 2, 1tr into 3rd of 3ch. Turn.

Rep last row 4[5:5] times more. 20 sts. Fasten off.

Right sleeve

1st piece Work as given for 2nd piece of left sleeve and fasten off.

2nd piece Work as given for 1st piece of left sleeve, but do not fasten off.

Next row Work in main patt across 64[70:76] sts of 2nd piece, 2ch, then with RS of work facing, patt across 37 sts of 1st piece. Turn. 103[109:115] sts. Complete as given for left sleeve from ** to end.

To make up

Press lightly under a damp cloth with a warm iron. Join shoulder seams. Set in sleeves. Join side and sleeve seams.

Neck edging Using No.2.50 (ISR) hook and with RS of work facing, rejoin yarn to top of right front neck and work 3 rows dc all round neck edge. Fasten off.

Left front border Using No.2.50 (ISR) hook and with RS of work facing, work 5 rows dc down left side of opening. Mark positions for 5 buttonholes on this border, first to come 1.5cm (½in) from base of opening and last 2 sts below top of neck with the others evenly spaced between.

Right front border Work as given for left front border, making buttonholes on 3rd row to correspond with markers by working 2ch and missing 2dc.
Catch down ends of borders to base of opening, right over left.

Sleeve opening border Using No.2.50 (ISR) hook and with RS of work facing, work 2 rows dc all round opening, working 3 buttonloops evenly spaced along cuff part of larger piece on 2nd row by making 3ch and missing 2dc.

Lower edging Using No.2.50 (ISR) hook and with RS of work facing, work 1dc into each of first 3 sts, *(ss, 5ch, ss, 5ch, ss, 5ch, ss) all into next st, 1dc into each of next 5 sts, *, rep from * to * 32[34:36] times more, 1dc into next st, rep from * to * 32[34:36] times more, (ss, 5ch, ss, 5ch, ss, 5ch, ss) all into next st, 1dc into each of last 3 sts. Join with a ss into first st. Fasten off. Press seams. Sew on buttons.

Next row 3ch, (1tr into next 2ch sp, 1tr into next tr) 16[17:18] times, 1tr into each of next two 2ch sp, (1tr into next tr, 1tr into next 2ch sp) 16[17:18] times, 1tr into 3rd of 5ch. Turn. 68[72:76] sts. Work 2 rows in tr.

OPEN LACE DESIGNS

Open lace designs

Open lace work is quick and easy to work in crochet as it is formed with large spaces between the stitches and so the pattern grows rapidly. Any type of yarn may be used and this will be determined by the nature of the work.

There are many uses for this type of crochet where an open effect is required. It can be used for entire garments but naturally these will need to be lined. More commonly strips of open lace work are used as insets especially on evening clothes where the laciness of the crochet looks most appropriate.

However these openwork designs do have everyday purposes as well. String bags, onion bags or simple cotton lace curtains for one of the windows in your home are examples of a few of the things that you can make once you have practised some of the samples of open lace work that are given below.

String stitch used as an insert on a bodice

Solomon's knot stitch

Using No. 3.00 (ISR) crochet hook and a fine yarn make 35ch loosely.

1st row Extend loop on hook for 2cm (¾ in), placing thumb of left hand on loop to keep it extended, yrh and draw through a loop, place hook from front to back under left hand vertical loop of stitch just worked, yrh and draw through a loop, yrh and draw through both loops on hook – called one Solomon st –, ss into 10th ch from last Solomon st, * 1ch, work 2 Solomon sts, ss into 5th ch from last Solomon st, rep from * to end. Turn.

2nd row 6ch, work 1 Solomon st, ss into st between first pair of Solomon sts on previous row, 1ch, * work 2 Solomon sts, ss into st between next pair of Solomon sts, rep from * ending with last ss into last of the turning ch of the previous row. Turn.

The last row is repeated throughout to create a very attractively lacy stitch with a 3-dimensional effect.

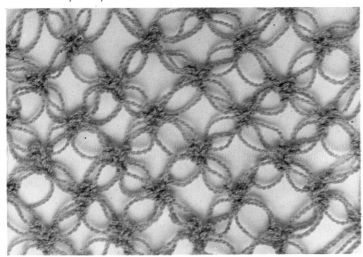

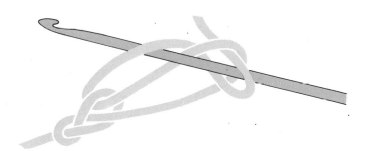

Working a Solomon's knot stitch.

Chain lace

Using No.3.00 (ISR) crochet hook and a fine yarn make 44ch.

1st row Into 12th ch from hook work 1dc, *8ch, miss next 3ch, 1dc into next ch, rep from * to end. Turn.

2nd row 8ch, 1dc into first 8ch loop, *8ch, 1dc into next loop, rep from * to end. Turn.

The last row is repeated throughout to form a very simple diamond shaped mesh.

It is an ideal stitch for an evening snood or a string bag like the one in our illustration.

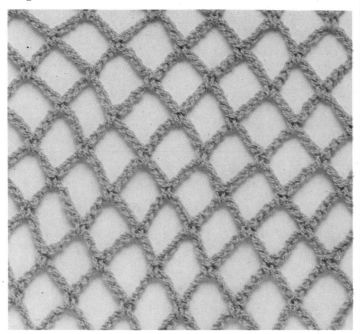

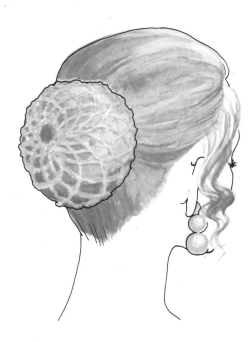

Chain lace used for a snood

To make a string bag

You will need one ball of parcel string, a brass curtain ring 3cm (1¼ inch) in diameter and a No.4.50 (ISR) crochet hook.

1st round Form a slip loop on the hook, 1dc into brass ring, *9ch, 1dc into ring, rep from * 21 times more, ss into first dc.

Next and all successive rounds Ss into first 4ch of next 9ch loop, 1dc into this loop, *9ch, 1dc into next loop, rep from * all round ending with 9ch, ss into first dc of the round. Turn.

When the bag is the required depth, fasten off and slot drawstrings through the spaces.

String stitch

Using No.2.50 (ISR) crochet hook and a fine yarn, make 43ch.

1st row Ss into 5th ch from hook, miss next ch, 1dc into next ch, *5ch, miss next 5ch, 1dc into next ch, 5ch, ss into dc last worked, 1dc into same ch as last dc, rep from * to end. Turn.

2nd row Ss to top of first 5ch loop, 6ch, ss into 5th ch from hook, 1dc into first loop, *5ch, 1dc into next 5ch loop, 5ch, ss into last dc worked, 1dc into same loop, rep from * to end. Turn.

The last row is repeated throughout to form the pattern.

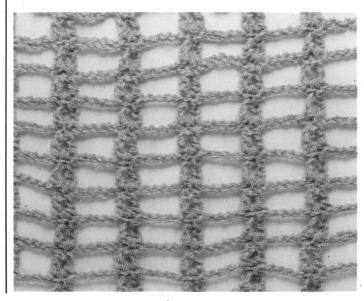

Mohair muffler

For a muffler about 30cm (12in) wide by 244cm (96in) long

Materials

150grm (5¼oz) of random coloured mohair yarn in a double knitting quality
One No. 4.50 (ISR) crochet hook

Muffler

Using the crochet hook make 20 Solomon's knots, drawing each loop up to a height of 2.5cm (1in).
Continue working in pattern until the work measures 244cm (96in) from the beginning. Fasten off.

Solomon's knot worked in mohair

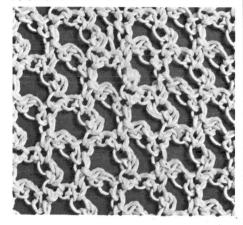

Solomon's knot worked in fine string

String shopping bag

Size

For a bag about 35cm (14in) wide by 40cm (16in) deep

Materials

2 balls of fine parcel string
One No. 3.50 (ISR) crochet hook

Bag

Using the crochet hook make 40 Solomon's knots, drawing each loop up to a height of 1.25cm (½in).
Continue in pattern until the work measures 81cm (32in) from the beginning.

Fasten off.
Make up the bag by folding it in half lengthwise. Join the side seams by over-sewing them, from the lower edge to within 15cm (6in) of the top edge.

Handle

Cut 12 lengths of string, each 91cm (36in) long for the handle.
Divide the string into 3 groups with 4 lengths in each and plait them together,

knotting each end.

Thread each plait through the last row at the top of the bag from the outer edge to the centre and tie the ends together to form a handle.

Complete the other handle in the same way.

Fringed shawl

Size

For a shawl measuring about 168cm (66in) across the top edge, excluding the fringe

Materials

100grm (3½oz) of 3 ply Botany Wool plus 25grm (1oz) extra for fringe
One No. 3.00 (ISR) crochet hook

Shawl

Using the crochet hook make 140 Solomon's knots, drawing each loop to a height of 1.25cm (½in), then shape the sides by working as follows:

Next row Miss knot on hook and next 4 knots, insert hook into centre of next knot and work 1dc, *make 2 knots, miss 1 knot along 1st row, 1dc into centre of next knot on 1st row, rep from * to end, working last dc into first ch.

Next row Make 3 knots, miss first knot, next unjoined knot and joined knot of last row, 1dc into centre of next unjoined knot of last row, *make 2 knots, miss next joined knot of last row, 1dc into centre of next unjoined knot of last row, rep from * to end.

Repeat the last row until 2 knots remain. Fasten off.

Cut lengths of yarn, each 40cm (16in) long.

Take 6 strands together at a time and knot into each space along side edges only.

Work 2 lines of fringing (see chapters on Trimmings and Braids later), each line 2.5cm (1in) below previous knots. Trim the fringe.

Solomon's knot worked in botany wool

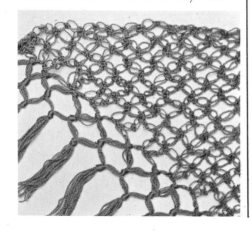

Solomon's knot stitch worked in 3-ply botany wool makes a gossamer shawl

FUR FABRICS AND LOOP STITCHES

Recently it has become very popular to represent fur fabrics with 'fun fur' fashions. In crochet this is equivalent to using loop stitch. Here we tell you how to work three basic loop stitches. The next section covers more advanced techniques.

Loop stitches give a very raised effect and form a solid, virtually windproof fabric which is ideal for cooler days. It is important not to underestimate the amount of yarn you will require for an item worked in loop stitches as this could be quite considerable.

Waistcoats, jackets and hats made entirely in loop stitch and bright paintbox colours are perfect for children's wear. Alternatively use the same stitches to give a 'fur' trimming effect on garments.

Clothes are not the only items you will come across in loop stitch. It is useful for making bathroom sets especially if a machine washable and quick drying yarn like Courtelle is used.

Loop stitch

This is loop stitch in its most usual form. It is worked into the fabric as you proceed in rows.

Using No.5.00 (ISR) crochet hook and a Double Knitting yarn, make 22ch.

1st row 1dc into 3rd ch from hook, work 1dc into every ch to end. Turn.

2nd row 1ch to count as first dc, miss first st of previous row, work a loop by inserting hook into next st, position yarn over 1st and 2nd fingers and extend yarn by lifting 2nd finger, draw through a loop as shown in diagram, then draw loop through

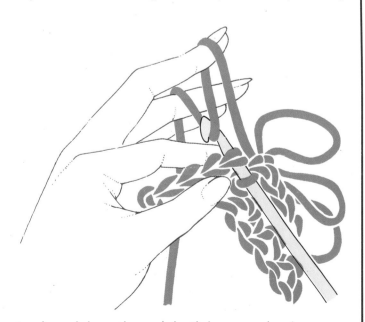

st, yrh and draw through both loops on hook, remove 2nd finger from loop, rep the action of making a

loop into every st to the end of the row, 1dc into the turning chain. Turn.

3rd row 1ch to count as first dc, miss first st of previous row, 1dc into every st to end, 1dc into the turning chain. Turn.

Repeat the 2nd and 3rd rows throughout to form the pattern.

Note You will see that the loops are on the back of the fabric as you are working. This is correct as you are making the loops from the wrong side of the work. The density of the loops can be altered by working them across the row on alternate stitches, and into the stitches between loops on following alternate rows.

Chain fur stitches

Again these chain loops are formed as part of the fabric. It has a close, curly fur effect that is reminiscent of many popular furs.

Using No.5.00 (ISR) crochet hook and a Double Knitting yarn, make 25ch.

1st row 1tr into 4th ch from hook, work 1tr into every ch to end. Turn.

2nd row 1ch to count as first dc, miss first st of previous row, *1dc into back loop only of next st, 10ch, rep from * to end of row, working last dc into the turning chain. Turn.

3rd row 3ch to count as first tr, missing the first st, work 1tr into every st of the last row worked in tr,

inserting the hook into the loop missed in the previous row of dc, 1tr into the turning chain. Turn.
Repeat the 2nd and 3rd rows throughout to form the pattern.

Cut fur stitch

Here the loops are added after the basic background —a mesh—has been worked.
Using No.5.00 (ISR) crochet hook and a Double Knitting yarn, make 25ch.
1st row 1dc into 3rd ch from hook, *1ch, miss next ch, 1dc into next ch, rep from * to end. Turn.
2nd row 1ch to count as first dc, 1dc into first 1ch sp, *1ch, 1dc into next 1ch sp, rep from * to last sp, 1ch, 1dc into the turning chain. Turn.
The 2nd row is repeated throughout.

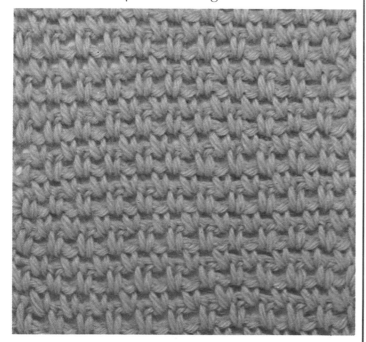

To add the loops Cut lengths of yarn as required (approximately 13 centimetres (*5 inches*) long).
Take two pieces of yarn together each time and fold in half, with right side of work facing, insert the crochet hook horizontally through the first dc in the mesh, place the two loops of yarn over the hook and draw through the work, place the four cut ends of yarn over the hook and draw through the two loops on the hook. Pull up tightly to secure. Repeat this process into every dc throughout the mesh.
Note As with loop stitch you can vary the amount of cut loops and their position on the fabric. See how attractive these loops can look and the different designs you can create if you work them in various colours, or in shades of one colour like our sample.

▼ *Hat in loop stitch and chain fur stitch on jacket*

'Fun fur' carriage cover

Color chart for cover

1 Square =1DC

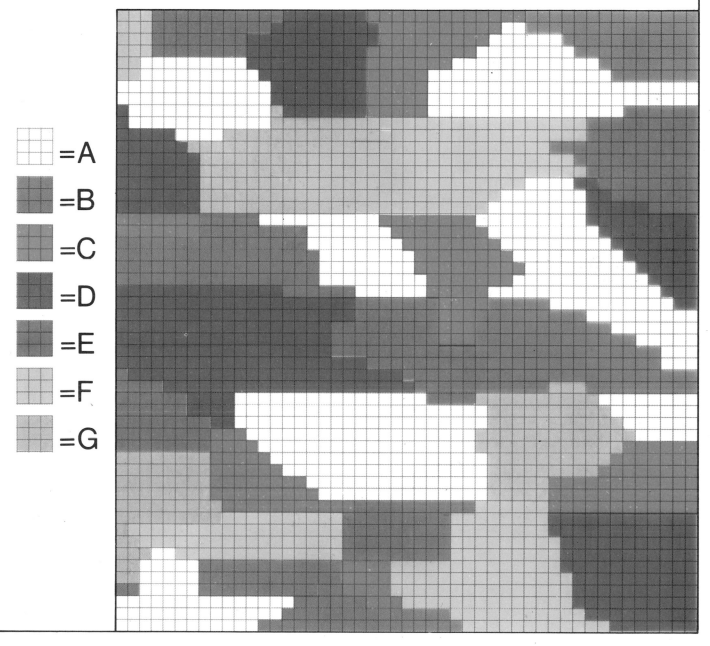

=A

=B

=C

=D

=E

=F

=G

Size
Crochet base measures 58.5cm × 34.5cm
(23in × 13½in)

Tension
13tr and 9 rows to 10cm (3.9in) worked on
No.4.00 (ISR) hook

Materials
10 × 20grm balls Wendy Courtellon

Double Knitting in main shade, A
3 balls each of contrast colours B, C, D,
E, F and G
One No.4.00 (ISR) crochet hook

Crochet base
Using No.4.00 (ISR) hook and A, make 50
ch.
1st row Into 4th ch from hook work 1tr,
1tr into each ch to end. Turn. 48tr.
2nd row 3ch to count as first tr, miss

first tr, 1tr into each tr, ending with 1tr
into 3rd of 3ch. Turn.
Rep last row 50 times more. Fasten off.

To make up
Cut rem balls of A and each ball of B, C,
D, E, F and G into 12.5cm (5in) lengths.
Following chart and using 2 strands of
yarn tog, knot round every tr in base.
Trim strands to desired length or leave
shaggy.

LOOPED BRAIDS AND EDGINGS

In this chapter we shall continue with more variations of the looped stitches you learnt in the last chapter. More advanced techniques are illustrated, including working with beads and we suggest how you might use these stitches.

Here the methods are used as a trim rather than an all over design because they are so decorative. To give the greatest contrast when using these trimmings on a crochet garment, the main stitches should be very basic such as double crochet or treble.

Accordion braid

This is formed by working many trebles into a small space on a background fabric of double treble to give a fluted effect.

Using No. 5.00 (ISR) crochet hook and a Double Knitting yarn, make 23ch.

1st row 1dtr into 5th ch from hook, work 1dtr into every ch to end. Turn.

2nd row 4ch to count as first dtr, miss first st in previous row, 1dtr into each st to end, 1dtr into the turning chain. Do not turn.

3rd row 3ch, work 6tr down side of first dtr, 1tr into st at base of this dtr, *work 7tr up side of next dtr in row, 1tr into st at top of this dtr, work 7tr down side of next dtr in row, 1tr into st at base of this dtr, rep from * to end of row. Fasten off.

Repeat the process on the first row of dtr that was worked.

This braid can be incorporated into a garment or applied to one that has been completed. It looks very effective round the outer edges of a long, simple evening coat as the bulkiness counteracts the length of the coat.

Accordion braid used to trim an evening coat

Triple loops worked over a bar

This is an unusual technique for making very thick loops. To be most effective it should be worked into the garment you are making as single rows or no more than three rows at the most. You could try spacing single rows at varying distances as in our illustration.

Work until the point in your garment where you wish to include triple loops, ending with a right side row.

Take a separate ball of yarn and wind it in a single strand over a piece of wood several times – a rule or a rug wool gauge used for cutting yarns for rug making and which has a groove down one side is ideal.

Next row Holding the wool-covered rule or gauge behind your work, begin at opposite end to ball of yarn, *insert hook into next st, then insert hook behind first 3 loops on rule, yrh and draw beneath the 3 loops of yarn and through the st of the previous row, yrh and draw through both loops on hook, rep from * to end of row, taking care to remove the yarn from the rule in consecutive order.

Remove the rule from the loops and cut the loop yarn at the end of the row. Work one row in double crochet before starting another triple loop row.

Vertical beaded loops

These are ideal for working a jabot around the front opening of an evening top.

Make sure that you buy beads that have the correct size hole for the yarn that you are using. Usually the beads will already be threaded on a coarse string when you purchase them, but you will need to transfer them on to the crochet yarn with which you will be working before you start work. To do this, make an overhand knot in one end of the bead thread, place the crochet yarn through this knot as in the diagram and carefully slide the beads from the thread on to the crochet yarn. Work to the position where a beaded row is required, ending with a right side row.

Next row Ss into the first st, *yrh and draw through a loop extending it for 15cm (6in), push up the required number of beads on the yarn and draw through the extended stitch, draw the enlarged st over the beaded loop and pull yarn tightly to secure (there is now no loop on the hook), insert hook into next st, yrh and draw through a st, ss into next st, *, rep from * to * until the required number of beaded loops have been worked. Use this same method to work beaded fringes, varying the number of beads used in a loop to give different depths.

ARAN CROCHET
BASIC STITCHES

Aran crochet

Aran is usually considered to be a knitting technique, but in this and following chapters we explain how you can achieve a similar effect working in crochet. It is a satisfying technique for those who prefer to crochet, giving quicker results and the same range of garments and items for the home can be made.

Traditional Aran work is usually seen in natural or off-white shades of yarn, but today many wool manufacturers make a special Aran yarn, which is very thick, in a variety of shades. The samples here explain how to work the basic patterns in crochet, which resemble the knitted versions quite closely.

Sample 1

Rib stitch This is the crochet version of the knitted rib. The fabric would be used from side to side across a garment, so that the foundation chain forms the side seam rather than the hem. If you are making a garment, this stitch is suitable for the welt. Using a smaller hook size than used for the rest of the garment, i.e. No.5.00 (ISR), make a length of chain to give the required depth of rib.

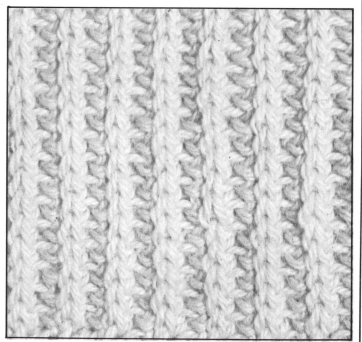

1st row Into 3rd ch from hook work 1dc, 1dc into each ch to end. Turn.
2nd row 1ch to count as first dc, miss first st, 1dc into each st to end, placing the hook into the horizontal loop under the normal ch loop of the dc, 1dc into turning ch. Turn.

Repeat the 2nd row throughout until the rib is the width of the garment.

To begin work on the main part of the garment, the ribbed fabric is turned so that the ridges run vertically. The loops formed by the row ends are then used as a basis for the first row of the main fabric. A larger hook, No.5.50 (ISR), is used for the main part and it may be

necessary to increase the number of stitches by working 2dc into some loops. In the following photograph the rib stitch is shown complete, followed by several rows of double crochet. This forms the basis of many Aran styles.

Sample 2

The following attractive stitches could be used as an all-over pattern or in a panel within an Aran design.

Even moss stitch Make a length of chain with multiples of 2 stitches.

1st row Miss first ch, ss into next ch, *1htr into next ch, ss into next ch, rep from * to end. Turn.

2nd row 1ch, miss first st, *1htr into next st, ss into next st, rep from * ending with last ss worked into turning ch. Turn.

The 2nd row is repeated throughout.

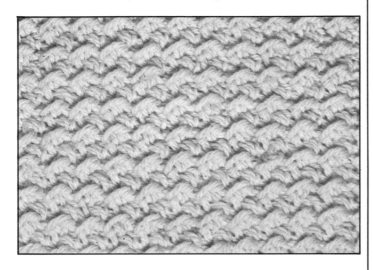

Uneven moss stitch Make a length of chain and work 1st and 2nd rows as given for even moss stitch.

3rd row 2ch to count as first htr, miss first st, ss into next st, *1htr into next st, ss into next st, rep from * to end, 1htr into turning ch. Turn.

4th row As 3rd.

5th row As 2nd.

6th row As 2nd.

The 3rd to 6th rows are repeated throughout.

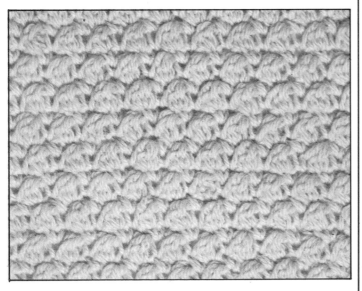

Sample 3

Even berry stitch Make a length of chain with multiples of 2 stitches.

1st row Into 3rd ch from hook work 1dc, 1dc into each ch to end. Turn.

2nd row 1ch to count as first ss, miss first st, *yrh and insert hook into next st, yrh and draw through a loop, yrh and draw through first loop on hook, yrh and insert hook into same st, yrh and draw through a loop, yrh

and draw through all 5 loops on hook, 1ch to secure st – called berry st –, ss into next st, rep from * ending with last ss worked into turning ch. Turn.

3rd row 1ch to count as first dc, miss first st, *ss into next berry st, 1dc into next ss, rep from * to end. Turn.

4th row 1ch to count as first ss, *1 berry st into next ss, ss into next dc, rep from * to end. Turn.

The 3rd and 4th rows are repeated throughout.

Uneven berry stitch Make a length of chain and work 1st to 3rd rows as given for even berry stitch.

4th row 1ch to count as first ss, 1 berry st into first dc, ss into next ss, *1 berry st into next dc, ss into next ss, rep from * to end. Turn.

5th row As 3rd.

The 2nd to 5th rows are repeated throughout.

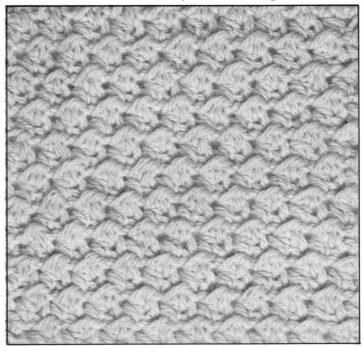

RAISED DESIGNS

We have already shown you how to work the basic background effects necessary for Aran crochet, where the double crochet or treble stitches are very important. Here you will see how the background can be decorated with raised designs which are added after the main fabric has been completed. Practise our samples first on a piece of double crochet fabric before starting your own designs.

Sample 1

Raised lines may run horizontally, vertically or diagonally. For all samples of raised work begin at the lower edge and hold the crochet hook on top of the crochet (i.e. right side of work) with the incoming yarn held in the normal way, under the work. Using No.5.50 (ISR) hook, make a slip loop on the hook, insert hook into first hole on the foundation chain, yrh and draw through a loop drawing it through loop on hook, *insert hook into same hole as last st, yrh and draw through a loop (2 loops on hook), insert hook into next hole above last insertion, yrh and draw through a loop drawing it through both loops on hook – called one raised double crochet –, rep from * to end of line.

Other crochet stitches, such as slip stitch or treble, may be substituted instead of the raised double crochet, depending on the depth of stitch required.

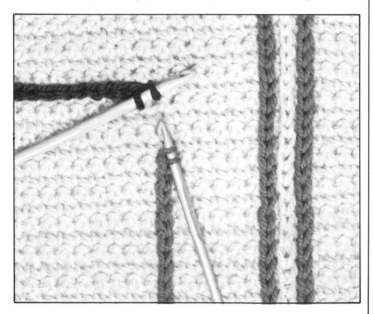

Sample 2

This sample depicts a variety of designs worked on a double crochet background. From left to right across the design there are 2 vertical rows of double crochet, then working from the diagram there is a row of twisted raised double crochet (work black line first), 2 lines of twisted double crochet which form a diamond pattern, another line of twisted raised double crochet and finally, 2 more vertical lines of crochet.

These designs could be used as a pattern panel on a garment, or on a household article as with the cushion cover the instructions for which we give below.

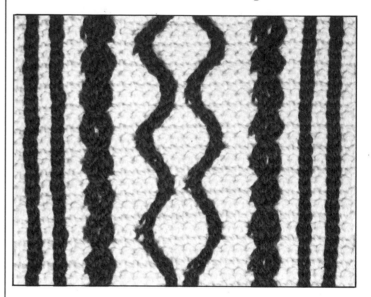

Aran Cushion cover
Size
56cm (*22in*) × 38cm (*15in*), excluding fringe

Tension
13 sts and 8 rows to 10cm (*3.9in*) over tr worked on No.4.00 (ISR) crochet hook

Materials
10 × 50grm balls Emu Aran
One No.4.00 (ISR) crochet hook
One No.5.50 (ISR) crochet hook
0.70 metres (¾ *yard*) cotton lining material
Kapok for filling
1 × 50cm (*20in*) zip fastener

Cushion cover (make 2)
Using No.4.00 (ISR) hook make 72ch loosely.
1st row Into 4th ch from hook work 1tr, 1tr into each ch to end. Turn. 70tr.
2nd row 3ch to count as first tr, miss first tr, 1tr into each tr, ending with last tr into 3rd of 3ch. Turn.
Rep last row 28 times more. Fasten off.
Surface crochet This can be worked on either both sides or only one side as required. Using No.5.50 (ISR) hook and double yarn throughout, follow the chart and work in raised slip stitch following the direction

of the arrows throughout, noting that in row C the cable patt should first be worked by following the arrows, then in the opposite direction indicated by the dots.

To make up

With WS tog and using No.5.50 (ISR) hook and double yarn, join 2 short sides and 1 long side by working a row of dc through both thicknesses, working 1dc into each tr, 1dc into each row end and 3dc into each corner. On 4th side, work in dc along one side only leaving opening for zip. Sew in zip. Make up cushion pad to required size using lining material and fill with kapok. Insert into cushion cover.

Fringe Cut yarn into 30.5cm (*12in*) lengths and using 3 strands tog, knot through each dc along short edges.

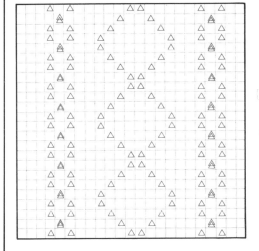

☐ = one space between double crochet

△ = one raised double crochet

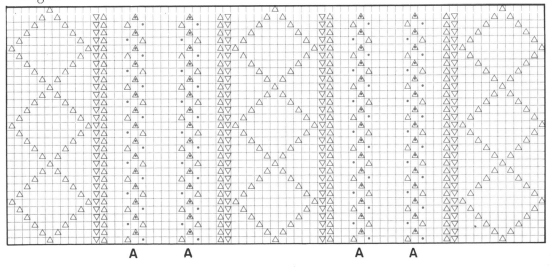

☐ = one space between trebles

△ = one raised slip stitch

= one raised slip stitch in opposite direction to arrows

BERRY STITCH MOTIFS

This chapter shows in detail how berry stitch, which was previously explained as an all-over design, can be worked into motifs on a double crochet background. The motifs are then outlined with raised double crochet to form a panel which could be incorporated into an Aran style garment.

Sample 1

This illustrates one method of grouping berry stitch. Using No.5.50 (ISR) hook and an Aran yarn, make a length of chain with multiples of 8+4 stitches.

1st row Into 3rd ch from hook work 1dc, 1dc into each ch to end. Turn.

2nd row 1ch to count as first dc, miss first st, 1dc into each st to end. Turn.

3rd row 1ch, miss first st, 1dc into each of next 3 sts, *ss into next st, yrh and insert into next st, yrh and draw through a loop, yrh and draw through first loop on hook, yrh and insert into same st, yrh and draw through a loop, yrh and draw through all loops on hook, 1ch to secure st – called berry st –, ss into next st, 1dc into each of next 5 sts, rep from * ending last rep with 1dc into each of next 4 sts. Turn.

4th row 1ch, miss first st, 1dc into each of next 3 sts, *1dc into next ss, ss into next berry st, 1dc into next ss, 1dc into each of next 5 sts, rep from * ending last rep with 1dc into each of next 4 sts. Turn.

5th row 1ch, miss first st, 1dc into each of next 2 sts, * ss into next dc, berry st into next dc, ss into next ss, berry st into next dc, ss into next dc, 1dc into each of next 3 sts, rep from * to end. Turn.

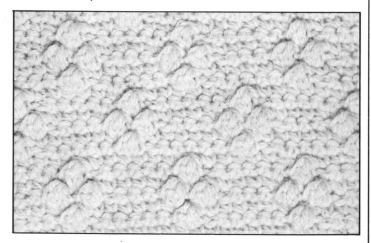

6th row 1ch, miss first st, 1dc into each of next 3 sts, *ss into next berry st, 1dc into next ss, ss into next berry st, 1dc into each of next 5 sts, rep from * ending last rep with 1dc into each of next 4 sts. Turn.

7th–8th rows As 3rd–4th rows.

9th row 1ch, miss first st, berry st into next dc, ss into next dc, *1dc into each of next 5 sts, ss into next dc, berry st into next dc, ss into next dc, rep from * to end. Turn.

10th row 1ch, miss first st, ss into next berry st, *1dc into each of next 7 sts, ss into next berry st, rep from * ending with 1dc into last st. Turn.

11th row 1ch, miss first st, *ss into next ss, berry st into next dc, ss into next dc, 1dc into each of next 3 sts, ss into next dc, berry st into next dc, rep from * to last 2 sts, ss into next ss, 1dc into last st. Turn.

12th row 1ch, miss first st, 1dc into next ss, ss into next berry st, *1dc into each of next 5 sts, ss into next berry st, 1dc into next ss, ss into next berry st, rep from * to last 3 sts, ss into next berry st, 1dc into next ss, 1dc into last st. Turn.

13th–14th rows As 9th–10th rows.

The 3rd to 14th rows are repeated to form the pattern.

Sample 2

This is a sample design where berry stitches in a diamond pattern have been included in a double crochet background and then the entire design has been emphasised with lines of raised double crochet. The technique of working raised double crochet was explained in detail previously and in our sample the lines are worked in varying colours to give them definition.

Using No.5.50 (ISR) hook and an Aran yarn, make 23ch.

1st row Into 3rd ch from hook work 1dc, 1dc into each ch to end. Turn.

Continue working in double crochet until one row before the position for starting berry stitch motif.

Next row Work across first 7 sts marking last st with a coloured thread, work across next 7 sts – this is the pattern area for the berry st motif, work across last 8 sts marking first st with a coloured thread. Turn.

1st patt row Work to marked position, 1dc into each of next 2 sts, ss into next st, berry st into next st, ss into next st, 1dc into each of next 2 sts, work to end. Turn.

Note From this point the instructions only refer to the centre 7 sts involved in the berry st design.

2nd patt row 1dc into each of next 3 sts, ss into next st, 1dc into each of next 3 sts.

3rd patt row 1dc into next st, (ss into next st, berry st into next st) twice, ss into next st, 1dc into next st.

4th patt row 1dc into each of next 2 sts, (ss into next st, 1dc into next st) twice, 1dc into next st.

5th patt row Ss into next st, (berry st into next st, ss into next st) 3 times.

6th patt row 1dc into next st, (ss into next st, 1dc into next st) 3 times.

7th–8th patt rows As 3rd–4th rows.

9th–10th rows As 1st–2nd rows.

Continue working in double crochet for the required depth, making more motifs if required. Complete the design by working the lines in raised double crochet from the chart.

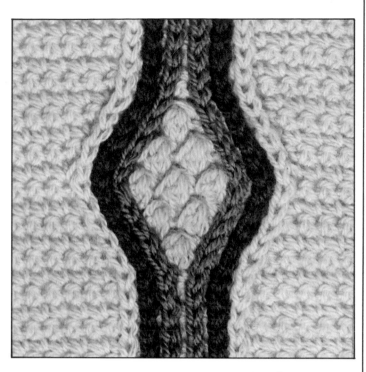

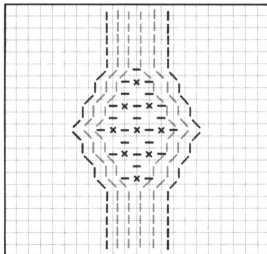

KEY

Each vertical line on each square = one double crochet
Each horizontal line on each square = one row
x = one berry stitch in place of a double crochet stitch
– = one slip stitch in place of a double crochet stitch
| = one raised double crochet worked vertically
/ = one raised double crochet worked diagonally

Sample 3

This is a variation on the previous sample with an enlarged berry stitch motif and double lines of raised double crochet which cross each other.

Work in same way as sample 2, marking a centre panel to cover 7 sts. Repeat 1st–6th patt rows, 3rd–6th, 3rd–4th and then 1st and 2nd rows. Use the chart to work the lines of raised double crochet.

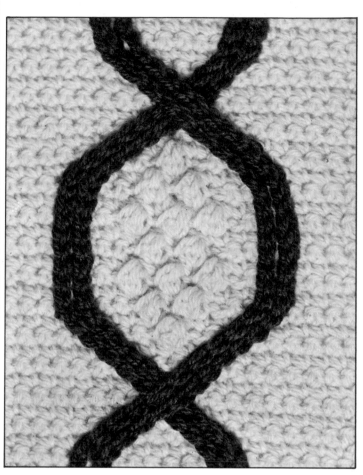

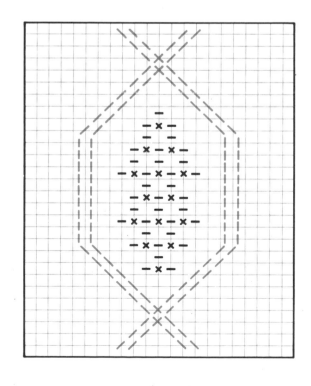

IRISH CROCHET
BASIC TECHNIQUES

Irish crochet

Irish crochet, also known as Honiton crochet, is a form of lace which originated as an imitation of the Guipure laces of Spain. The lace background and various motifs, such as the rose, leaf, shamrock plus other flowers and curves, are both major characteristics of this work.

This introductory chapter to the craft will cover some of the techniques for working the background and also a selection of some of the more simple motifs. The motifs may be applied directly on to the background or the lace mesh may be worked around the motif.

The samples shown here were worked in a No.5 cotton yarn with a No.2.00 (ISR) crochet hook. When you understand the basic techniques, try experimenting with some more unusual yarns and see what different effects may be achieved. All the net backgrounds seen here would make attractive evening shawls, especially if you work in one of the new mohair yarns.

Sample 1

To work the net background Make 50ch loosely.

1st row Into 10th ch from hook work 1dc, *6ch, miss 3ch, 1dc into next ch, rep from * to end of row. Turn.

2nd row 9ch, 1dc into first ch sp, *6ch, 1dc into next ch sp, rep from * to end of row. Turn.

The 2nd row is repeated throughout.

To work the rose motif Wrap the yarn 20 times round a pencil.

1st round Remove yarn carefully from the pencil, work 18dc into the ring. Join with a ss into first dc.

2nd round 6ch, miss 2dc, 1htr into next dc, *4ch, miss 2dc, 1htr into next dc, rep from * 3 times more, 4ch. Join with a ss into 2nd of 6ch.

3rd round Into each 4ch sp work 1dc, 1htr, 3tr, 1htr and 1dc to form a petal. Join with a ss into first dc.

4th round Ss into back of nearest htr of 2nd round, *5ch, passing chain behind petal of previous round, ss into next htr of 2nd round, rep from * 5 times more.

5th round Into each 5ch sp work 1dc, 1htr, 5tr, 1 htr and 1dc. Join with a ss into first dc.

6th round Ss into back of ss of 4th round, *6ch, passing chain behind petal of previous round, ss into next ss of 4th round, rep from * 5 times more.

7th round Into each 6ch sp work 1dc, 1htr, 6tr, 1htr and 1dc. Join with a ss into first dc. Fasten off.

Sample 2

To work the net background Make 58ch loosely.

1st row Into 16th ch from hook work 1dc, 3ch, 1dc into same ch as last dc, *9ch, miss 5ch, 1dc into next ch, 3ch, 1dc into same ch as last dc, rep from * to end of row. Turn.

2nd row 13ch, 1dc into first ch sp, 3ch, 1dc into same sp, *9ch, 1dc into next ch sp, 3ch, 1dc into same sp,

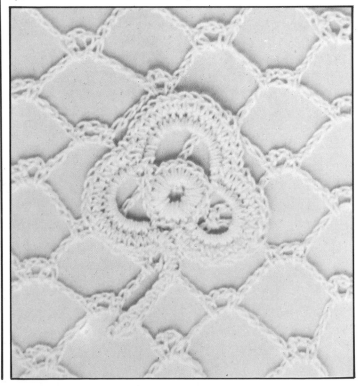

rep from * to end of row. Turn.
The 2nd row is repeated throughout.
To work the motif Wrap yarn 12 times round a pencil.
1st round Remove yarn carefully from the pencil, work 18dc into the ring. Join with a ss into first dc.
2nd round 8ch, miss 4dc, ss into next dc, 10ch, miss 4dc, ss into next dc, 8ch, miss 4dc, ss into next dc, work 12ch for stem, into 3rd ch from hook work 1dc, 1dc into each of next 9ch, turn.
3rd row Into first ch sp work 16dc, 20dc into next ch sp and 16dc into next ch sp. Turn.
4th row 3ch to count as first tr, miss first dc, 1tr into each dc to end of row. Fasten off.

Sample 3

To work the net background This background incorporates an attractive picot design. Make 47ch loosely.
1st row Work 4ch, ss into 4th ch from hook – called a picot –, 2ch, into 12th ch from picot work 1dc, *4ch, work a picot, 2ch, miss 4ch, 1dc into next ch, rep from * to end of row. Turn.
2nd row 6ch, work a picot, 2ch, 1dc into first ch sp, *4ch, work a picot, 2ch, 1dc into next ch sp, rep from * to end of row. Turn.
The 2nd row is repeated throughout.
To work the motif Wrap yarn 14 times round little finger of left hand.
1st round Remove yarn carefully from finger, work 38dc into the ring. Join with a ss into first dc.
2nd round *9ch, miss 6dc, ss into next dc, rep from * 4 times more, ss into each of next 3dc.
3rd round Into each 9ch sp work 12dc, work 14ch for stem, into 3rd ch from hook work 1dc, 1dc into each of next 11ch. Join with a ss into first dc.
4th round 3ch to count as first tr, miss first dc, 1tr into each dc on all 5 loops. Fasten off.

Sample 4

Here our sample has the same net background as sample 2, but it is worked in an ordinary parcel string and the raffia motif is made in the same way as the motif on sample 3. Use different coloured motifs to decorate a string hold-all.

Sample 5

Use the rose motif described in sample 1 to decorate a wedding veil. Our rose is worked in an extremely fine yarn and has beads sewn on to the motif over the background. The net here is a commercial one, but you could, with time and patience, make a valuable family heirloom if you worked your veil in a crochet net.

ADVANCED DESIGNS

To continue our series about Irish crochet we have ideas for a more complicated background net, also several different motifs.

The crochet lace background could be used for a scarf or evening shawl, made either into a stole shape or a large triangle trimmed with a fringe. Instead of using traditional cotton for Irish crochet try using mohair, lurex or a novelty cotton for an unusual effect. By working the motifs illustrated here you will learn the two techniques which are most common in this type of work. They both give a raised look to the work but by different means. One is working over several thicknesses of yarn and the other way is to insert the hook into the horizontal loop under the two loops where the hook is usually placed.

1st row Into 4th ch from hook work a ss – one picot formed –, 8ch, ss into 4th ch from hook, 2ch, 1dc into 8th ch from first picot worked, *6ch, ss into 4th ch from hook, 8ch, ss into 4th ch from hook, 2ch, miss 4ch, 1dc into next ch, rep from * to end. Turn.

2nd row 9ch, ss into 4th ch from hook, 8ch, ss into 4th ch from hook, 2ch, 1dc into first ch sp (i.e. between the 2 picots), *6ch, ss into 4th ch from hook, 8ch, ss into 4th ch from hook, 2ch, 1dc into next ch sp, rep from * to end. Turn.

The 2nd row is repeated throughout.

To work the rose motif Repeat the instructions given for the rose in the last chapter, do not fasten off but continue as follows:

Next round *7ch, passing chain behind petal of

Shawl incorporating net background, rose and leaf motifs

The samples in this chapter were worked in a very fine cotton yarn, No.25, and a fine crochet hook, but the size of the hook will vary depending on the sort of yarn you use.

Sample 1
To work the net background Make 57ch loosely.

previous round ss between the 2dc of next adjoining petals, rep from * 5 times more.

Next round Into each 7ch sp work 1dc, 1htr, 8tr, 1htr, 1dc. Join with a ss into first dc. Turn work.

Next round 1ch to count as first dc, miss first st, work 1dc into each st all round placing the hook into the horizontal loop behind the st in the previous row – this st gives a raised effect on the right side of the work. Fasten off.

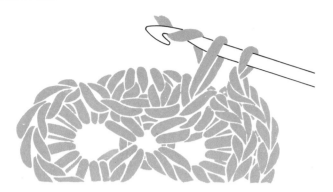

To work the leaf motif All the double crochet stitches from a given point in the pattern are worked over four thicknesses of yarn to give a ridged effect. Cut four lengths of yarn, each 40.5cm (*16in*) long, and when the first dc to be worked in this way is indicated, place the yarn behind the work on a level with the stitch into which the hook is to be placed.

Make 16ch. Into 3rd ch from hook work 1dc, 1dc into each ch to last ch, 5dc into last ch to form tip of leaf, then work 1dc into each st on other side of chain. Work 3dc over the 4 thicknesses of yarn, still working over the yarn and continuing towards tip of leaf, work 1dc into each of next 12dc, working into back loop only of each st. Turn work, 1ch, miss first dc, working down one side of leaf and up the other side, work 1dc into each dc to within 4dc of tip of leaf. Turn work, *1ch, miss first st, 1dc into each dc of previous row to last 4dc of row and working 3dc into dc at base of leaf. Turn work. *. Repeat from * to * until the leaf is the required size.

Sample 2
Wrap yarn 14 times round a pencil.
1st round Remove yarn carefully from pencil, work 21dc into ring. Join with a ss into first dc.
2nd round 1ch to count as first dc, miss first st, 1dc into each dc all round. Join with a ss into first ch.
3rd round 1ch to count as first dc, miss first dc, 1dc into each of next 6 sts, (12ch, 1dc into each of next 7 sts) twice, 14ch. Join with a ss into first ch.
4th round 1ch to count as first dc, miss first dc, 1dc into each of next 4 sts, (22dc into next 12ch sp, 1dc into each of next 5 sts) twice, 24dc into next 14ch sp. Join with a ss into first ch.
5th round Ss into each of next 4 sts, *4ch, miss 2 sts, ss into next st, *, rep from * to * 6 times more, miss next 3 sts, ss into each of next 3 sts, rep from * to * 7 times, miss next 3 sts, ss into each of next 3 sts, rep from * to * 8 times. Join with a ss into first ss.
6th round 1ch to count as first dc, miss first st, 1dc into each of next 2 sts, (6dc into next 4ch sp) 7 times, ss into next st, work 18ch for stem, into 3rd ch from hook work 1dc, 1dc into each of next 15ch, ss into next st on main motif, (6dc into next 4ch sp) 7 times,

1dc into each of next 3 sts, (6dc into next 4ch sp) 8 times. Join with a ss into first ch. Fasten off.

Sample 3
Make 40ch.
1st row Into 3rd ch from hook work 1dc, 1dc into each ch to last ch, 5dc into last ch. Do not turn.
2nd row 1dc into each ch on opposite side of 1st row. Turn.
3rd row The petals are worked individually down each side of the stem beginning from the tip where the last dc was worked as follows: *12ch, ss into st at base of ch, 3ch, miss 2dc, ss into next dc, turn, work 25tr into 12ch sp, ss into first dc on row 1, turn, 1ch to count as first dc, miss first tr, 1dc into each tr round petal, ss into same ss as last ss – one petal has been completed –, rep from * to give the required number of petals noting that when the 25tr have been worked, the ss is placed in front of the previous petal by inserting the hook into the 3rd dc up from the base of the petal being worked. Fasten off.
To complete the other side, rejoin yarn at the tip and work the petals in the same way, but join the last of the 25tr behind the previous petal.

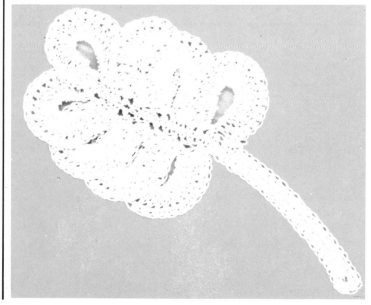

COMBINING MOTIFS AND BACKGROUNDS

During our previous chapters on Irish crochet instructions have been given for working the background and motifs separately. This chapter will deal with the alternative techniques of producing the background and motifs together.

Sample 1

This is a six-sided figure where the net background has been worked around the central motif. The shapes may eventually be joined together to form a whole fabric (the chapter on Square and Wheel Motifs gives the method) which would make an attractive bedcover or lampshade covering.

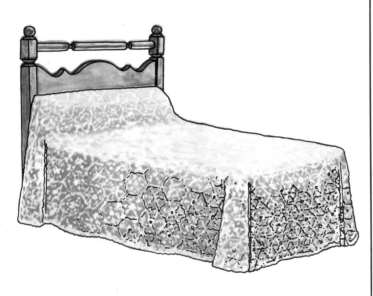

To work the sample Using a No.2.00 (ISR) crochet hook and a No.25 cotton yarn, make a rose motif as in preceding chapter.

Next round Ss into each of next 3 sts of first petal, *(5ch, miss 2 sts, ss into next st) twice, 5ch, miss 3 sts, ss into next st, rep from * 5 times more.

Next round Ss into each of next 2 sts, 6ch, *1dc into next 5ch sp, 5ch, rep from * 16 times more. Join with a ss into 2nd of 6ch.

Next round *Into next 5ch sp work 1dc, 1htr, 5tr, 1htr and 1dc, (5ch, 1dc into next 5ch sp) twice, 5ch, rep from * 5 times more. Join with a ss into first dc.

Next round Ss into each of next 5 sts, 6ch, (1dc into next 5ch sp, 5ch) 3 times, *1dc into centre tr of next petal gr, (5ch, 1dc into next 5ch sp) 3 times, 5ch, rep from * 4 times more. Join with a ss into 2nd of 6ch.

Next round Ss into each of next 2 sts, 6ch, *1dc into next 5ch sp, 5ch, rep from * 22 times more. Join with a ss into 2nd of 6ch.

Next round Ss into each of next 2 sts, 6ch, (1dc into next 5ch sp, 5ch) twice, into next 5ch sp work 1dc, 1htr, 5tr, 1htr and 1dc, *(5ch, 1dc into next 5ch sp) 3 times, 5ch, into next 5ch sp work 1dc, 1htr, 5tr, 1htr and 1dc, rep from * 4 times more, 5ch. Join with a ss into 2nd of 4ch.

Next round Ss into each of next 2 sts, 6ch, 1dc into next ch sp, 5ch, 1dc into next ch sp, 5ch, 1dc, into centre tr of next petal gr, *(5ch, 1dc into next ch sp) 4 times, 5ch, 1dc into centre tr of next petal gr, rep from * 4 times more, 5ch, 1dc into next ch sp, 5ch. Join with a ss into 2nd of 6ch.

Next round Ss into each of next 2 sts, 6ch, *1dc into next ch sp, 5ch, rep from * 28 times more. Join with a ss into 2nd of 6ch.

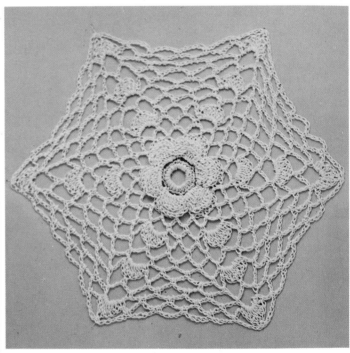

Next round Ss into each of next 2 sts, 6ch, 1dc into next ch sp, 5ch, into next ch sp work 1dc, 1htr, 5tr, 1htr, and 1dc, *(5ch, 1dc into next ch sp) 4 times, 5ch, into next ch sp work 1dc, 1htr, 5tr, 1htr and 1dc, rep from * 4 times more, (5ch, 1dc into next ch sp) twice, 5ch. Join with a ss into 2nd of 6ch.

Next round Ss into each of next 2 sts, 6ch, 1dc into next ch sp, 5ch, 1dc into centre tr of next petal gr, *(5ch, 1dc into next 5ch sp) 5 times, 5ch, 1dc into centre tr of next petal gr, rep from * 4 times more, (5ch, 1dc into next ch sp) 3 times, 5ch. Join with a ss into 2nd of 6ch. Fasten off.

Sample 2

The technique shown here is the method of working motifs and placing them on to paper so that a chain stitch may be worked to join the motifs together to form a fabric.

To work the circle Wrap yarn 20 times round a pencil.

1st round Remove yarn carefully from pencil, work 24dc into circle. Join with a ss into first dc.

2nd round 8ch, miss 2dc, *1tr into next dc, 5ch, miss 2dc, rep from * 6 times more. Join with a ss into 3rd of 8ch.

3rd round 3ch to count as first tr, 3tr into first ch sp, 4ch, ss into 4th ch from hook – ca!led 1 picot –, 4tr into same ch sp, 1 picot, *(4tr, 1 picot) twice into next ch sp, rep from * 6 times more. Join with a ss into 3rd of 3ch. Fasten off.

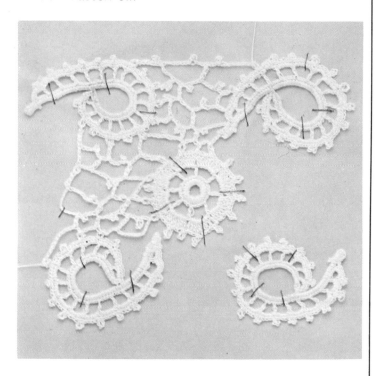

To work the curve Cut ten lengths of yarn, each 18cm (7in) long. Work 60dc over yarn. Turn work and leave extra yarn to hang freely.

Next row 1ch, ss into 2nd dc, 3ch, miss 3dc, 1htr into next dc, (3ch, miss 3dc, 1tr into next dc) 5 times, (3ch, miss 2dc, 1tr into next dc) 8 times, (3ch, miss 2dc, 1htr into next dc) 3 times, 3ch, ss into last dc. Join with a ss into dc below 3rd tr worked at beg of row to give a circle plus a small length of work. Turn.

Next row Into first ch sp work 5dc, (4dc into next ch sp, 1 picot) 16 times, 4dc into next ch sp, double back the extra 10 lengths of yarn and work 4dc very tightly over the double length, 1dc into end loop, 1ch. Fasten off working yarn. Pull ten lengths of yarn tight to neaten, then cut away.

To join the motifs Make the desired number of motifs and tack on to a firm paper background. The green tacking stitches may be seen in the illustration and further tacks, rather than pins which tend to fall out, should be used as the filling-in progresses.

Our sample shows a circle and four curves, but any of the previous motifs which you have learnt could be incorporated in this method of working. Only half the filling-in has been completed so that the working method may be clearly seen.

A dress pattern of an evening bodice could be used as the paper backing and then the various motifs would be joined together to give the appearance of lace. It would then be necessary to make a lining for this lace.

Chain stitches are used for the filling-in which was started at the top right hand corner of the work. At random intervals a picot is worked by making four chain and slip stitching into the first of these. It is easiest to work in lines to and fro, so joining the motifs together and slip stitching back across some chain stitches where necessary or even breaking off the yarn and rejoining it at a new position on the work. When all the motifs are joined, the tacks may be removed and all the cut ends of yarn should be neatened on the wrong side of the work.

IRISH MOTIFS ON SQUARES

Our illustration shows a long evening skirt which is made up of simple crochet squares some of which are decorated with Irish crochet motifs. To make the skirt, which has no side seams or opening, work 80 squares with double knitting yarn and a No.5.00 (ISR) crochet hook as described later in this chapter. The squares are joined, using the same method as described in the chapter on Square and Wheel Motifs, into ten lines of eight squares each.

Use the crochet motifs, also described in this chapter and worked with the same yarn and crochet hook, to decorate various motifs and sew them on to the squares with a matching yarn using tiny stitches. Neaten the waist with a round of loosely worked quadruple trebles and then slot elastic, dyed to a matching shade if necessary, through the trebles. Two motifs may be placed at the centre front of the waistband to act as buckles.

To work the square motif Make 6ch. Join with a ss into first ch to form a circle.

1st round 3ch to count as first tr, work 19tr into the circle. Join with a ss into 3rd of 3ch.

2nd round 1ch to count as first dc, 1htr into next st, 1tr, 3ch, and 1tr into next st, 1htr into next st, 1dc into next st, *1dc into next st, 1htr into next st, 1tr, 3ch and 1tr into next st, 1htr into next st, 1dc into next st, rep from * twice more. Join with a ss into first ch.

3rd round 3ch to count as first tr, 1tr into each of next 2 sts, into corner 3ch sp work 2tr, 3ch and 2tr, *1tr into each of next 6 sts, into corner 3ch sp work 2tr, 3ch and 2tr, rep from * twice more, 1tr into each of next 3 sts. Join with a ss into 3rd of 3ch.

4th round 3ch to count as first tr, 1tr into each of next 4 sts, into corner 3ch sp work 2tr, 3ch and 2tr, *1tr into each of next 10 sts, into corner 3ch sp work 2tr, 3ch and 2tr, rep from * twice more, 1tr into each of next 5 sts. Join with a ss into 3rd of 3ch.

5th round 3ch to count as first tr, 1tr into each of next 6 sts, into corner 3ch sp work 2tr, 3ch and 2tr, *1tr into each of next 14 sts, into corner 3ch sp work 2tr, 3ch and 2tr, rep from * twice more, 1tr into each of next 7 sts. Join with a ss into 3rd of 3ch. Fasten off.

This gives a firm crochet square, as used in samples 1 and 2, where the corners are emphasised by a diagonal line of holes. Samples 3 and 4 have the same square as a basis, but are made more solid by replacing the 3ch at each corner with 1ch.

Sample 1

To work the wheel motif Wrap yarn 20 times round first finger of left hand.

1st round Remove yarn carefully from finger, work 20dc into circle. Join with a ss into first dc.

2nd round 12ch, into 3rd ch from hook work 1dc, work 11dc over complete length of chain instead of into each ch, miss next dc on circle, ss into next dc, *10ch, join with a ss into 6th dc up from circle of last 'petal', 1ch, work 12dc over the complete chain, miss next dc on circle, ss into next dc, rep from * 7 times

more, 10ch, join with a ss into 6th ch up from circle of last 'petal', 1ch, work 6dc over the complete chain, join with a ss into free end of first 'petal', work 6 more dc over complete chain. Join with a ss into circle. Fasten off.

Sample 2

This is known as the Clones knot and it is often seen in Irish lace. Here we use a very different yarn to the traditional as it is easier to work with, but you will need to practise before achieving a perfect knot.

To work the knots Make 10ch. Hold the length of chain firmly between thumb and first finger of left hand, *yrh, bring hook towards you, under the length of chain and draw through a loop, rep from * approx 18 times, noting that the yarn passing over the hook and length of chain should be loosely but evenly placed to give a good looped knot. When the required number of loops have been worked, yrh and draw through all the loops on the hook, ss into the ch just behind the looped knot. Continue by making as many lengths of chain and knots as required.

A stem may be added to complete the motif, by working 14ch after the last knot has been completed, into 3rd ch from hook work 1dc, work 14dc over complete length of chain, ss into last knot. Fasten off. Arrange the knots in position on the square and stitch in position.

Sample 3

This is a simple design achieved by making several small rings.

To work the rings Wrap yarn 12 times round first finger of left hand.

Next round Remove yarn carefully from finger, work 14dc into circle. Join with a ss into first dc. Fasten off. Make as many rings as required, then work a stem to complete the design.

To work a stem Make 14ch. Into 3rd ch from hook work 1dc, work 14dc over the complete length of chain. Fasten off.

Arrange the rings and stem on the square to give the desired effect and sew in place.

Sample 4

This is known as coiled work. Take 8 thicknesses of yarn, approx 57cm (*20in*) long, to form a filling core. We worked approx 25dc over the entire core, but you can experiment with any number you desire, then take the beginning of the work and twist up and behind the hook to form a circle, ss into 5th dc worked, continue by working another 25dc over the core and make it into a circle as before.

Continue in this way until the desired shape is achieved. Fasten off yarn and arrange in place on the square.

Glittering Irish crochet bolero

Sizes

To fit 81.5/91.5[94/101.5]cm (32/36[37/40]in) bust
Length to centre back, 40.5[43]cm (16[17]in)
Sleeve seam, 30.5cm (12in)
The figures in brackets [] refer to the 94/101.5cm (37/40in) size only

Tension

4½ shells and 16 rows to 10cm (3.9in) over patt worked on No.2.50 (ISR) crochet hook

Materials

10[11] × 20grm balls Wendy Minuit Lurex
One No.2.50 (ISR) crochet hook
One button

Note

It is easier to work with Minuit Lurex if the ball of yarn is first placed on a central spool. This can be done by rolling up a piece of card, about 12.5cm (5in) square, and securing the end with sticky tape

Jacket

Using No.2.50 (ISR) crochet hook make 90[99]ch and beg at neck edge.
Base row Into 3rd ch from hook work 1dc, 1dc into each ch to end. Turn. 89[98] dc.
1st inc row 1ch to count as first dc, 1dc into each of next 7dc, *2dc into next dc, 1dc into each of next 8dc, rep from * to end, working last dc into turning ch. Turn. 98[107]dc.
Next row 1ch, *1dc into next dc, rep from * to end. Turn.
2nd inc row (buttonhole row) 1ch, 1dc into each of next 2dc, 3ch, miss 3dc, 1dc into each of next 2dc, *2dc into next dc, 1dc into each of next 9[10]dc, rep from * to end. Turn. 107[116]dc.
Next row 1ch, 1dc into each dc to end, working 3dc into 3ch loop of previous row. Turn.
3rd inc row 1ch to count as first dc, 1dc into each of next 7dc, *2dc into next dc, 1dc into each of next 10[11]dc, rep from *

to end. Turn. 116[125]dc.
Next row 1ch, 1dc into each dc to end. Turn.
Commence lace patt.
Base row 1ch to count as first dc, 1dc into each of next 6dc for right front border, *5ch, miss 2dc, 1dc into next dc, rep from * to last 7dc, turn and leave these 7dc for left front border. 34[37] 5ch loops.
1st row 1ch, *into next 5ch loop work (2dc, 3ch, ss into last dc to form picot, 3dc, 1 picot, 2dc) – called 1 shell –, ss into next dc, rep from * to end, working 1dc into last dc. Turn.
2nd row 7ch, 1dc into centre dc between first 2 picots, *5ch, 1dc into centre dc between 2 picots on next shell, rep from * to end, 3ch, 1dtr into last dc. Turn.
3rd row 1ch to count as first dc, into next 3ch loop work (1dc, 1 picot, 2dc), ss into next dc, *1 shell into next 5ch loop, ss into next dc, rep from * to end, ending with 2dc, 1 picot, 2dc into 7ch loop, 1dc into 4th of 7ch. Turn.
4th row 1ch to count as first dc, *5ch, 1dc into centre dc between 2 picots on next shell, rep from * to end, 3ch, 1dtr into last dc. Turn.
These 4 rows form patt, noting that on subsequent 1st patt rows the first shell will be worked into 3ch loop and last dc will be worked into 3rd of 5ch loop. Rep them once more, then first of them again.
Shape yoke
**1st inc row Patt 6[7] loops, (always counting ½ loops at ends of rows as 1 loop), (5ch, miss next picot and 2dc, 1dc into ss between shells, 5ch, 1dc between next 2 picots – called inc 1), patt 6[6] loops, inc 1, patt 7[8] loops, inc 1, patt 6[6] loops, inc 1, patt to end. 39[42] loops.
Patt 3 rows without shaping.
2nd inc row Work as given for 1st inc row, working 11[12] loops in centre-back instead of 7[8] loops. 43[46] loops.
Patt 3 rows without shaping.
3rd inc row Patt 3[4] loops, *inc 1, patt 5 loops, rep from * ending last rep with 3[5] loops.
Patt 3 rows without shaping.

4th inc row Patt 3[5] loops, *inc 1, patt 5 loops, rep from * ending last rep with 3[5] loops.
Patt 3 rows without shaping.
5th inc row Patt 2[3] loops, *inc 1, patt 5 loops, rep from * ending last rep with 1[3] loops. 68[71] loops.
Patt 3 rows without shaping.
Divide for underarm
Next row Patt 12[13] loops, *work 15[18]ch, miss 11[12] shells, 1dc between next 2 picots, *, patt 19[20] loops, rep from * to * once more, patt to end. Turn.
Next row Patt 12[13] loops, *1dc into each of next 15[18]ch, *, patt 19[20] loops, rep from * to * once more, patt to end. Turn.
Next row Patt 12[13] loops, *5ch, miss first of 15[18]dc at underarm, 1dc into next dc, (5ch, miss 3dc, 1dc into next dc) 3[4] times, 5ch, 1dc between next 2 picots, *, patt 18[19] loops, rep from * to * once more, patt to end. Turn. 51[56] loops.
Keeping patt correct, cont without shaping until 13[15] picot rows in all have been worked from underarm. Fasten off.
Sleeves
Using No.2.50 (ISR) hook and with WS of work facing, rejoin yarn to centre dc at 15 underarm dc for 1st size and between 2 centre dc of 18dc for 2nd size.
Next row (5ch, miss 3dc, 1dc into next dc) once[twice], 5ch, 1dc into next dc, (5ch, 1dc between next 2 picots) 11[12] times, 5ch, 1dc into next dc before underarm, (5ch, miss 3dc, 1dc into next dc) twice. Turn. 16[18] loops.
Cont in patt until 14 picot rows in all have been worked from underarm, ending with a picot row.
Next row (inc) Patt 1 loop, inc 1 as given for yoke, patt 5[6] loops, inc 1, patt 6[7] loops, inc 1, patt to end. Turn. 19[21] loops.
Patt 7[9] more rows without shaping.
Fasten off.

To make up

Do not press. Join sleeve seams.
Edging Using No.2.50 (ISR) hook and with WS of left front facing, rejoin yarn to 7dc at neck, 1ch, 1dc into each dc to end. Turn.
Next row 1ch, 1dc into each dc to end. Turn.
Rep this row until border, slightly stretched, fits down left front to lower edge. Fasten off.
Work other side in same way. Sl st borders into place.
With RS of work facing, rejoin yarn to right front at neck edge and work 1 row ss all round neck edge. Fasten off.
Sew on button to correspond with buttonhole.

Irish motif cushions

Sizes
Each cushion measures 40.5cm (*16in*) square

Tension
Brown and orange motif measures 7.5cm (*3in*) square worked on No.2.00 (ISR) crochet hook

Turquoise and lemon motif measures 11.5cm (*4½in*) between widest points worked on No.2.00 (ISR) crochet hook

Materials
Both cushions 1 × 20grm ball Twilley's Lyscordet in each of two colours, A and B
One No.2.00 (ISR) crochet hook
0.45 metres (*½yd*) of 0.90 metre (*36in*) wide gingham material
40.5cm (*16in*) square cushion pad

Brown and orange motifs
1st motif
Using No.2.00 (ISR) hook and A, make 8ch. Join with a ss into first ch to form a circle.

1st round 4ch, leaving last loop of each on hook work 2dtr into circle, yrh and draw through all loops on hook – called 1st cluster –, *4ch, leaving last loop of each on hook work 3dtr into circle, yrh and draw through all loops on hook – called 1 cluster –, rep from * 6 times more, 4ch. Join with a ss to top of 1st cluster. Break off A.

2nd round Join B with a ss into any 4ch loop, work 1st cluster into this loop, (4ch and 1 cluster) twice into same loop, *3ch, 1dc into next 4ch loop, 3ch, 1 cluster into next 4ch loop, (4ch and 1 cluster) twice into same loop, rep from * twice more, 3ch, 1dc into next 4ch loop, 3ch. Join with a ss to top of first cluster. Break off B.

3rd round Join A with a ss to next 4ch loop, 1dc into same loop, *9ch, 1dc into next 4ch loop, (5ch, 1dc into next 3ch loop) twice, 5ch, 1dc into next 4ch loop,

rep from * 3 times, omitting last dc. Join with a ss into first dc.

4th round Using A work *7tr, 5ch and 7tr into 9ch loop, 1dc into next 5ch loop, 3dc, 3ch and 3dc into next 5ch loop, 1dc into next 5ch loop, rep from * 3 times more. Join with a ss into top of first tr. Fasten off.

2nd motif
Work as given for 1st motif until 3rd round has been completed.

4th round Work 7tr into first 9ch loop, 2ch, ss into corresponding 5ch loop on 1st motif, 2ch, 7tr into same 9ch loop on 2nd motif, 1dc into next 5ch loop, 3dc into next 5ch loop, 1ch, ss into corresponding 3ch loop on 1st motif, 1ch, 3dc into same 5ch loop on 2nd motif, 1dc

into next 5ch loop, 7tr into next 9ch loop, 2ch, ss to corresponding 5ch loop on 1st motif, 2ch, 7tr into same 9ch loop on 2nd motif, complete as given for 1st motif. Fasten off.

Make and join the 3rd and 4th motifs in the same way so that they form a square.

5th motif
Work as given for 1st motif, using B instead of A and A instead of B and joining to one free side of 1st motif on 4th round.

6th motif
Work as given for 5th motif and join on the 4th round to other free side of 1st motif, also joining to 5th motif at one corner.

7th and 8th motifs

Work as given for 5th motif, but join to the two free sides of 3rd motif and to each other at one corner.

Small flowers

Using A only, work as given for 1st motif until 1st round has been completed.

2nd round Work 3dc, 3ch and 3dc into each 4ch loop to last loop, 3dc into last loop, 1ch, ss to free 5ch loop of motif of opposite colour, 1ch, 3dc into same 4ch loop. Join with a ss to first dc. Fasten off. Make 3 more motifs in A and 2 in B.

To make up

Cut a piece of gingham 86.5cm (*34in*) square, fold in half and seam along 3 edges, leaving 1.5cm (½*in*) turnings. Turn to RS and insert a piece of card into the case to make pinning the motifs easier. Pin crochet in position on cover, then sew using a matching colour. Place pad in cover, turn in raw edges and oversew the seam.

Turquoise and lemon motifs
1st motif

Using No.2.00 (ISR) hook and A, make 8ch. Join with a ss into first ch to form a circle.

1st round 6ch to count as first tr and 3ch, 1tr into circle, *3ch, 1tr into circle, rep from * 3 times more, 3ch. Join with a ss into 3rd of 6ch.

2nd round *Into next 3ch loop work 1dc, 1htr, 3tr, 1htr and 1dc, rep from * all round.

3rd round 5ch, *working across back work 1dc round stem of next tr in 1st round, 5ch, rep from * 4 times more. Join with a ss round last stem, taking in first 5ch.

4th round *Into next 5ch loop work 1dc, 1htr, 5tr, 1htr and 1dc, rep from * to end.

5th round *7ch, 1dc into back of dc between petals of previous round, rep from * all round, ending with 7ch, 1dc into back of next dc between petals, taking in the base of the 7ch.

6th round Into next 7ch loop work 1dc, 1htr, 7tr, 1htr and 1dc, rep from * all round. Join with a ss into first dc. Break off A.

7th round Join in B to dc between petals, 1dc into same place, *8ch, 1dc into 4th of 7tr of next petal, 8ch, 1dc between petals, rep from * all round. Join with a ss into first dc.

8th round Ss into first 4ch, 1dc into 8ch loop, *12ch, 1dc into next 8ch loop, 1dc into next 8ch loop, rep from * omitting dc at end of last rep. Join with a ss into first dc.

9th round *1dc into each of next 6ch, 3ch, 1dc into each of next 6ch, 1dc between 2dc of previous round, rep from * to end. Join with a ss into first dc. Fasten off.

2nd motif

Work as given for 1st motif until 8th round has been completed.

9th round 1dc into each of first 6ch, 1ch, ss into 3ch loop on 1st motif, 1ch, 1dc into each of next 6ch on 2nd motif, work as given for 1st motif, joining as before on the next 3ch loop, complete as given for 1st motif. Fasten off.

Make 7 more motifs, joining as before into 3 rows with 3 motifs in each.

Small motif

Using No.2.00 (ISR) hook and A, make 5ch. Join with a ss into first ch to form a circle.

1st round 3ch, 11tr into circle. Join with a ss into 3rd of 3ch.

2nd round 1dc into sp between 3ch and next tr, *8ch, miss next 2 sp between tr, 1dc into sp between next 2tr, rep from * to end. Join with a ss into same sp as first dc.

3rd round Ss into first 4ch, 1dc into 8ch loop, *6ch, 1dc into join of large motifs, 6ch, 1dc into next 8ch loop on small motif, rep from * 3 times more, working last dc into first dc.

Fasten off. Make 3 more small motifs and join to large motifs in the same way.

To make up

Complete as given for other cushion.

91

COLOURED PATTERNS
ZIGZAG STRIPES

Zig-zag crochet designs
The technique of working this very attractive form of patterning is very different to those learnt in previous chapters. Crochet formed in this way with a double knitting yarn gives a very decorative, thick fabric which is suitable for jackets and jerkins. The same technique could be worked in Lurex for evening bags and belts, or in raffia yarns for more casual accessories. Instructions for working the technique and several variations on the design are given here.

Sample 1
Two colours of double knitting yarn, A and B, have been used for this sample. Using No.3.50 (ISR) hook and A, make a chain with multiples of 10+2 stitches.
1st row Into 3rd ch from hook work 1dc, 1dc into each ch to end. Turn.
2nd row 1ch to count as first dc, miss first st, 1dc into each st, ending with last dc into turning ch. Turn.
3rd–6th rows As 2nd. Do not break off A.
7th row Using B, 1ch to count as first dc, *1dc into next st missing 1 row, noting that each time the hook is inserted into a stitch missing a row, the yarn forming the loop on the hook must be extended to meet the

previous st of the working row, 1dc into next st missing 2 rows, 1dc into next st missing 3 rows, 1dc into next st missing 4 rows, 1dc into next st missing 5 rows, 1dc into next st missing 4 rows, 1dc into next st missing 3 rows, 1dc into next st missing 2 rows, 1dc into next st missing 1 row, 1dc into next st, rep from * to end. Turn.
8th–12th rows Using B, as 2nd.
13th row 1ch (this does not count as first st), 1dc into first st missing 5 rows, *1dc into next st missing 4 rows, 1dc into next st missing 3 rows, 1dc into next st missing 2 rows, 1dc into next st missing 1 row, 1dc into next st, 1dc into next st missing 1 row, 1dc into next st missing 2 rows, 1dc into next st missing 3 rows, 1dc into next st missing 4 rows, 1dc into next st missing 5 rows, rep from * to end. Turn.

14th–18th rows Using A, as 2nd.
The 7th–18th rows inclusive are repeated throughout.
Note It is a good idea at the beginning of a row when changing colour to wind the working colour around the yarn not in use in order to make a neat edge to the work.

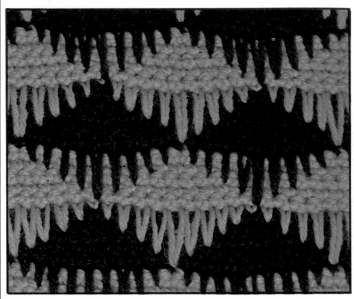

Sample 2
Here we have used three colours of a double knitting yarn, A, B and C. Using No.3.50 (ISR) hook and A, make a chain with multiples of 14+4 stitches.
1st–6th rows As 1st–6th rows of sample 1. Do not break off A.

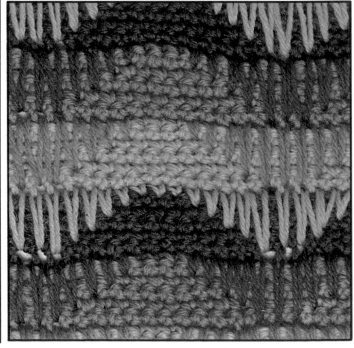

7th row Using B, 1ch to count as first dc, 1dc into each of next 2 sts, *1dc into next st missing 1 row, 1dc into next st missing 2 rows, 1dc into next st missing 3 rows, 1dc into next st missing 4 rows, 1dc into each of next 3 sts missing 5 rows, 1dc into next st missing 4 rows, 1dc into next st missing 3 rows, 1dc into next st missing 2 rows, 1dc into next st missing 1 row, 1dc into each of next 3 sts, rep from * to end. Turn.

8th–12th rows Using B, as 2nd row of sample 1. Do not break off B.

13th–18th rows Using C, as 7th–12th rows. Do not break off C.

19th–24th rows Using A, as 7th–12th rows. The 7th–24th rows are repeated throughout.

Sample 3

The four colours of double knitting yarn used here are denoted as A, B, C and D. Using No.4.50 (ISR) hook and A, make a chain with multiples of 6+1 stitches.

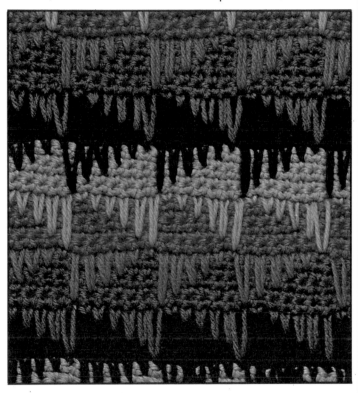

1st–6th rows As 1st–6th rows of sample 1. Do not break off A.

7th row 1ch to count as first dc, *1dc into next st missing 1 row, 1dc into next st missing 2 rows, 1dc into next st missing 3 rows, 1dc into next st missing 4 rows, 1dc into next st missing 5 rows, 1dc into next st, rep from * to end, omitting 1dc at end of last rep. Turn.

8th–12th rows Using B, as 2nd row of sample 1. Do not break off B.

13th row Using C, 1ch (this does not count as first st), *1dc into first st missing 5 rows, 1dc into next st missing 4 rows, 1dc into next st missing 3 rows, 1dc into next st missing 2 rows, 1dc into next st missing 1 row, 1dc into next st, rep from * to end. Turn.

14th–18th rows Using C, as 2nd row of sample 1. Do not break off C.

19th–24th rows Using D, as 7th–12th rows. Do not break off D.

25th–30th rows Using A, as 13th–18th rows.
The 7th–30th rows inclusive form the pattern and colour sequence for this design.

Sample 4

Shiny and matt raffia in four colours, A, B, C and D have been used for this unusual sample. Using No.3.50 (ISR) hook and A, make a chain with multiples of 6+2 stitches.

1st–4th rows As 1st–4th rows of sample 1. Do not break off A.

5th row Using B, 1ch (this does not count as first st), 1dc into first st, *1dc into next st missing 1 row, 1dc into next st missing 2 rows, 1dc into next st missing 3 rows, 1dc into next st missing 2 rows, 1dc into next st missing 1 row, 1dc into next st, rep from * to end. Turn.

6th–8th rows Using B, as 2nd row of sample 1. Do not break off B.

9th row Using C, 1ch (this does not count as first st), 1dc into first st missing 3 rows, *1dc into next st missing 2 rows, 1dc into next st missing 1 row, 1 dc into next st, 1dc into next st missing 1 row, 1dc into next st missing 2 rows, 1dc into next st missing 3 rows, rep from * to end. Turn.

10th–12th rows Using C, as 2nd row of sample 1. Do not break off C.

13th–16th rows Using D, as 5th–8th rows. Do not break off D.

17th–20th rows Using A, as 9th–12th rows.
The 5th–20th rows inclusive are repeated throughout.

CHEVRON DESIGNS AND BRAIDS

More zig-zag designs in crochet

A different kind of zig-zag design which is very simple to work is illustrated in this chapter. Both wavy lines and pronounced zig-zags are formed by this method, either to give an all-over patterned fabric or a strip of crochet braid.

If double knitting yarn is used, this crochet work makes beautiful bed covers, rugs and cushion covers or could be used as a pattern on a fashion garment such as a jacket where a scalloped edge is required as a design feature. More unusual yarns, string and raffia in particular, could be used to make bags, belts and shoe uppers.

Our samples show different stitches for you to experiment with before starting an article of your choice.

Sample 1

Using No.4.50 (ISR) hook and double knitting yarn in various colours, make a length of chain with multiples of 17 + 4 stitches.

1st row Into 4th ch from hook work 3tr, **1tr into each of next 5ch, *yrh and insert hook into next ch, yrh and draw through a loop, yrh and draw through first 2 loops on hook, yrh and insert hook into next ch, yrh and draw through a loop, yrh and draw through first 2 loops on hook, yrh and draw through all 3 loops on hook – called dec 1tr –, *, rep from * to * twice more, 1tr into each of next 5ch, 4tr into next ch, rep from ** to end. Turn.

2nd row 3ch to count as first tr, miss first 2 sts, 3tr into next st, *1tr into each of next 5 sts, dec 3tr over next 6 sts, 1tr into each of next 5 sts, 4tr into next st, rep from * ending last rep with 4tr into 3rd of 3ch. Turn.

Repeat 2nd row throughout, alternating the colours as required. You will see that the pattern gives a flowing, wavy line.

Sample 2

This design, which gives a very ribbed zig-zag pattern, has been worked throughout in four rows each of two colours of double knitting yarn, A and B. Using No.4.50 (ISR) hook and A, make a length of chain with multiples of 16 + 4 stitches.

1st row Insert hook into 3rd ch from hook, yrh and draw through a loop, insert hook into next ch, yrh and draw through a loop, yrh and draw through all 3 loops on hook, **1dc into each of next 6ch, 3dc

into next ch, 1dc into each of next 6ch, *insert hook into next ch, yrh and draw through a loop, *, rep from * to * twice more, yrh and draw through all 4 loops on hook – called dec 2dc –, rep from * to end. Turn.

Note From this point, insert hook into back loop only of each st throughout.

2nd row 2ch, insert hook into st at base of ch, yrh and draw through a loop, insert hook into next st, yrh and draw through a loop, yrh and draw through all loops on hook, *1dc into each of next 6 sts, 3dc into next dc, 1dc into each of next 6 sts, dec 2dc over next 3 sts, rep from * ending last rep by working into 2nd of 2ch. Turn. The 2nd row is repeated throughout the design.

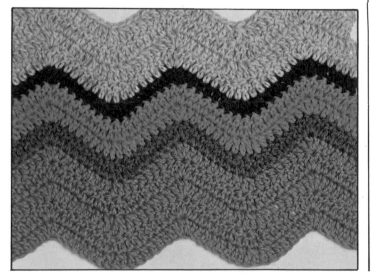

94

Sample 3

Two colours of a double knitting yarn, A and B, have been used for this sample. Using No.4.50 (ISR) hook and A, make a length of chain with multiples of 13 + 6 stitches.

1st row Yrh and insert into 4th ch from hook, yrh and draw through a loop, yrh and draw through first 2 loops on hook, *yrh and insert into next ch, yrh and draw through a loop, yrh and draw through first 2 loops on hook, *, rep from * to *, yrh and draw through 4 loops on hook, **1tr into each of next 4ch, 4tr into next ch, 1tr into each of next 4ch, rep from * to * 4 times, yrh and draw through all 5 loops on hook – called dec 3tr –, rep from ** to end, 2ch. Fasten off A. Do not turn.

2nd row Join B to 3rd of 3ch at beg of previous row, 1ch to count as first dc, 1dc into front loop of each st to end. Fasten off B. Do not turn.

3rd row Join A to first ch at beg of previous row, 3ch, working into back loop only of each st in previous alternate row, *yrh and insert into next st, yrh and draw through a loop, yrh and draw through first 2 loops on hook, *, rep from * to * twice more, yrh and draw through all loops on hook, **1tr into each of next 4 sts, 4tr into next st, 1tr into each of next 4 sts, dec 3tr over next 4 sts, rep from ** to end, 2ch. Fasten off A. Do not turn.

The 2nd and 3rd rows complete the design and should be repeated throughout.

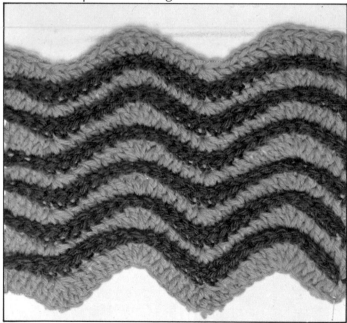

Sample 4

Sometimes zig-zag designs require at least one straight edge, as on a belt. Here our sample illustrates this method of work with two zig-zag lines between the straight edges. Two colours of a double knitting yarn, A and B, have been used so that it is easy to distinguish between the straight lines and zig-zag.

Using No.4.50 (ISR) hook and A, make a length of chain with multiples of 13 + 4 stitches. The 4 extra chains are not turning chains but are for the 4 slip stitches at each end of the pattern repeat.

1st row Miss first ch, ss into each of next 3ch, *1dc into next ch, 1htr into next ch, 1tr into next ch, 1dtr into next ch, 1tr tr into next ch, 1dtr into next ch, 1tr into next ch, 1htr into next ch, 1dc into next ch, ss into each of next 4ch, rep from * to end. Turn. Break off A.

2nd row Join B to first st, 3ch, *yrh and insert into next st, yrh and draw through a loop, yrh and draw through first 2 loops on hook, *, rep from * to * twice more, yrh and draw through all loops on hook, **1tr into each of next 4 sts, 4tr into next st, 1tr into each of next 4 sts, rep from * to * 4 times, yrh and draw through all loops on hook, rep from ** to end. Turn.

3rd row As 2nd, working 4tr group between 2nd and 3rd tr of 4tr group of previous row. Fasten off B.

4th row This shows how to end a zig-zag design with a straight edge. Join A to last st worked in previous row, 4ch to count as first tr tr, *1dtr into next st, 1tr into next st, 1htr into next st, 1dc into next st, ss into each of next 4 sts, 1dc into next st, 1htr into next st, 1tr into next st, 1dtr into next st, 1tr tr into next st, rep from * to end. Fasten off.

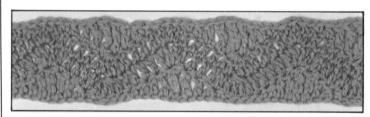

Sample 5

Here is one of the many interesting effects that can be achieved using the techniques here. Make two lengths of crochet by working the first two rows as given for sample 2, using only 4dc between each increase and decrease. Then twist the lengths around each other to give this plaited effect which could be used as a braid or a belt.

Crochet dress with chevron skirt

Sizes

To fit 81.5[86.5:91.5:96.5:101.5]cm (32[34:36:38:40]in) bust
Length to shoulder, 95[96.5:98:99:100.5] cm (37½[38:38½:39:39½]in)
Long sleeve seam, 40.5[42:42:43:43]cm (16[16½:16½:17:17]in)
Short sleeve seam, 10cm (4in)
The figures in brackets [] refer to the 86.5 (34), 91.5 (36), 96.5 (38) and 101.5cm (40in) sizes respectively

Tension

20 sts and 24 rows to 10cm (3.9in) over dc worked on No.3.50 (ISR) crochet hook

Materials

Dress with long sleeves 18[19:20:21:22] × 1oz balls Lee Target Motoravia 4 ply or 17[18:19:20:21] × 20grm balls Lee Target Duo 4 ply Crepe Tricel Nylon in main shade, A
6[6:6:7:7] × 1oz balls or 6[7:8:9:9] × 20grm balls of contrast colour, B
Dress with short sleeves 16[17:18:19:20] × 1oz balls Lee Target Motoravia 4 ply or 15[16:17:18:19] × 20grm balls Lee Target Duo 4 ply Crepe Tricel Nylon in main shade, A
4[4:5:5:6] × 1oz balls or 5[6:6:7:8] × 20grm balls of contrast colour, B
One No.3.00 (ISR) crochet hook
One No.3.50 (ISR) crochet hook
One No.4.00 (ISR) crochet hook
1 × 55cm (22in) zip fastener

Dress

(worked in one piece to underarm)
Using No.4.00 (ISR) hook and A, make 244[260:276:292:308] ch for entire lower edge.
1st row (RS) Into 4th ch from hook work 1tr, *1tr into each of next 6ch, miss 3ch, 1tr into each of next 6ch, 3tr into next ch, rep from * ending last rep with 2 tr into last ch instead of 3. Turn.
2nd row 3ch to count as first tr, 1tr into st at base of ch, *1tr into each of next 6tr, miss 2tr, 1tr into each of next 6tr, 3tr into next tr, rep from * ending last rep with 2tr into 3rd of 3ch instead of 3. Turn.
The 2nd row forms the patt. Cont in patt until work measures 15cm (6in) from beg.
Next row 3ch, miss first tr, 1tr into each of next 6tr, *miss 2tr, 1tr into each of next 13tr, rep from * to last 9tr, miss 2tr, 1tr into each of next 6tr, 1tr into 3rd of 3ch. Turn.
Next row 3ch, 1tr into st at base of ch, *1tr into each of next 5tr, miss 2tr, 1tr into each of next 5tr, 3tr into next tr, rep from * ending last rep with 2tr into 3rd of 3ch. Turn.
The last row forms the patt. Cont in patt until work measures 30.5cm (12in) from beg.
Next row 3ch, miss first tr, 1tr into each of next 5tr, *miss 2tr, 1tr into each of next 11tr, rep from * to last 8tr, miss 2tr 1tr into each of next 5tr, 1tr into 3rd of 3ch. Turn.
Next row 3ch, 1tr into st at base of ch, *1tr into each of next 4tr, miss 2tr, 1tr into each of next 4tr, 3tr into next tr, rep from * ending last rep with 2tr into 3rd of 3ch. Turn.
Cont in patt as now set until work measures 45.5cm (18in) from beg.
Next row 3ch, miss first tr, 1tr into each of next 4tr, *miss 2tr, 1tr into each of next 9tr, rep from * to last 7tr, miss 2tr, 1tr into each of last 4tr, 1tr into 3rd of 3ch. Turn.
Next row 3ch, 1tr into st at base of ch, *1tr into each of next 3tr, miss 2tr, 1tr into each of next 3tr, 3tr into next tr, rep from * ending last rep with 2tr into 3rd of 3ch. Turn.
Cont in patt as now set until work measures 53.5cm (21in) from beg, ending with a WS row. Change to No.3.50 (ISR) hook.

Shape waist

1st row 1ch to count as first dc, miss first st, *1dc into next tr, 1htr into next tr, 1tr into next tr, 1dtr into each of next 2tr, 1tr into next tr, 1htr into next tr, 1dc into next tr, miss next tr, rep from * to end working 1dc into 3rd of 3ch. Turn. 122[130:138:146:154] sts.
2nd row (eyelet hole row) 3ch to count as first tr, miss first st, 1tr into next st, *1ch, miss next st, 1tr into each of next 3 sts, rep from * to end. Turn.
3rd row 1ch to count as first dc, miss first st, work 1dc into each tr and ch sp to end. Turn.
4th row 1ch to count as first dc, miss first st, 1dc into each dc to end. Turn.
Join in B. Using B, rep 4th row twice. Using A, rep 4th row twice. The last 4 rows form the stripe patt for the bodice which is repeated throughout.

Shape bodice

Next row 1ch, miss first st, 1dc into each of next 28[30:32:34:36]dc, 2dc into each of next 2dc, 1dc into each of next 60[64:68:72:76]dc, 2dc into each of next 2dc, 1dc into each of next 29[31:33:35:37]dc. Turn.
Next row Work in dc.
Next row 1ch, miss first st, 1dc into each of next 29[31:33:35:37] sts, 2dc into each of next 2dc, 1dc into each of next 62[66:70:74:78]dc, 2dc into each of next 2dc, 1dc into each of next 30[32:34:36:38]dc. Turn.
Cont inc 4dc in this way on foll alt rows until there are 138[146:158:166:178] sts, then on every foll 4th row until there are 166[174:186:194:206] sts. Cont without shaping until work measures 78.5cm (31in) from beg, ending with a WS row.

Divide for back and front armholes

Next row 1ch, miss first st, 1dc into each of next 38[40:43:45:48]dc, turn.
Cont on these 39[41:44:46:49] sts for left back.
Next row 1ch, miss first 2 sts, 1dc into each dc to end. Turn.
Next row 1ch, miss first st, 1dc into each dc to last 2dc, miss next dc, 1dc into last st. Turn.
Rep last 2 rows 3[3:4:4:5] times more. 31[33:34:36:37] sts. Cont without shaping until armhole measures 16.5[18:19:20.5: 21.5]cm (6½[7:7½:8:8½]in) from beg, ending at back edge.

Shape shoulder

Next row Patt to last 8 sts, turn.
Next row Ss into each of next 8[10:11: 13:14] sts, patt to end. Fasten off.
With RS of work facing, return to main part, miss 5 sts for underarm, rejoin yarn to next st and work 1ch, 1dc into each of next 77[81:87:91:97]dc, turn. Cont on these 78[82:88:92:98] sts for front.
Next row 1ch, miss first 2 sts, 1dc into each dc to last 2dc, miss next dc, 1dc

into last st. Turn.

Rep last row 7[7:9:9:11] times more. 62[66:68:72:74] sts. Cont without shaping until work measures 14 rows less than back to shoulder shaping.

Shape neck

Next row Patt across 23[25:26:28:29] sts. Turn.

Next row 1ch, miss first 2 sts, patt to end. Turn.

Next row Patt to last 2 sts, miss next dc, 1dc into last st. Turn.

Rep last 2 rows twice more, then first of them again. 16[18:19:21:22] sts. Cont without shaping until work measures same as back to shoulder, ending at armhole edge.

Shape shoulder

Next row Ss into each of next 8 sts, patt to end. Fasten off.

With RS of work facing return to rem sts at front, miss centre 16 sts for front neck, rejoin yarn to next st, 1ch, patt to end. Turn. Complete to match first side of neck, reversing shapings.

With RS of work facing return to main part, miss 5 sts for underarm, rejoin yarn to next st, 1ch, patt to end for right back. Complete to match left back, reversing shapings.

Long sleeves

Using No.3.00 (ISR) hook and A, make 39 [41:43:45:47]ch.

1st row Into 3rd ch from hook work 1dc, 1dc into each ch to end. Turn. 38[40:42:44:46] sts.

2nd row 1ch to count as first dc, miss first st, 1dc into each dc to end, finishing with last dc into turning ch. Turn.

Join in B. Using B, rep 2nd row twice. Using A, rep 2nd row twice more. These 4 rows form the stripe patt which is repeated throughout. Cont in patt until work measures 5cm (2in) from beg. Change to No.3.50 (ISR) hook. Cont in patt, inc one dc at each end of next and every foll 6th row until there are 60[64:68:72:76] sts. Cont without shaping until work measures 40.5[42:42:43:43]cm (16[16½:16½:17:17]in) from beg.

Shape top

1st row Ss into each of next 4 sts, 1ch, patt to last 3 sts, turn.

2nd row Patt to end. Turn.

3rd row 1ch, miss 2 sts, 1dc into each st to last 2 sts, miss next dc, 1dc into last st. Turn.

Rep 2nd and 3rd rows until 36[36:40:40: 44] sts rem, then rep 3rd row until 14 sts rem. Fasten off.

Short sleeves

Using No.3.50 (ISR) hook and A, make 53[57:61:65:69]ch.

1st row Into 3rd ch from hook work 1dc, 1dc into each ch to end. Turn. 52[56:60: 64:68] sts.

2nd row As 2nd row of long sleeves. Join in B and working in stripe sequence as given for bodice, inc one dc at each end of next and every foll 6th row until there are 60[64:68:72:76] sts. Cont without shaping until work measures 10cm (4in) from beg.

Shape top

Work as given for long sleeves.

To make up

Press each piece according to manufacturer's instructions. Join shoulder and sleeve seams. Set in sleeves.

Neck edging Using No.3.00 (ISR) hook and A, work 5 rows dc evenly round neck edge.

Sew in zip, joining rem back seam. Using 6 strands of A tog, make a twisted cord approx 152.5cm (60in) long and thread through eyelet holes at waist. Press seams.

CHECK PATTERNS

Check patterns in crochet

Effective check crochet patterns in one or more colours may be worked which, because of the method used, form a thick fabric suitable for warm outer garments such as coats, jackets and skirts. The stitches used to form the checks pass over previous rows so forming a double fabric in some designs. Some of the designs may be reversible and this should be taken into account when deciding on the kind of garment which you are going to make.

Double knitting yarn and a No.4.50 (ISR) crochet hook are recommended for the samples which you see illustrated. Samples 2 and 3 are worked from one side, therefore the crochet could be worked in continuous rounds without turning the work or breaking the yarn at the end of each row. This technique would be ideal for making a skirt as it would avoid any side seams.

Sample 1

Make 26ch.

1st row Into 4th ch from hook work 1tr, 1tr into each ch to end. Turn. 24tr.

2nd row 3ch to count as first tr, miss first tr, (1tr into next tr inserting the hook from the front of the work horizontally from right to left under the vertical bar of the tr in the previous row so that the hook is on the front of the work) 3 times, (1tr into next tr inserting the hook from the back of the work from right to left over the vertical bar of the tr in the previous row so that the hook is on the back of the work) 4 times, cont in this way working 4tr to the front and 4tr to the back of the work to the end of the row, working last tr into 3rd of the 3ch. Turn.

3rd row As 2nd.

4th row 3ch to count as first tr, miss first tr, work 1tr to the back of each of the next 3tr, work 1tr to the front of each of the next 4tr, cont in this way so reversing the check effect to the end of the row, working the last tr into 3rd of the 3ch. Turn.

5th row As 4th.

Rows 2 to 5 form the pattern and are repeated throughout.

Sample 2

This is worked in 2 colours, A and B. With A, make 26ch.

1st row Into 3rd ch from hook work 1dc, 1 dc into each ch to end. 25dc. Fasten off yarn. Do not turn.

Note Unless otherwise stated, work into the back loop only of each st to end of design.

2nd row Join B to beg of previous row, 1ch to count as first dc, miss first st, 1dc into each st to end. Fasten off yarn. Do not turn work.

3rd and 4th rows As 2nd.

5th row Join A to beg of previous row. 1ch to count as first dc, miss first st, insert hook under horizontal front loop of next st, yrh and draw through a loop, (insert hook under horizontal front loop of st immediately below st just worked into, yrh and draw

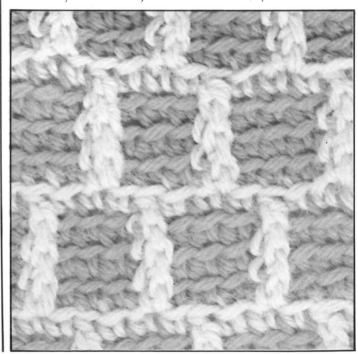

through a loop) 3 times, (yrh and draw through first 2 loops on hook) 4 times – 1 connected quad tr has been worked –, *1dc into each of next 3 sts, 1 connected quad tr into next st, rep from * to last 2 sts, 1dc into each of next 2 sts. Fasten off yarn. Do not turn work.

6th to 8th rows As 2nd.

9th row Join A to beg of previous row, 1ch to count as first dc, miss first st, 1dc into each of next 3 sts, *1 connected quad tr into next st, 1dc into each of next 3 sts, rep from * to last st, 1dc into last st. Fasten off yarn. Do not turn.

Rows 2 to 9 form the pattern and are repeated throughout.

Sample 3

Three colours are used for this sample, A, B and C. Unless otherwise stated, insert the hook into the back loop only of each st. With A, make 26ch.

1st row Into 3rd ch from hook work 1dc, 1dc into each ch to end. 25dc. Fasten off yarn. Do not turn.

2nd row Join A to beg of previous row. 1ch to count as first dc, miss first st, 1dc into each st to end. Fasten off yarn. Do not turn.

3rd row As 2nd.

4th row Join B to beg of previous row. 1ch to count as first dc, miss first st, 1dc into next st, yrh 3 times, insert hook under horizontal front loop of next st in 4th row below, yrh and draw through a loop, (yrh and draw through first 2 loops on hook) 4 times – 1 surface tr tr has been worked –, 1 surface tr tr into each of next 2 sts, *1dc into each of next 3 sts, 1 surface tr tr into each of next 3 sts, rep from * to last 2 sts, 1dc into each of next 2 sts. Fasten off yarn. Do not turn.

5th and 6th rows With B, as 2nd.

7th row Join C to beg of previous row. 1ch to count as first dc, miss first st, 1dc into each of next 4 sts, *1 surface tr tr into each of next 3 sts, 1dc into each of next 3 sts, rep from * to last 2 sts, 1dc into each of last 2 sts.

Fasten off yarn. Do not turn.

8th and 9th rows With C, as 2nd.

10th to 12th rows With A, as 4th to 6th rows.

13th to 15th rows With B, as 7th to 9th rows.

16th to 18th rows With C, as 4th to 6th rows.

Rows 1 to 18 form the pattern and colour sequence for this sample.

Sample 4

Two colours, A and B, are used for this sample. With A, make 22ch.

1st row Into 3rd ch from hook work 1dc, 1dc into each ch to end. Turn. 21dc.

2nd row 1ch to count as first dc, miss first dc, 1dc into front loop only of each st to end. Turn. Fasten off yarn.

3rd row Join in B. 2ch to count as first htr, miss first st, 1htr into each st to end placing hook under both loops. Fasten off yarn. Do not turn.

4th row Join A to beg of previous row. 1ch to count as first dc, (1dtr into front loop only of next st in 3rd row below) twice, 1dc into back loop only of next 3 sts, *1dtr into each of next 3 sts placing the hook as before, 1dc into back loop only of next 3 sts, rep from * to last 3 sts, 1dtr into each of next 2 sts, 1dc into last st. Fasten off yarn. Do not turn work.

5th row As 3rd.

6th row Join A to beg of previous row. 1ch to count as first dc, 1dc into back loop only of next 2 sts, *(1dtr into front loop only of next st in 3rd row below) 3 times, 1dc into back loop only of next 3 sts, rep from * to end. Fasten off. Do not turn.

7th row As 3rd.

Rows 4 to 7 form the pattern.

CROCHET WITH LEATHER AND SUEDE

In this chapter we have used circular leather motifs and crochet stitches together to give some interesting results. This type of work lends itself especially to the making of belts, bags, jerkins and waistcoats. A firm, good quality leather, suede or grain skin should be chosen to withstand the pull of the crochet work. Most local handicraft shops will sell off-cut leather pieces suitable for this purpose. First mark the shape on the wrong side of the skin by drawing round a circular object with a pencil. Cut out the circles with a sharp pair of scissors to avoid making a rough edge. You will need a special tool, called a leather punch, to make the holes which must be evenly spaced around the circle, but not too near the edge. Also make sure that the holes are the correct size to take the yarn and crochet hook which you are using.

We have used various sized circles decorated with a double knitting yarn, string and a lurex yarn, and a No.2.00 (ISR) crochet hook. There are a number of methods for working crochet round leather circles which are demonstrated here, together with instructions for joining the circles.

Sample 1

This illustrates a 4cm (1½in) leather circle with the holes cut out ready for work to commence.

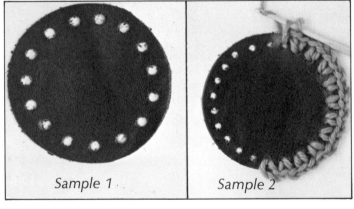

Sample 1   Sample 2

Sample 2

This is a 5.5cm (2¼in) circle with the surrounding crochet in progress.

To work the crochet Hold the leather circle so that the right side is facing you and place the working yarn behind the circle, insert hook through any hole, yrh and draw through hole, yrh and draw through loop on hook, 2ch, *insert hook into next hole, yrh and draw yarn through hole, yrh and draw. yarn through both loops on hook – 1dc has been worked into the hole –, 1ch, rep from * until the circle is complete. Join with a ss into first ch to neaten. Fasten off.

Sample 3

The double crochet edging round this circle is now complete.

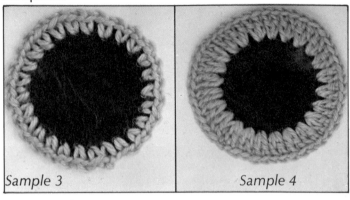

Sample 3   Sample 4

Sample 4

Using the same technique as described in sample 2, work 3ch at the beginning of the edging and work 1tr into the same hole, *2tr into next hole, rep from * to the end of the circle. Join with a ss into 3rd of 3ch. Fasten off.

Sample 5

Here is a grouping of circles ranging in sizes from 2.5cm (1in) to 5.5cm (2¼in). The surrounding stitches vary in depth to give a 'clam' appearance.

Begin by working 2ch into the first hole, 1dc into each of next 2 holes with 1ch between them, then continue by working 2 sts into each hole and increase the stitch depth by working into the same number of holes in each of htr, tr and dtr, then decrease the st size in the same way. The number of sts in each group will have to be varied according to the size of the circle and number of holes.

Samples 6, 7, 8 and 9 show a more experimental way to edge the leather. These would make ideal edgings for a plain leather jerkin.

Sample 6
1st round Beg with 2ch and 1dc into first hole, 2dc into each hole all round. Join with a ss into 2nd of 2ch.
2nd round 2ch, (yrh and insert into st at base of ch, yrh and draw through a loop extending it for 1cm ($\frac{3}{8}$in), twice, yrh and draw through all 5 loops on hook, 1ch, miss next st, *yrh and insert into next st, yrh and draw through a loop extending it for 1cm ($\frac{3}{8}$in), (yrh and insert into same st as last, yrh and draw through an extended loop) twice, yrh and draw through all 7 loops on hook, 1ch, miss next st, rep from * to end of circle. Join with a ss into 2nd of 2ch.
3rd round 1ch to count as first dc, *2dc into next sp between bobbles, 1dc into top of next bobble, rep from * to end, 2dc into next sp. Join with a ss into first ch. Fasten off.

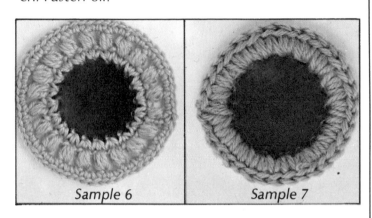

Sample 6   *Sample 7*

Sample 7
Cut 8 thicknesses of yarn to fit all round the outer edge of the circle.
Next round Working over 8 thicknesses of yarn to produce a rounded effect, commence with 2ch and 1dc into first hole, 2dc into each hole to end of round. Join with a ss into 2nd of 2ch. Fasten off.

Sample 8
Two colours, A and B, were used for this sample.
1st round Using A, beg with 3ch and 1tr into first hole, 2tr into each hole to end of round. Join with a ss into 3rd of 3ch.
2nd round Join in B. Work 1dc into each st, working from left to right (i.e. working backwards round circle) instead of right to left. Fasten off.

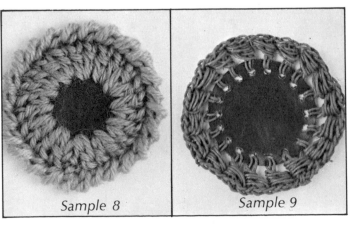

Sample 8   *Sample 9*

Sample 9
Green parcel string was used for this sample.
1st round Beg with 4ch into first hole, (yrh and take hook in front of chain, round to the back and yrh) 3 times, yrh and draw through all 7 loops on hook, 1ch, *1tr into next hole, (yrh and take hook in front of tr, round to the back and yrh) 3 times, yrh and draw through all 7 loops on hook, 1ch, rep from * to end of round. Join with a ss into 3rd of 4ch. Fasten off.

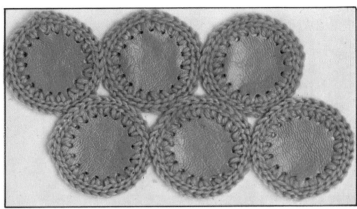

Sample 10
1st round Beg with 2ch, then work 1dc and 1ch into each hole to end of round. Join with a ss into 2nd of 2ch.
2nd round Ss into back loop only of each st to end of round.
To join the circles At the point where two circles are to be joined on the 2nd round, insert the hook into the next st of the circle on which you are working and then into any stitch of the circle to be joined, yrh and draw though all loops on hook. In our sample three stitches were used at each joining point. Our circles were all the same size, but if there are a variety of sizes then they may be joined in the same way.

Sample 11
This gold belt illustrates the method of edging used in sample 7. Twelve circles, each 5cm (2in) in diameter were used to fit a 68.5cm (27in) waist. Work round half the circle in crochet before joining on to the next circle, and when the complete length has been worked, the return crochet is worked on the second half of each circle.
Brass rings are used as a fastening with a cord worked in double chain threaded through to link them.

LEATHER OR PVC PROJECTS

The technique of working crochet around leather circles was dealt with in the last chapter, and now we shall show you more ideas for using this technique with a variety of shapes and materials.

PVC is an interesting fabric to work with as it has a very glossy surface which is a good contrast to most crochet yarns. Also it has the additional advantage that it can be cut without the edges fraying in the same way as leather. There are two types of PVC which are available, one with and one without a light backing fabric, and both are suitable to use.

To make the satchel

You will need four pieces of PVC, two measuring 20.5cm (8 inches) by 26.5cm (10½ inches) for the outer piece and lining and another two measuring 40.5cm (16 inches) by 26.5cm (10½ inches). The larger piece is for the back and folds over to form the flap, and should have all the corners rounded. Only the corners of the lower edge of the smaller piece (front) need to be rounded.

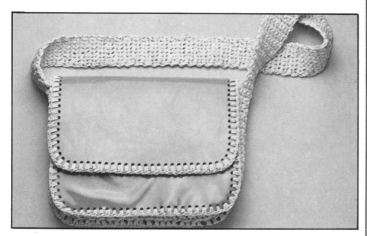

A middle layer of thick bonded interfacing is stuck with an adhesive suitable for fabric between the outer PVC and the lining. The three layers are then treated as one. Holes are punched evenly all round the PVC pieces at least 0.5cm (¼ inch) in from the edge.

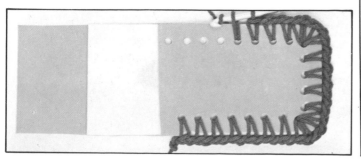

The back and front are linked with a crochet gusset which extends to form the handle.

To work the gusset Using No.4.00 (ISR) crochet hook and a very strong knitting yarn or string (we used a fine ribbon similar to Russia braid), make 9ch.

Next row Into 3rd ch from hook work 1dc, 1dc into each ch to end. Turn.

Next row 1ch to count as first dc, 1dc into each st to end. Turn.

Rep last row until work measures 145cm (57 inches) from beg. Fasten off. Join 2 short ends to form a circle.

To work the edging and join the sections together Begin with a slip loop on the hook and hold the bag section with RS towards you, insert hook from front to back into first hole at right hand side of flap, yrh and draw through a loop, yrh and draw through both loops on hook – 1dc has been worked into the hole –, *1ch, work 1dc into next hole, rep from * to halfway down first long side (i.e. where back begins), then join bag on to gusset by placing hook through next hole as before and also through edge of gusset and complete the st in the normal way, cont in this way until all the back and flap section has been worked. Work round the front section and join to the gusset in the same way.

To make the leather belt

The same techniques have been incorporated into the making of a belt. According to the size required, you will need approximately ten rectangles of leather each 4.5cm (1¾ inches) by 6.5cm (2½ inches). In addition a strong bonded interfacing is again stuck to the wrong side of each shape.

To work the crochet Using a No.3.50 (ISR) hook, a lurex yarn and with the RS of the shape facing you, insert the hook from front to back into a hole, yrh and draw through hole, yrh and draw through a loop – 1ch has been worked –, *insert hook into next hole, yrh and draw through hole, yrh and draw through first loop on hook, yrh and draw through both loops on hook, rep from * all round shape, working 3 sts into each corner hole. Fasten off and neaten ends.

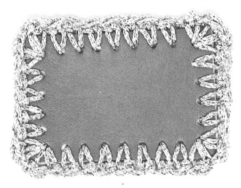

To join the shapes Place two shapes with right sides together so that the chain of each stitch is uppermost on the right side to give a pronounced ridge effect and sew together.

To fasten the belt Two large eyelets, available at most chain stores, have been placed at either side of the centre front opening. A double chain tie has been made to lace through the eyelets, but this must be made long enough to allow the belt to open sufficiently to allow the wearer to slip the belt over her hips. Four loops of beads have been added to each end of the tie to decorate them.

To make the slippers

Another use for this form of patchwork is the attractive slippers which are so easy to make and fit a size 5–6 foot. The pattern for the upper is divided into five shapes and each piece is cut out in suede and in a heavy bonded interfacing, which is then stuck to the suede. Holes are then punched all round each shape.

To work the crochet Using No.3.50 (ISR) crochet hook, a chenille yarn (or any other type of heavy yarn) and with the RS of the shape facing you, insert hook into hole from front to back, yrh and draw through hole, yrh and insert into same hole, yrh and draw through a loop, yrh and draw through all 4 loops on hook, cont in this way all round shape, working 3 sts into each corner hole.

To join the shapes together When the 5 shapes are complete, sew them firmly together on the wrong side. A lining fabric can also be hemmed into place at this stage, if you wish.

The insole is cut out in a plastic fabric and has a bonded interfacing backing stuck to it. Holes are punched all round the sole. The stitches described for the suede shapes are worked into the holes, noting that 1ch should be worked between the stitches at the heels and toes, also that the upper should be joined to the insole between the marked positions by inserting the hook into the upper and then into the insole, completing the stitch in the normal way. At this point the completed work is then stuck to a main rubber sole with a suitable adhesive. These instructions are repeated for the second sandal, making sure that the pattern pieces are reversed.

Graph pattern for slippers

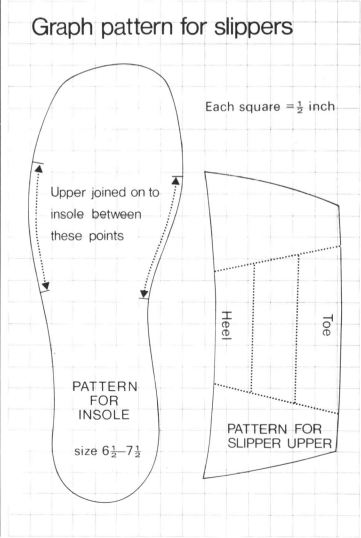

Each square = ½ inch

Upper joined on to insole between these points

PATTERN FOR INSOLE

size 6½–7½

Heel

Toe

PATTERN FOR SLIPPER UPPER

COVERED RINGS
BASIC TECHNIQUES

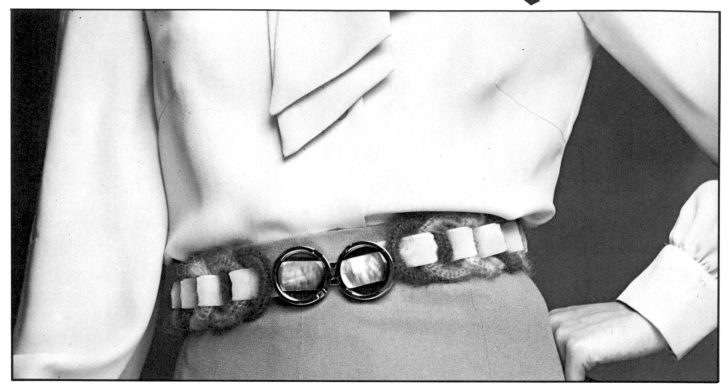

Crochet covered rings can be used in a variety of ways such as for belt fastenings and window hangings. There are several different methods of covering rings, some of which have already been illustrated, such as covering with a looped or button-hole stitch or with crochet stitches.

This chapter develops the technique further and shows what can be done by using several rings on a belt. All types of curtain rings, obtainable from the haberdashery counters of large stores, are suitable. The type of yarn is dependent upon the item being made, but most yarns can be used. The crochet hook should be one size smaller than usual in order to obtain a close stitch, which will cover the ring completely.

To make the belt

For a belt which is approximately 71cm (28in) long, you will need 23 rings with a 4cm (1½in) diameter, five different shades of mohair yarn, a length of 2.5cm (1in) wide velvet ribbon, a clasp and a No.3.00 (ISR) crochet hook.

Before starting work on covering the ring note that the cut end of yarn at the beginning can be laid along the ring and worked over in order to neaten it Remember to keep the stitches close together so that the ring is completely covered. Hold the yarn in the left hand in the usual way and place the ring over the yarn and hold between the thumb and first finger of the left hand, insert the hook from front to back into the centre of the ring, yrh and draw through a loop, place the hook over the top of the ring, yrh and draw yarn through loop on hook, *insert hook from front to back into the centre of the ring, yrh and draw through a loop, place hook over top of the ring, yrh and draw through both loops on hook, rep from * until the ring is completely covered. Join with a ss into first st. Break off the yarn and darn in the cut end.

Slot ribbon through the rings as shown in the diagram to form a continuous belt and attach the clasp to either end.

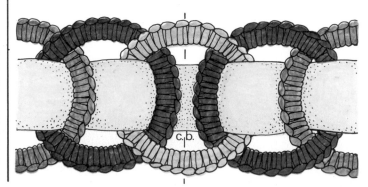

Alternative methods of working and joining rings suitable for belts

(a) Here the method of work is the same as that used for the belt rings, except that the rings are covered and joined continously in one operation. Using No.3.00 (ISR) hook, a double knitting yarn and 3.5cm ($1\frac{1}{4}in$) diameter rings, you should work 14 stitches as previously explained to cover half the ring, then work the same number of stitches in a semi-circle around the next ring and so on until the required number of rings are joined and half covered in crochet. Work completely round the last ring and continue back along the other side of the rings.

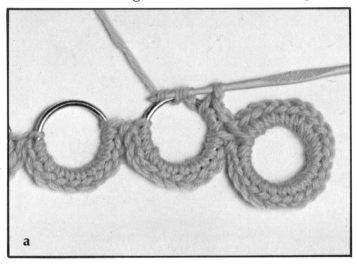

a

(b) Using No.3.00 (ISR) crochet hook, a cotton yarn and 3.5cm ($1\frac{1}{4}in$) rings, work in the same way as given

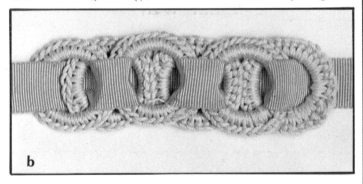

b

for the belt and cover each ring individually. Thread petersham ribbon through the rings as shown in the diagram.

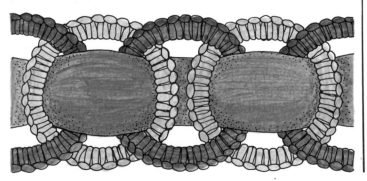

Alternative methods of covering individual rings

Each ring here is 5cm (2in) in diameter and a No.3.00 (ISR) hook is used for all the work.

(a) Here 34 stitches worked in raffia yarn are needed to cover the ring. The raffia gives a distinct chain edging to the circumference.

(b) Chenille yarn gives a softer appearance to this ring. You will need to work 46 stitches to cover the ring completely. The reverse side of the work is illustrated as this gives a more looped stitch.

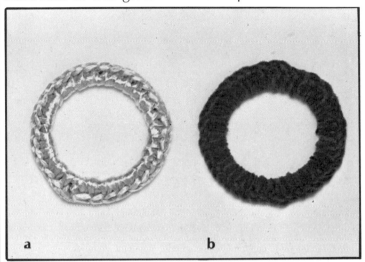

a   b

(c) Two rounds in two different yarns are worked over this ring. Using a double knitting yarn work 50 stitches into the ring as given for the belt. Lurex yarn is used for the 2nd round where double crochet is worked into each stitch in the 1st round, working from left to right instead of from right to left.

(d) Work in the same way as the previous sample until the 1st round has been completed. For the 2nd round, instead of working into all the stitches of the previous round, the hook is inserted into the centre of the ring at various intervals. In this sample, using Lurex yarn, work, *1dc into each of next 3 sts, 1dc inserting hook into centre of ring, 1dc into each of next 3 sts, 3dc inserting hook into centre of ring, repeat from * to end of round. Join with a ss into first st. Fasten off.

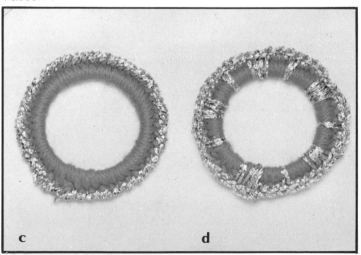

c   d

LARGE CIRCULAR MOTIFS

In this chapter, by telling you how to work our attractive window hanging, we shall increase your knowledge of working circular motifs and combine it with two new techniques which you will learn from these instructions. These are: the method of covering a large ring and making loops so that crochet work may be attached to the ring; and the method of making small circles by wrapping yarn round the fingers to form the basis of the ring.

Window hangings are a popular continental form of decoration. Usually white yarn is used for this form of work as many of the designs are based on snowflake patterns. Once you know the new methods of working described in this chapter, use them with the various techniques and stitches which we have dealt with in previous chapters and you will be able to design your own circular motifs.

To cover the ring

The most suitable ring to use is a plastic covered lamp shade ring. Ours is 30.5cm (*12in*) in diameter and the plastic will prevent rust marks from appearing and spoiling the white yarn.

Work **eleven** pairs of reversed half hitch knots, making a picot between each group of **eleven** knots by leaving 1.5cm ($\frac{1}{2}$in) of yarn free before working the next knot. Continue in this way until 24 picots have been made, join to first knot and fasten off. The covered ring will next be needed in the final round of the crochet work.

To work the window hanging

Using No.2.00 (ISR) hook and a cotton yarn, wrap yarn 20 times round first two fingers of your left hand, insert hook under all the strands of yarn, yrh and draw through a loop which is your working st.

1st round 1ch to count as first dc, work 47dc into the circle of yarn. Join with a ss into first ch.

2nd round 3ch, 1tr into same place as ss, *11ch, miss 5dc, leaving the last loop of each on hook, work 2tr into next dc, yrh and draw through all 3 loops on hook, rep from * 6 times more, 11ch. Join with a ss into 3rd of the 3ch.

3rd round *13dc into next 11ch sp, ss into top of pair of tr in previous round, rep from * 7 times more.

4th round **Ss into each of next 5dc, 5ch, miss 3dc, yrh 4 times and insert hook into next dc, yrh and draw through a loop, (yrh and draw through first 2 loops on hook) 5 times – called a quad tr–, *8ch, work a ring as foll: wrap yarn 10 times round second finger of left hand, insert hook under all the strands of yarn, yrh and draw a loop through the working st on the hook, remove yarn from finger, work 23dc into the circle, join with a ss into first st, (10ch, miss next 5dc on ring, ss into next dc) twice, 8ch, ss into top of pair of quad tr at base of previous 8ch, *, 17ch, 1 quad tr into 5th dc of next sp, miss 3dc, 1 quad tr into next dc, rep from * to *, work 5ss down side of next quad tr, ss into each of next 5dc of sp, 21ch, into 3rd ch from hook work 1dc,

1dc into each ch just worked, **, rep from ** to ** 3 times more. Join with a ss into first ss of round. Fasten off.

5th round *Rejoin yarn into the top of the length of ch just worked, 6ch, 6dc into first 10ch sp above next ring, 6dc into next 10ch sp above same ring, 5ch, leaving the last loop of each on hook work 3tr into next 17ch sp, yrh and draw through all 4 loops on hook, 5ch, (6dc into next 10ch sp above ring) twice, 6ch, ss into top of next length of 20ch, rep from * 3 times more.

6th round *1ch, 6dc into next 6ch sp, ss into each of next 12dc, (6dc into next 5ch sp) twice, ss into each of next 12dc, 7dc into next 6ch sp, rep from * 3 times more working 7dc at beg of each rep instead of 1ch, 6dc. Join with a ss into first ch.

7th round 3ch to count as first tr, 1tr into same place, *5ch, miss next 4 sts, leaving the last loop of each on hook work 2tr into next st, yrh and draw through all 3 loops on hook, rep from * all round, ending with 5ch. Join with a ss into 3rd of the 3ch.

8th round This is the round where the crochet motif is joined into the circle. Work 1ch, 5dc into first 5ch sp, 6dc into each sp to end of round, *at the same time* after every 10th dc, remove hook from working loop, insert it into picot on ring from front to back, reinsert hook into working loop and draw through picot. Join with a ss into first ch.

A window hanging

Our last chapter dealt with the basic techniques involved in working large circular motifs which are popularly used as window hangings. The intricate design shown here involves three more complicated techniques in crochet. These are the method of covering a narrow tube, enclosing spheres with crochet and a different method of covering and joining the centre motif into the ring.

Follow our step by step instructions for making the window hanging and learn these new methods. You will also find them useful for other forms of crochet work as the spheres could be used as a decorative fringe on a lampshade.

Once again a plastic covered lampshade ring, 30.5cm (12in) in diameter, was used for the large circle. Also used were a fine cotton yarn and a No.2.00 (ISR) crochet hook.

To cover the tube
Make a slip loop on the hook. * Holding the tube between thumb and first finger of left hand and having the yarn behind the tube, insert hook inside tube from top to lower edge, yrh and draw through tube taking hook behind tube, yrh and draw through both loops on hook, rep from * 47 times more. Join with a ss into first st. Fasten off.

Move the chain ridge formed by the previous row to give a zig-zag pattern with 3 points at each edge of the tube.

To work the centre motif
1st round Join yarn into one of the zig-zag points, *6ch, ss into next point at same edge, rep from * twice more.

2nd round 12dc into first 6ch sp, 12ch into each of next 2 sp.

3rd round *6ch, miss 5 sts, ss into next st, rep from * 5 times more.

4th round Work 1dc into each dc worked on 2nd round. 36dc. Join with a ss into first dc.

5th round *4ch, ss into next 6ch sp, 4ch, ss into 6th dc of previous round (i.e. behind the joining point of two 6ch sp), rep from * 5 times more.

6th round Work 5dc into each 4ch sp all round. Join

with a ss into first dc.

7th round 9ch, miss 4dc, ss into next dc, ss into next to last ch just worked, *7ch, miss 4dc, ss into next dc, ss into next to last ch just worked, rep from * 9 times more, 5ch. Join with a ss into 2nd of first 9ch.

8th round Work 7dc into each 5ch sp all round. Join with a ss into first dc.

9th round 3ch to count as first tr, 2tr into st at base of ch, *7ch, miss 6dc, 2dtr into next dc, 7ch, miss 6dc, 3tr into next dc, rep from * 4 times more, 7ch, miss 6dc, 2dtr into next dc, 7ch, miss 6dc. Join with a ss into 3rd of first 3ch.

10th round 1ch to count as first dc, 1dc into each of next 6 sts, 10ch, miss 8 sts, *1dc into each of next 11 sts, 10ch, miss 8 sts, rep from * 4 times more, 1dc into each of next 4 sts. Join with a ss into first ch. Fasten off.

Rejoin yarn into one of the zig-zag points at the other end of the tube and repeat 1st to 10th rounds, so giving a 3-dimensional effect to the work.

To cover the small spheres

These are made from a crochet casing filled with cotton wool which forms a firm ball shape approximately 4cm (1½ in) in diameter. You will need six balls for our window hanging.

Using the same yarn and crochet hook, leave a length of yarn 35cm (14in) long and then make 3ch. Join with a ss into the first ch to form a circle.

1st round 1ch to count as first dc, work 9dc into circle. Join with a ss into first ch.

2nd round 1ch to count as first dc, 2dc into next dc, *1dc into next dc, 2dc into next dc, rep from * to end. Join with a ss into first ch. 15dc.

3rd round 2ch to count as first cluster st, *yrh and insert into next dc, (yrh and draw through a loop extending it for 1cm (⅜in)) 4 times, yrh and draw through all loops on hook – called 1 cluster st, 1ch to secure the st, rep from * into each dc all round. Join with a ss into 2nd of the 2ch.

4th round 2ch to count as first cluster st, work 1 cluster st and 1ch into each cluster st all round. Join with a ss into 2nd of the 2ch.

Taking care that the right side of the work is on the outside, insert the cotton wool into the ball at this point.

5th round *1ch, (yrh and insert into next cluster st, yrh and draw through a loop) twice, yrh and draw through all 5 loops on hook – thus dec 1dc, rep from * all round. Join with a ss into first ch.

6th round 1ch to count as first dc, 1dc into each st of previous round. Join with a ss into first ch.

Thread yarn carefully through each st of last round and draw through the last st on the hook. Leave a length of yarn 35.5cm (14in) long for attaching sphere on to work.

To cover the ring and join in the centre motif

To work the covering of our lampshade ring, we used a No.3.00 (ISR) crochet hook and a slightly thicker cotton. First place a slip loop on to the crochet hook, keeping the yarn behind the ring, insert the hook into the ring from top to lower edge, yrh and draw through both loops on hook. Repeat this stitch until the ring is completely covered. You will need 258 stitches if you are using the same size ring as we are. Fasten off.

Next round Rejoin yarn into any st and draw through yarn thus making a st, work 1dc into each st all round. Join with a ss into first st.

Next round *36ch, miss 42dc, ss into next dc, rep from * 5 times more.

Next round Ss into each of next 2ch, 3ch, 1tr into st at base of 3ch, (2ch, miss next 2ch, leaving the last loop of each on hook work 2tr into next ch, yrh and draw through all 3 loops on hook – called a joint tr) 5 times, 1ch, remove hook from working loop and insert it from back to front into any of the 10ch sp of 10th round of either section of centre motif, * pick up working loop and work 1ch, miss 2ch, (a joint tr into next ch, 2ch, miss 2ch) 5 times, a joint tr into next ch, miss 2ch, a joint tr into next ch, (2ch, miss 2ch, a joint tr into next ch) 5 times, remove hook from working loop and insert it into next 10ch sp of *same* section as before, *, rep from * to * 4 times more, pick up working loop and work 1ch, miss 2ch, (a joint tr into next ch, 2ch, miss 2ch) 5 times, a joint tr into next ch. Join with a ss into 3rd of the 3ch.

To join the spheres

Using the 10ch sp of the other section of the centre motif, attach one end of the sphere firmly to the centre of the space. At the other end of the sphere, crochet 4ch and attach to the point where two joint treble meet at the point of a star on the ring.

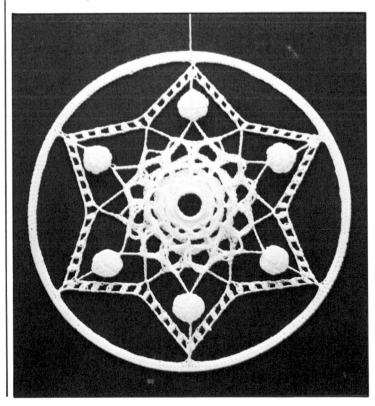

CROCHET ON NET

Crochet on net

This is an unusual and unexpected use for crochet – working on to net to give a design, which can eventually be built up to give the appearance of lace. However, the samples in this chapter demonstrate the basic techniques and are worked in straight lines, but they need to be practised before attempting anything more complicated.

Several types of net are available, usually made from nylon, silk or rayon. Although coloured nets are easy to obtain, white is the most popular colour, especially as it can be very wide which is ideal for wedding veils. For beginners the usual commercial net is rather fine to work with at first, so for our samples we have used one with a larger hole. Work with a No.2.00 (ISR) hook and a double knitting yarn when practising. If the larger holed net for practising is difficult to obtain, we suggest using the plastic net covering for oranges and other fruits which is often found in supermarkets.

You may find it easier to work the crochet if the net is first placed into an embroidery ring. In this way the net is held taut in the ring, and this will make the insertion of the hook much easier.

Sample 1

The chain on net is the first basic stitch, and all the other designs are variations on this, therefore it is important to master this technique first. Place the net firmly in the ring. Begin working from the outer edge of the ring and plan to work in an upward direction. This is the easiest way to start, but when you are more familiar with this technique you will be able to work in all directions. Holding yarn under net on ring and hook over net on ring, insert hook into one hole, yrh and draw through a loop, *insert hook into next hole above as shown in the diagram, yrh and draw through

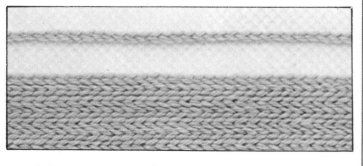

a loop, drawing it through loop already on hook – one chain st has been worked over one hole in the net –, rep from * for the required length.

Note It is important to keep your chain stitches fairly loose, otherwise the net will pucker and not lie flat.

Sample 2

Chain stitch is used again, but the hook is placed into alternate holes.

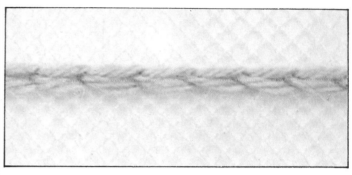

Sample 3

This is worked in the same way as sample 2, but in 8 rows of 4 colours to give a striped block. The chain is worked backwards and forwards, turning the ring for each new row and only cutting the yarn when changing colours.

Sample 4

Straight lines have been used again here, but a zig-zag effect has been achieved by, *working 8 sts into alternate diagonal holes in a left to right direction, then another 8 sts into alternate diagonal holes in a right to left direction, rep from * for the required length. Two rows have been worked in a variety of colours, leaving a space of two rows of holes between each new colour.

Sample 5

Here a variety of stitches have been worked using the same technique. First place the net in the ring as given for sample 1.

(a) Insert hook into one hole on the edge of the ring,

and again work upwards, yrh and draw through a loop extending it to reach 3rd hole on right, insert into this hole, yrh and draw through a loop drawing it through loop on hook, *insert hook into adjacent hole above last st on left, yrh and draw through a loop extending it as before, insert hook into 3rd hole on the right, yrh and draw through all loops on hook, rep from * to end of line.

(b) Following the diagram work in a similar way to previous sample, extending the stitches alternately two and three spaces to the right.

(c) You will see from the diagram that this sample has been worked over 3 sts in a zig-zag direction.

(d) Two rows of sts as given for sample (a) have been worked side by side (i.e. work one row as explained for sample (a), then turn the ring so that the completed row is on the right and work a second row like the first so that the chain sts are worked in adjacent rows).

Sample 6

These stitches are all a zig-zag variation of chain stitch.

(a) Place net in ring as given for sample 1. Working upwards as before, insert hook into hole at left edge, yrh and draw through a loop, miss one hole on the right, insert hook into next hole on the right, yrh and draw through a loop drawing it through loop on hook, *insert hook into next hole above last st on the left, yrh and draw through a loop drawing it through loop on hook, miss one hole on the right, insert hook into next hole above last st on the right, yrh and draw through a loop drawing it through loop on hook, rep from * to end of line.

(b) This is worked in the same way as sample (a), but slightly more spaced (i.e. there is one hole missed between each st worked on the left and the right).

(c) Here is another variation where the hook is inserted to give a diamond effect.

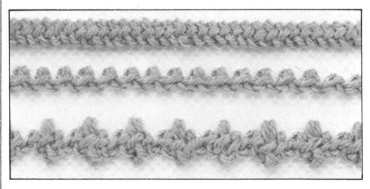

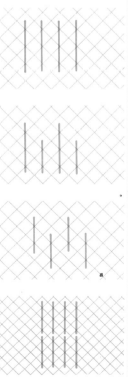

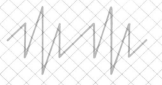

CROCHET ON RUG CANVAS

Crochet on rug canvas

Stitches on all varieties of canvas are usually worked with a needle, but many interesting effects will be illustrated in this chapter using crochet techniques.

In the last chapter, we demonstrated how crochet is worked on to net where the holes do not come immediately above each other, but to either side on each new row. With canvas, however, the holes are immediately next to and above each other and so designs can easily be worked out on ordinary squared graph paper.

Both double and single weave canvas can be used for this technique and very delicate work can be achieved by using a finer canvas which has more holes to the square inch. Choose a hook which will easily enter the holes in the canvas and a yarn which will completely cover the weave when the stitches are worked. Too fine a yarn used with a thick canvas will result in unsightly gaps.

No frame is necessary if you are using a stiff canvas. If a large amount of work is required and a finer canvas is being used, a slate or traditional embroidery frame is recommended, which can be obtained from any good crafts supplier or shop. For our samples we have used an ordinary rug canvas, a chunky knitting yarn and a No.3.50 (ISR) crochet hook. This combination of materials is suitable for making shoulder bags, holdalls and stool or chair seats.

Sample 1

At the top of the sample a straight line of chain stitch has been worked in every adjacent hole. This was worked upwards from the lower edge of the canvas and then turned to give a horizontal line of stitches. Two lines have been completed and the third is in the process of being worked.

To work the stitches Holding the yarn under the canvas in the normal way and the hook above the right side of the canvas, insert hook into one hole on the line of canvas to be worked, yrh and draw loop through hole, *insert hook into next hole upwards, yrh and draw through a loop drawing it through loop on hook, rep from * for the required length of chain.

To the left of the photograph the same chain stitches have been worked vertically. The canvas can be turned at the end of every row in order to keep working in an upwards direction.

The remaining sample shows chain stitches worked into a zig zag design. Again work up the canvas and follow the chart which shows where to insert the hook.

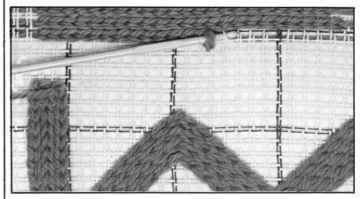

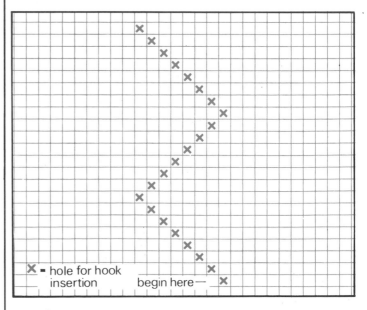

X = hole for hook insertion   begin here—

Sample 2

This is a square design worked in chain stitch which can be enlarged to form one pattern, or a number of smaller squares can be used together as motifs.

Each new round of our sample has been worked in a different colour and yarn, including raffene. Follow the diagram for the order of working, beginning with the 1st round which is worked over four holes at the centre.

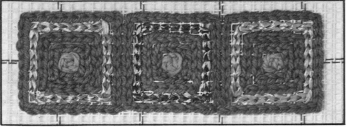

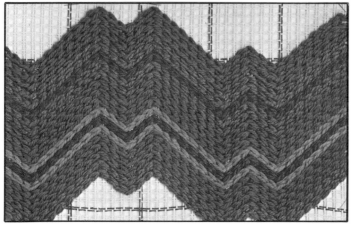

○ = 1st round

□ = 2nd ,,

△ = 3rd ,,

◇ = 4th ,,

▽ = 5th ,,

Sample 3

This is an imitation of Florentine embroidery, the zig zag stitchery which is often seen on canvas. Careful colour selection is necessary and the work can be made much more effective by varying the number of rows worked in each colour. The chart illustrates our design, but it is quite easy to adapt your own ideas into zig zag patterns.

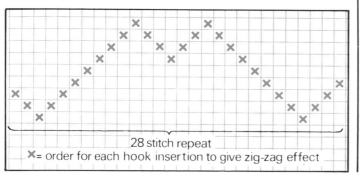

28 stitch repeat
×= order for each hook insertion to give zig-zag effect

Sample 4

This illustrates three stitches which could be used on rug canvas in place of chain stitch. Follow the instructions given to learn how to work these stitches.

a) Holding the yarn and hook as given for sample 1 and working in an upwards direction, insert hook into one hole on the line of work, yrh and draw through a loop, insert hook into next hole up, yrh and draw through a loop drawing it through loop on hook, *insert hook into next hole up on 2nd row to the left, yrh and draw through a loop extending it to meet the next hole above last st worked on the right, insert hook into that hole, yrh and draw through a loop drawing it through both loops on hook, rep from.* for the required length.

b) Holding the yarn and hook as given for sample 1 and working in an upwards direction, insert hook into one hole on the line of work, yrh and draw through a loop, insert hook into next hole up, yrh and draw through a loop drawing it through loop on hook, insert hook into next hole up on 2nd row to the left, *yrh and draw through a loop extending it to meet the next hole above last st worked on the right, insert hook into that hole, yrh and draw through a loop drawing it through both loops on hook, *, – one long st has been worked –, insert hook into next hole up on the next row to the left and rep from * to * so forming a short st, cont working a long and a short st alternately to end of the line. Turn work and repeat a second line of crochet opposite the first, working a long st next to a short st and a short st next to a long st.

c) Holding the yarn and hook as given for sample 1 and working in an upwards direction, insert hook into one hole on line of work, *insert hook into next hole up to the left, yrh and draw through a loop drawing it through loop on hook, insert hook into next hole to the right, yrh and draw through a loop drawing it through loop on hook, rep from * for the required length.

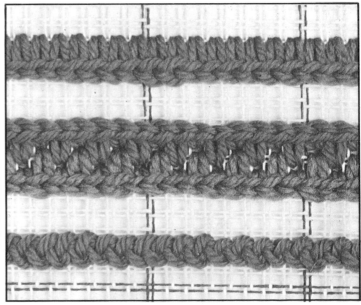

EMBROIDERY ON CROCHET

Crochet plus stitchery

A background of simple crochet lends itself attractively to decorative stitchery and many of the traditional embroidery stitches can be worked on to crochet fabrics.

To work the crochet background This is a basic mesh which is quick and simple to work. You can vary the size of the mesh by working a smaller or larger crochet stitch with more or less chain stitches between as required. Any yarn may be used, but for these samples we have used a No. 3.50 (ISR) crochet hook and a double knitting yarn. Make a length of chain with multiples of 4 plus 11 stitches.

1st row Into 11th ch from hook work 1dtr, *3ch, miss next 3ch, 1dtr into next ch, rep from * to end. Turn.

2nd row 7ch to count as first dtr and 3ch, miss first dtr, 1dtr into next dtr, *3ch, 1dtr into next dtr, rep from * ending with last dtr into 4th of turning ch. Turn.

Rep the 2nd row for the required depth of work. Throughout these samples we have used an embroidery stitch which is a form of darning. Again any yarn can be used, but choose it carefully and work a trial piece before commencing work as stitches can look entirely different depending on the yarn used. Many varied and attractive designs can be made using this basic stitch technique including table linen, bedcovers and curtains. A more delicate effect can be made by using a finer cotton yarn and a smaller sized crochet hook.

Sample 1

Here is a design which is suitable for an all-over pattern. Certain squares in the background have been

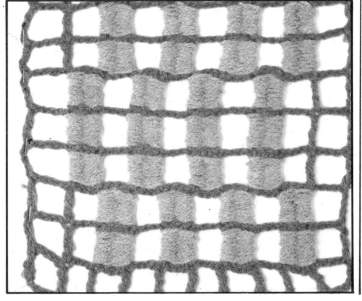

filled in with the darning or weaving stitch as shown in the diagram. The chart shows which squares are to be filled in.

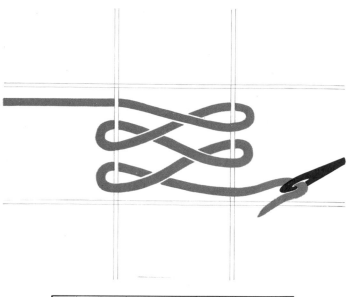

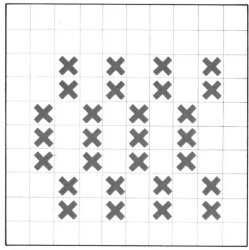

X = sq. to be filled in with 'darning' stitch

Sample 2

This basic background has a shaped edge so that the finished piece of work could be used as a window pelmet or an edging on a roller blind.

To work the background Work 3 rows as given for the basic background.

4th row Ss over first 4 sts so dec one square, 7ch, patt to end. Turn.

5th row Patt to last square, turn so dec one square.

6th row 8ch to count as first dtr of this row and space at end of next row, ss into each of first 4ch, 3ch, patt to end. Turn.

7th row Patt to end, working last dtr into final ss of previous row so inc one square. Turn.

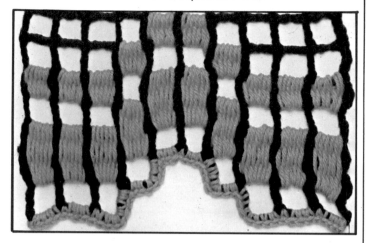

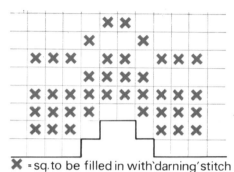

✕ = sq. to be filled in with 'darning' stitch

8th row 10ch so inc one square, 1dtr into first dtr, patt to end. Turn.

9th-10th row Patt to end. Turn.

These 10 rows form the basic shape which can be repeated for the required length.

Darn the appropriate squares as shown in the chart and then, using the same yarn as for the darning, complete the shaped edge by working 3dc into each square and 1dc into each dtr or corner of a square.

Sample 3

Circular motifs have been added to the basic background. Using two strands of a 4 ply yarn together,

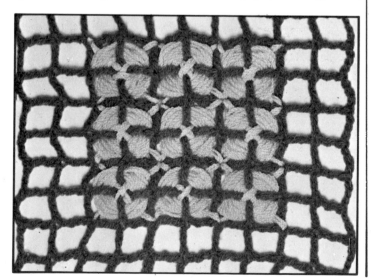

thread the motifs over four squares as shown in the diagrams. The photograph shows the motifs worked over adjacent groups of four squares.

Sample 4

Here a single flower motif has been worked on to a basic background using a chunky yarn. After working the four basic lines as shown in the diagram twice, the thread is woven round the centre by passing the needle (under the blue line, over the green, under the red and over the brown) six times in all. All the cut ends of yarn should then be neatened on the wrong side of the work.

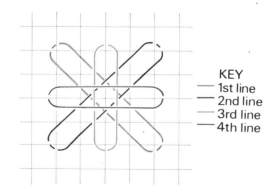

KEY
— 1st line
— 2nd line
— 3rd line
— 4th line

115

MORE EMBROIDERY DESIGNS

This is a continuation of our chapter about weaving designs on to a crochet mesh background. We also give instructions for working an unusual and decorative shawl, which is simple to make and employs the techniques shown in recent chapters. Practise the samples shown here before starting work on the shawl.

Sample 1

To work the background Using No.3.00 (ISR) crochet hook and a 4 ply yarn, make a length of chain with multiples of 4 + 11 stitches.

1st row Into 11th ch from hook work 1dtr, *3ch, miss 3ch, 1dtr into next ch, rep from * to end. Turn.

2nd row 7ch to count as first dtr and 3ch, miss first sp, 1dtr into next dtr, *3ch, 1dtr into next dtr, rep from * ending with last dtr into 4th of turning ch. Turn.

The 2nd row is repeated throughout.

To work the flower Using double thickness of a contrasting yarn and a large blunt-eyed bodkin, follow the diagram and work the yarn through the crochet mesh.

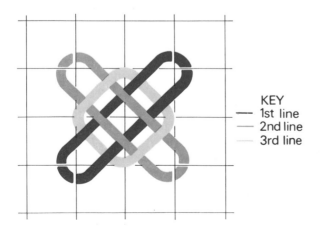

KEY
— 1st line
— 2nd line
— 3rd line

Sample 2

Work the mesh as given for sample 1, weave the flower with a double thickness of contrasting yarn following the diagram for sample 4 on previous page.

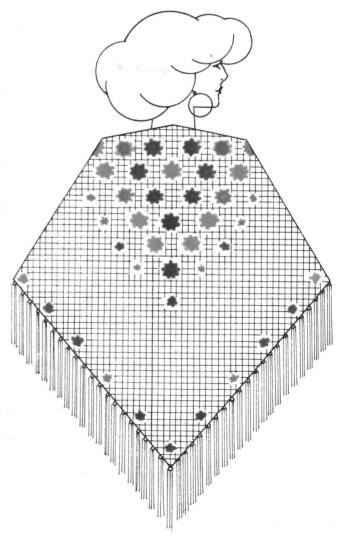

Crochet shawl

Size

Triangle measures approx 114.5cm (*45in*) across top and 76cm (*30in*) from centre of top edge to point

Tension

5ch sp and 6 rows to 7.5cm (*3in*) over patt worked on No.3.00 (ISR) crochet hook

Materials

12 × 25grm balls Twilley's Cortina
Oddments of six contrasting colours
One No.3.00 (ISR) crochet hook

Shawl

Using No.3.00 (ISR) hook and A, make 327ch loosely.
1st row Into 11th ch from hook work 1dtr, *3ch, miss 3ch, 1dtr into next ch, rep from * to end. Turn. Eighty 3ch sp.
2nd row 7ch to count as first dtr and 3ch, miss first sp, 1dtr into next dtr, *3ch, 1dtr into next dtr, rep from * ending with last dtr into 4th of turning ch. Turn.
3rd and 4th rows As 2nd.
5th row (dec row) 7ch to count as first dtr and 3ch, miss first sp, (1dtr into next dtr) twice – i.e. miss the 3ch between dtr, so dec one sp –, *3ch, 1dtr into next dtr, rep from * to last 2 sp, 1dtr into next dtr, 3ch, 1dtr into 4th of turning ch. Turn. 2 sp decreased.
6th and 7th rows As 2nd.
8th row As 5th.
Cont in this way, dec 2 sp on every foll alt row, until 46 sp rem, then on every row until 2 sp rem. Fasten off.

To make up

Using the contrasting colours apply motifs as shown in the diagram. Care should be taken to keep all the cut ends neatly finished on the wrong side of the work.
Fringe Cut 10 strands of yarn each 33cm (*13in*) long, fold in half and using crochet hook pull folded end through first space at side of shawl, pull cut ends through loop thus made and pull tight to form a knot. Rep these knots into each space along 2 sides of the triangle. Trim fringe to an equal length.

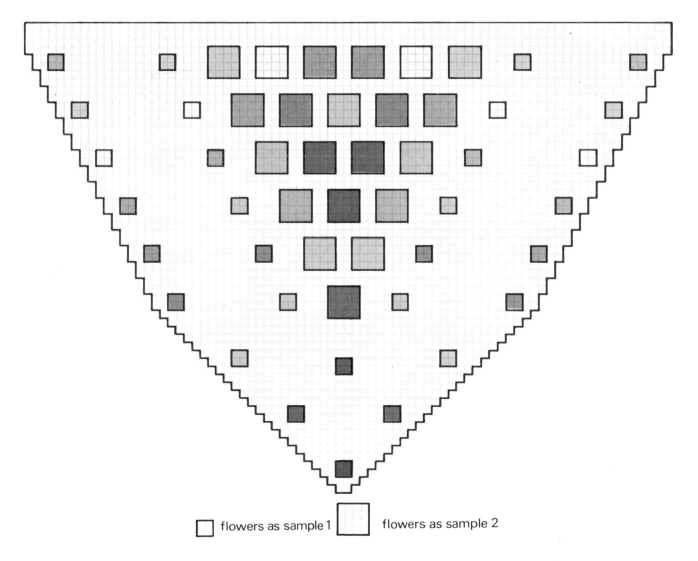

☐ flowers as sample 1   ☐ flowers as sample 2

BEADED DESIGNS

Beaded designs may easily be incorporated into the crochet work during the process of making an article. There are numerous types of beads, normally made of glass, china or wood, which are available from most large multiple stores.

The size of beads varies dramatically, but any type can be used for this kind of work providing that the hole in the bead is large enough to take the yarn which is being used. To thread the beads on to the yarn, see the second chapter on Loopy Stitches. Each bead is positioned so that it forms part of a design and care must be taken to see that the beads are placed on the right side of the work.

It should be remembered that the beads are quite heavy if they are used in large quantities. Therefore small articles are really the most suitable, or isolated areas to form a border pattern. These articles would need to be lined to strengthen the work and to take the weight of the beads.

Beads are particularly popular for evening wear. Very attractive patterns using beads may be designed and applied to evening waistcoats and bags, or as a border design around the hem of a long evening coat or skirt. There are two distinct methods of applying the beads. One way is to thread the beads on to the yarn which you will be using, before you start working. The bead is then pushed up and positioned as it is required and the following stitch is then worked in the usual way. This technique is illustrated in samples 1 and 2. Another method, used in sample 3, is to thread the beads on to a separate ball of yarn. When a bead row is being worked, the yarn on either side of the bead is caught into place during the working of the crochet, by looping the working yarn round the yarn holding the beads. Our samples show some simple designs which follow the methods described above. If you practise these samples from our instructions you will soon become familiar with the art of beaded crochet.

Sample 1

Using a fine yarn and No.2.50 (ISR) crochet hook, make 40ch.

1st row Into 3rd ch from hook work 1dc, 1dc into each ch to end. Turn.

2nd-7th rows 1ch to count as first dc, 1dc into each dc to end. Turn.

8th row 1ch to count as first dc, 1dc into each of next 6 sts, *push up one bead, placing it at back of the work which will be the right side, 1dc into next st − called 1 Bdc −, 1dc into each of next 7 sts, rep from * 3 times more. Turn.

9th row 1ch to count as first dc, 1dc into each of next 6 sts, *noting that beads are placed at the front of the work, 1Bdc into each of next 2 sts, 1dc into each of next 6 sts, rep from * 3 times more. Turn.

10th row 1ch to count as first dc, 1dc into each of next 5 sts, *1Bdc into each of next 3 sts, 1dc into each of next 5 sts, rep from * 3 times more, ending last rep 1dc into each of next 6 sts. Turn.

11th row 1ch to count as first dc, 1dc into each of next 5 sts, *1Bdc into each of next 4 sts, 1dc into each of next 4 sts, rep from * 3 times more, ending last rep 1dc into each of next 5 sts. Turn.

12th row 1ch to count as first dc, 1dc into each of next 4 sts, *1Bdc into each of next 5 sts, 1dc into each of next 3 sts, rep from * twice more, 1Bdc into each of next 5 sts, 1dc into each of next 5 sts. Turn.

13th row As 11th.

14th row As 10th.

15th row As 9th.

16th row 1ch to count as first dc, 1dc into each of next 2 sts, *1Bdc into next st, 1dc into each of next 3 sts, rep from * 8 times more. Turn.

17th row 1ch to count as first dc, 1dc into each of next 2 sts, *1Bdc into each of next 2 sts, 1dc into each of next 6 sts, rep from * 3 times more, 1Bdc into each of next 2 sts, 1dc into each of next 2 sts. Turn.

18th row 1ch to count as first dc, 1dc into next st, *1Bdc into each of next 3 sts, 1dc into each of next 5 sts, rep from * 3 times more, 1Bdc into each of next 3 sts, 1dc into each of next 2 sts. Turn.

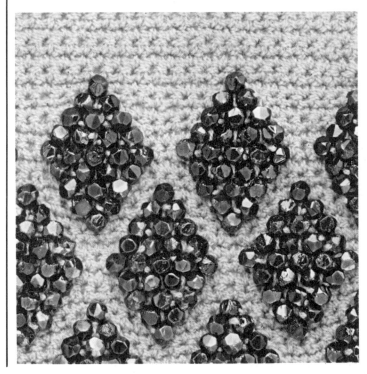

19th row 1ch to count as first dc, 1dc into next st, *1Bdc into each of next 4 sts, 1dc into each of next 4dc, rep from * 3 times more, 1Bdc into each of next 4 sts, 1dc into last st. Turn.

20th row 1ch to count as first dc, *1Bdc into each of next 5 sts, 1dc into each of next 3 sts, rep from * 3 times more, 1Bdc into each of next 5 sts, 1dc into last st. Turn.

21st–24th rows As 19th–16th rows in that order. The 9th row is then repeated to complete the pattern and start the next diamond shape.

Sample 2

Using a cotton yarn and No.2.50 (ISR) crochet hook, make 40ch.

1st row Into 3rd ch from hook work 1htr, 1htr into each ch to end. Turn.

2nd row 2ch to count as first htr, 1htr into each of next 6 sts, *push up one bead, placing it at back of work which will be the right side, 1htr in the next st – called 1Bhtr –, 1htr into each of next 7 sts, rep from * 3 times more. Turn.

3rd row 2ch to count as first htr, *1htr into each of next 5 sts, 1Bhtr into next st, 1htr into next st, 1Bhtr into next st, rep from * 3 times more, 1htr into each of next 6 sts. Turn.

4th row 2ch to count as first htr, 1htr into each of next 4 sts, *1Bhtr into next st, 1htr into each of next 3 sts, rep from * 7 times more, 1Bhtr into next st, 1htr into each of next 2 sts. Turn.

5th row 2ch to count as first htr, 1htr into each of next 3 sts, *1Bhtr into next st, 1htr into each of next 5 sts, 1Bhtr into next st, 1htr into next st, rep from * 3 times more, 1htr into each of next 3 sts. Turn.

6th row 2ch to count as first htr, 1htr into each of next 2 sts, *1Bhtr into next st, 1htr into each of next 7 sts,

rep from * 3 times more, 1 Bhtr into next st, 1htr into each of next 3 sts. Turn.

7th–10th rows As 5th–2nd rows in that order. The 2nd to 10th rows form the pattern.

Sample 3

Wooden beads, approximately 2cm ($\frac{3}{4}$in) long were used for this sample. Thread them on to a separate ball of yarn.

Using a cotton yarn and No.3.00 (ISR) crochet hook, make 33ch.

1st row Into 3rd ch from hook work 1dc, 1dc into each ch to end. Turn.

2nd–8th rows 1ch to count as first dc, 1dc into each dc to end. Turn.

9th row 1ch to count as first dc, 1dc into next st, *hold the yarn with the beads behind the work, place the working yarn round the yarn holding the beads, work 1dc into next st, work 1dc into each of next 3 sts using the main yarn, push up one bead into position behind the work, *, rep from * to * 9 times more, ending last rep with 1dc into each of next 2 sts. Turn. Cut off yarn holding beads.

10th row Work in dc.

11th row 1ch to count as first dc, 1dc into each of next 3 sts, rep from * to * of 9th row to complete the row. The 9th and 11th rows show the sequence of working the beads so that they lie in alternate spaces. You may make your own designs by using this sequence but remember that the beads are always placed from the opposite side of the work, so that you will have to cut the yarn after each bead row.

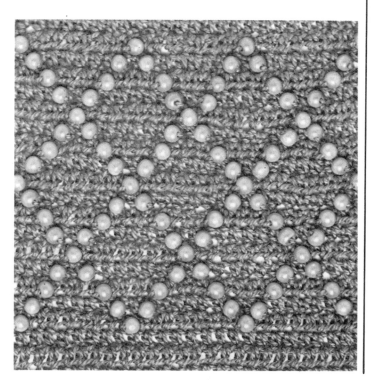

NEEDLE WEAVING
BASIC DESIGNS

Crochet with needle weaving

This chapter gives instructions for working a crochet background into which various materials may be woven to give a solid fabric. The background is formed by working in trebles with one chain separating them, and on subsequent rows the trebles are worked into those in the previous row to give a straight vertical line. The chains of each space or the trebles worked between the spaces form bars either over or under which the weaving threads may pass, according to the design.

A crochet hook or bodkin is used to pass the threads vertically, horizontally or diagonally across the fabric, breaking off the yarn after each row. It is interesting to experiment with different yarns and ribbons for weaving. We have used four thicknesses of the same yarn, rug wool, various ribbons and strips of plastic. Strips of fur could be used to give a more expensive-looking fabric.

The weaving threads help to keep the crochet in position, and as the fabric formed is thick and warm, it is especially suitable for outer garments such as jackets, coats, scarves and skirts. The fabric made by this technique is also ideal for cushions and rugs.

Follow the instructions for our samples before experimenting with your own designs and yarns.

Sample 1

This is the basic open background for needle weaving. Using No.4.00 (ISR) hook and a double knitting yarn, make 30ch.

1st row Into 6th ch from hook work 1tr, *1ch, miss next ch, 1tr into next ch, rep from * to end. Turn.

Note A firmer fabric is produced by placing the hook under three loops of each tr, instead of the normal one or two loops.

2nd row 4ch to count as first tr and 1ch, miss first ch sp, 1tr into next tr, *1ch, miss next ch sp, 1tr into next tr, rep from * to end, working last tr into 4th of 5ch. Turn.

The 2nd row is repeated throughout, noting that each subsequent row will end with last tr worked into 3rd of 4ch.

One attractive item to make entirely in this stitch is a bag. It is quick and easy to work in one piece which is folded in half and seamed at the sides. A line of crochet chain gathers the top edges and at the same time joins them to wooden handles.

Sample 2

Work a basic background as given for sample 1. Ribbon, 0.5cm ($\frac{1}{4}in$) wide, is then woven vertically through the spaces.

1st weaving row Take the ribbon under the ch of the foundation row and through into the first space, *miss the next space up and insert ribbon from front to back into the next space up, take ribbon from back to front into the next space up, *, rep from * to * to end of fabric.

2nd weaving row Insert ribbon from front to back into first space of next row, then take ribbon from back to front into second space, rep from * to * of 1st weaving row to end of fabric.

3rd weaving row Insert ribbon from front to back into second space of next row, then take ribbon from back to front into third space, rep from * to * of 1st weaving row to end of fabric.

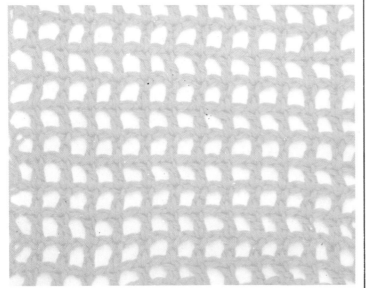

The 3 weaving rows are repeated vertically across the fabric.

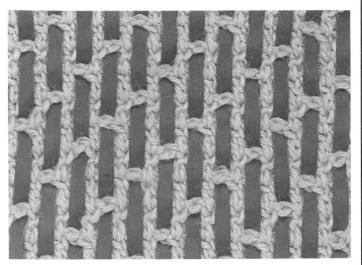

Sample 3

Green parcel string has been used for the background of this sample. Using No.5.00 (ISR) hook make 31ch.

1st row Into 7th ch from hook work 1dtr, *1ch, miss next ch, 1dtr into next ch, rep from * to end. Turn.

2nd row 5ch, miss next sp, 1dtr into next dtr, *1ch, 1dtr into next dtr, ending with last dtr into 5th of 6ch. Turn.

The 2nd row is repeated throughout, noting that each subsequent row will end with last tr worked into 4th of 5ch.

2cm (¾ in) wide petersham ribbon is woven horizontally through each space in the first row, and then through alternate spaces in the next row.

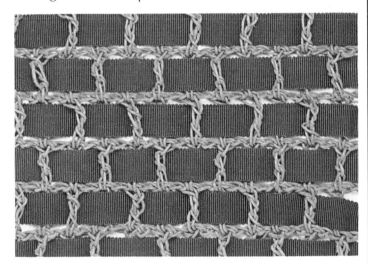

Sample 4

Work a basic background as given for sample 1.
There are two types of weaving involved in this design. Firstly thick rug wool is placed vertically round each treble stitch working up the fabric. Instead of working in and out of the crochet fabric, the rug wool is placed under each treble from left to right working upwards on the first row and following

alternate rows. On the remaining rows the rug wool is threaded in the same way but it is passed from right to left.

Strips of plastic 0.5cm (¼ in) wide, matching the background colour, and ribbon 0.5cm (¼ in) wide, matching the rug wool are then woven alternately between each row of trebles. The plastic is threaded so that on the right side the strip passes completely over one space, whilst the ribbon goes into alternate spaces.

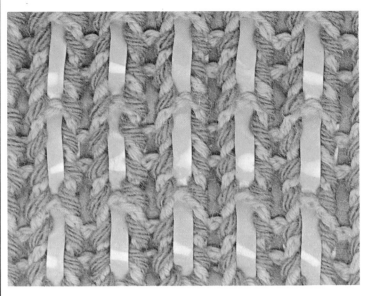

Sample 5

Work a basic background as given for sample 1.
The weaving is worked in two different colours, A and B, of double knitting yarn, using four thicknesses together each time. With A work into horizontal alternate spaces in the first row. Continue with A into each horizontal row throughout the fabric, alternating the spaces worked into with those in the previous row.

Colour B is woven vertically into each row in the same way as A, going in and out of the strands of A as well as the bars of the background fabric.

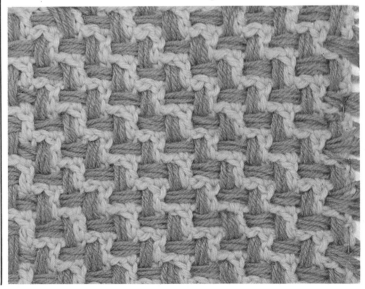

EXPERIMENTAL TECHNIQUES

The basic methods of needle weaving were dealt with in the last chapter, and now we shall illustrate some more experimental uses of this technique with different yarns and other ways of employing the weaving material.

Two of the samples are check fabrics worked into the basic background and these are thick and warm because of the method of working. Other samples are worked in alternative crochet stitches to form a background. Most of these samples of needle weaving are suitable for an all-over fabric, but some (such as sample 4) may be adapted to make an attractive border for a jacket or long skirt.

Sample 1

To work the background This is worked in two colours of double knitting yarn, A and B. Using No.4.50 (ISR) hook and A, make 30ch.

1st row Into 6th ch from hook work 1tr, *1ch, miss 1ch, 1tr into next ch, rep from * to end. Turn.

2nd row 4ch to count as first tr and 1ch, miss 1 ch sp, 1tr into next tr, *1ch, miss 1ch sp, 1tr into next tr, rep from * finishing with last tr into 5th of 6ch. Turn.

Join in B and rep 2nd row twice more, noting that on subsequent rows the last tr is worked into 3rd of 4ch. Continue in this way, working 2 rows in each colour, for the required length.

To work the weaving Using 4 thicknesses of A together, weave in and out of each vertical space in the first row. Then using A again, work into each space in the next row alternating where the yarn passes over or under a bar. Alternating A and B, repeat this process in two row stripes throughout the fabric.

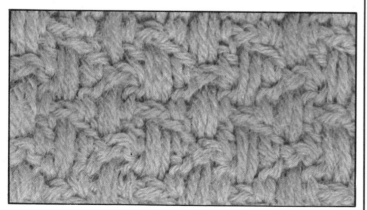

Sample 2

To work the background This is worked in three colours of double knitting yarn, A, B and C. Using No.4.50 (ISR) hook make a background as given for sample 1, but work one row in A, two rows in B and

three rows in C. Note also that colours A and C will have to be cut at the end of the line so that the yarn will be in the correct position for the repeat of colour sequence.

To work the weaving This is worked in the same way as sample 1, but work one vertical line in A, two lines in B and three lines in C.

Sample 3

Two colours of double knitting yarn are used for this sample, colour A for the background and B for the needle weaving.

To work the background Using No.4.50 (ISR) hook and A, make 27ch.

1st row Into 5th ch from hook work 4tr leaving last loop of each on hook, yrh and draw through all loops on hook, 1ch, miss 1ch, 1dc into next ch, *1ch, miss 1ch, into next ch work 4tr leaving last loop of each on hook, yrh and draw through all loops on hook, 1ch, miss 1ch, 1dc into next ch, rep from * to end. Turn.

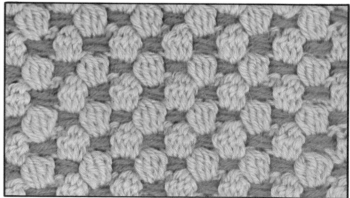

2nd row 3ch, into first dc work 3tr leaving last loop of each on hook, yrh and draw through all loops on hook, 1ch, *1dc into top of next 4tr gr, 1ch, into next dc work 4tr leaving last loop of each on hook, yrh and draw through all loops on hook, 1ch, rep from *

finishing with last 4tr gr into turning ch. Turn.

3rd row 2ch, * into next dc work 4tr leaving last loop of each on hook, yrh and draw through all loops on hook, 1ch, 1dc into top of next 4tr gr, 1ch, rep from * to end omitting 1ch at end of last rep. Turn.

The 2nd and 3rd rows are repeated throughout.

To work the weaving Four thicknesses of colour B are placed horizontally across every row by weaving them under each four treble group and over each double crochet.

Sample 4

The crochet background illustrates an attractive stitch made up of blocks and spaces.

To work the background Using No.4.50 (ISR) hook and a double knitting yarn, make 29ch.

1st row Into 5th ch from hook work 2dtr, miss 2ch, 1dc into next ch, *3ch, miss 3ch, 3dtr into next ch, miss 2ch, 1dc into next ch, rep from * to end. Turn.

2nd row 4ch, 2dtr into first dc, 1dc into next 3ch sp, *3ch, 3dtr into next dc, 1dc into next 3ch sp, rep from * finishing with last dc into turning ch. Turn.

The 2nd row is repeated throughout.

To work the weaving Following the diagram, thread the ribbon and four thicknesses of yarn in alternate strips over the vertical bars formed by three chain in the background.

Sample 5

To work the background Using No.4.50 (ISR) hook and a mohair yarn, make 29ch.

1st row Into 7th ch from hook work 1dc, 2ch, miss next ch, 1tr into next ch, *2ch, miss next ch, 1dc into next ch, 2ch, miss next ch, 1tr into next ch, rep from* to end. Turn.

2nd row 3ch to count as first dc and 2ch, *1tr into next dc, 2ch, 1dc into next tr, 2ch, rep from * to end, working last dc into 3rd of turning ch. Turn.

3rd row 5ch to count as first tr and 2ch, 1dc into first tr, 2ch, 1tr into next dc, 2ch, rep from * to end, working last tr into 2nd of 3ch. Turn.

The 2nd and 3rd rows are repeated throughout.

To work the weaving Diagonal lines of alternate strips of velvet ribbon and four thicknesses of a contrasting shade of mohair are worked over the diagonal chain bars and under the treble stitches in each row.

This fabric is very light, warm and luxurious and would be very suitable for a long evening skirt, straight evening stole or travelling rug.

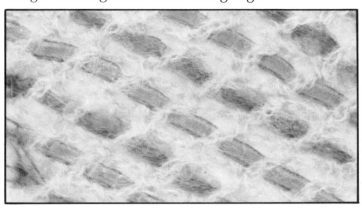

Sample 6

This beautiful evening belt is made very simply by following the needle weaving techniques. Using No.3.50 (ISR) hook and a lurex yarn, make a length of chain long enough to fit round your waist or hips minus combined diameters of the two rings used for fastening. Into the chain work 6 rows as given for the basic background in the previous chapter.

Two colours of Russia braid are threaded through the background to give a raised effect. Secure the ends of the belt over the fastening rings (ours are large brass rings, 5cm (2in) in diameter) and crochet a length of cord to bind the rings together.

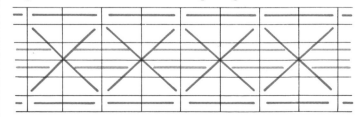

A woven crochet rug

Base row Into 6th ch from hook work 1tr, *1ch, miss 1ch, 1tr into next ch, rep from * to end. Turn. 95 sp.

1st row 3ch to count as first tr, *1tr into next tr, 1ch, rep from * to last sp, miss 1ch, 1tr into 4th of first 5ch. Turn. The last row forms patt. Rep last row 3 times more. Break off A. Cont in patt, working striped sequence of 5 rows B, 5 rows C and 5 rows A throughout. Rep striped sequence 6 times more. Fasten off.

To make up

Sew in ends. Press lightly under a dry cloth with a cool iron.

Weaving Cut 70 lengths of A, 60 lengths of B and 60 lengths of C, all 223.5cm (*88in*) long. Take 2 strands of A and, taking care not to twist strands, weave vertically over and under 1ch bars separating tr, beg with 1st row of sps and leaving 15cm (*6in*) hanging free. A firmer edge will be obtained if needle is passed through first ch on lower edge rather than into sp and also through final ch in top edge. Do not pull yarn too tightly, but weave at a tension that will leave 15cm (*6in*) hanging free at top edge. Work a further 4 rows in A weaving over alt bars to preceding row. Cont in

same way in striped sequence as given for rug.

Fringe Cut two 33cm (*13in*) lengths of colour required for each sp along both edges of rug. Fold strands to form a loop. Insert hook into first sp at lower edge, draw loop through, draw woven ends through loop then draw fringe ends through loop and draw up tightly. Rep along lower edge and upper edge, taking care to keep same side of rug uppermost while knotting fringe. Trim fringe.

Size
The finished dimensions of the travelling rug should measure 152.5cm x 132cm (60in x 52in), excluding fringe.

Tension
10tr and 10 sp and 10 rows to 14cm (5½in) over patt worked on No.6.00 (ISR) crochet hook

Materials
15 x 50grm balls Sirdar Wash'n'Wear Chunky Bri-Nylon Courtelle in main shade, A
13 balls each of contrast colours B and C
One No.6.00 (ISR) crochet hook
Large tapestry needle or bodkin

Note
To obtain an even background insert hook under 3 top strands of tr of previous row working into body of st

Rug
Using No.6.00 (ISR) hook and A, make 194ch.

CROCHET TRIMMINGS
INSERTIONS

Crochet as an insertion

An insertion is usually thought of as a decorative open work strip which joins two pieces of fabric together, so adding a pretty, patterned panel to a dress or down the side seams of trousers. In this chapter we deal with making straight insertions which are applied directly on to straight pieces of fabric, so working the crochet and joining the pieces together in one easy stage. Dress patterns with simple seams could easily employ this method, but remember that the crochet has a certain depth and therefore the appropriate amount should first be cut away from your pattern (i.e. half the width of the total insertion could be removed from both pattern pieces being joined). Before beginning work on a sample, turn under 5cm (2 inches) seam allowance or for a garment, press back the seam on the fitting line, then follow our instructions to learn the techniques and some interesting designs.

Sample 1

This sample shows the seam pressed back and ready for work to begin. As a crochet hook can not be inserted directly into the majority of dress fabrics, an even back stitch has been worked along the

fitting line (this has been emphasised in our sample by the use of green wool). The size of the sewing stitch should be large enough to allow the crochet hook to pass through it.

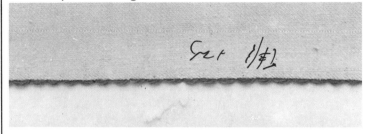

Sample 2

Here the first line of crochet is being worked. Make a slip loop on the hook, then working from right to left with the right side of the work facing, remove hook from loop and insert into first st on fabric, replace the loop on the hook and draw through the st on the fabric, 2ch, *insert hook into next sewing stitch, yrh and draw through a loop, yrh and draw through both loops (i.e. 1dc has been worked), 1ch, rep from * to end of work. Fasten off.

Note Our sample illustrates 1dc followed by 1ch, but if the back stitches are smaller there is no need for 1ch between stitches.

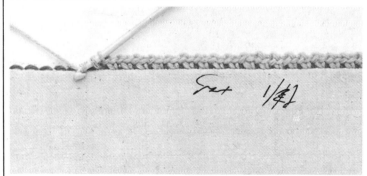

Sample 3

This is the completed insertion. First work along the edges of fabrics, A and B, as described in sample 2. With RS of work facing and working from right to left, insert hook into first ch of fabric A, work 5ch, slip hook out of st and insert into first ch of fabric B again with RS facing, *replace st on the hook and draw through the st on B, yrh 3 times, insert hook into next ch of fabric A, yrh and draw through a loop, (yrh and draw through first 2 loops on hook), 4 times – 1tr tr has been worked –, remove hook from st and insert into next ch on fabric B, rep from * to end. Fasten off yarn by replacing st and draw through the ch sp on fabric B, yrh and draw through, cutting end.

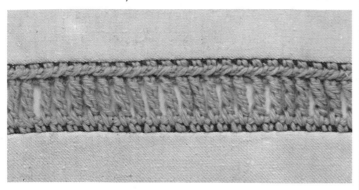

Note. When joining two pieces of fabric together in this way, it is important that the two rows of back stitches are exactly the same in size and number.

Sample 4

This sample has been made in the same way as sample 3, but a further development has been incorporated. A cord has been worked through pairs of tr tr – denoted as A and B. To do this, follow our diagram and place first tr tr – A over second tr tr – B and then take the cord under B and over A Repeat over each pair of tr tr. Here the insert has been used vertically as it would be in a trouser seam.

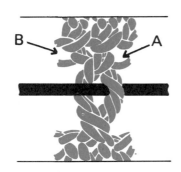

Sample 5

Work a row of dc along two pieces of fabric, A and B, as given for sample 2. To work the crochet joining the two pieces together, with RS of work facing and working from right to left, join yarn to first st on fabric A, work 9ch, slip hook out of st and insert hook into first st on fabric B again with RS of work facing, *replace the st on the hook and draw through the st on fabric B, yrh 8 times, insert hook into next st on fabric A, yrh and draw through a loop, (yrh and draw through first 2 loops on hook) 9 times – called 1tr8 –, remove st from hook and insert into next ch on

fabric B, rep from * to end. Fasten off yarn by replacing st on hook, then draw through the st on fabric B, yrh and draw through yarn, cutting off end. The diagram shows the method of threading cord through the stitches.

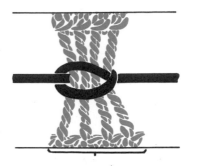

Sample 6

Work as given for sample 5, working 10ch at the beginning and working a 1tr9 by placing yrh 9 times and (yrh and draw through first 2 loops on hook) 10 times.

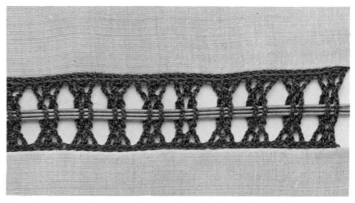

The diagram shows the method of working three rows of cord through the stitches.

EDGINGS

One of the neatest and most attractive ways of finishing off the outer edges of a garment, whether it is knitted or worked in crochet, is by using a crochet edging.

The edging may be worked in rounds or rows. It normally consists of only one row or round of crochet, but it may be necessary to work a foundation row or round of double crochet to give a firmer edge. These edgings are worked into the stitches round the outer edges of a garment or piece of crochet work after the main part has been completed and stitched together. Edgings can be either subtle or a feature of the design depending on the nature of the main work. A decorative edging can liven up a plain jacket, whilst a very simple edging may be all that is needed to neaten a heavily patterned piece of work. Choose a yarn that is applicable to the type of work you are doing. You will probably want to use the same yarn as you used for the rest of the garment, maybe in a different colour to add contrast. Should you want to make more of a feature of the edging however and use an entirely different yarn, remember the quality of the rest of the work, e.g. do not pick a thick, heavy yarn for delicate baby clothes.

There are an infinite number of edgings and below we give instructions for a number of the most unusual including basic picots, shells and clusters. One of these would be suitable for practically everything you can crochet from heavy outer garments to baby clothes and fine household linens.

Edging 1 Into first st work 1dc, *3ch, miss next st, 1dc into next st, rep from * to the end.

Edging 2 This is called crab stitch. It is simply double crochet into every stitch, but working from left to right instead of the normal right to left.

Edging 3 This is the most usual way of working a picot. Work 1dc into each of first 3 sts, *4ch, remove hook from st and insert it into first ch worked from front to back, pick up the st that was left and draw through the loop on the hook – 1 picot has been formed –, 1dc into each of next 3 sts, rep from * to end.

Edging 4 Here is a more decorative picot edging. Work 1dc into each of first 3 sts, *4ch, 1dc into 3rd ch from hook, 1ch, miss next st, 1dc into each of next 3 sts, rep from * to end.

Edging 5 The picots worked here form a very dense edge. Ss into first st, *4ch and work a picot into 4th ch from hook as described in edging 3, ss into next st, rep from * to end.

Edging 6 This is an easy way of making a looped edging. *Work 1dc into first st, extend loop on hook and transfer it to a No.1 knitting needle, keeping the needle at the back of the work, reinsert hook into last dc worked, yrh and draw through a loop, 1dc into next st, rep from * to end.

Edging 7 Ss into each of first 2 sts, *1dc into next st, 3ch, ss into same st where last dc was worked, ss into each of next 2 sts, rep from * to end.

Edging 8 The group of stitches in this edging form a decorative scallop shape. Work 3ch, into st at base of ch work (1htr, 1ch, 1tr, 1ch and 1dtr), *miss next 2 sts, ss into next st, (1htr, 1ch, 1tr, 1ch and 1dtr) into same st as ss, rep from * to end.

Edging 9 More loops, but this time formed by chain stitches. Work 1dc into first st, *3ch, ss into same st where last dc was worked, miss next st, 1dc into next st, rep from * to end.

Edging 10 The stitches in each group form a shell. Join in yarn and into 3rd st from hook work (2tr, 1ch, 1dtr 1ch, 2tr), *miss next 2 sts, ss into next st, miss next 2 sts, (2tr, 1ch, 1dtr, 1ch, 2tr) into next st, rep from * to end.

Edging 11 This edging gives an unusual geometric outline. *Work 7ch, into 3rd ch from hook work 1dc, 1htr into next ch, 1tr into next ch, 1dtr into next ch, 1tr tr into next ch, miss next 3 sts, ss into next st, rep from * to end.

Edging 12 Here a cluster of stitches gives an interesting variation. Work 2ch, miss first st, 1htr into next st, *(yrh and insert into the ch sp at right of htr just worked from front to back, yrh and draw through a loop) 3 times, yrh and draw through all 7 loops on hook, 1ch, miss next st, 1htr into next st, rep from * to end.

SIMPLE BRAIDS AND CORDS

Decoration plays an important part in fashion today, both for the fashions we wear and for those in the home. One type of decoration is to apply braids and cords to form an additional design. Here we shall tell you how to work a number of braids which are suitable for all types of garment.

A braid is usually considered to be a narrow piece of work made in a chosen yarn to complement the main garment which is then applied as a binding to cover or neaten a raw edge of fabric, or as a fashion detail. The colour, texture and width of the braid must be chosen carefully in conjunction with the fabric with which it is to be used and the trimming design must be worked out in relation to the whole garment so that it does not end up looking as though it has been added as an afterthought.

The cords illustrated in this chapter may be used for any form of tie lacing or decoration. Several strips of cord can be applied side by side to give a wider trim.

Sample 1

This is a simple cord made with a No.4.00 (ISR) hook and a double knitting yarn. Work a length of chain, and then slip stitch back along the length by placing the hook into the loop on the reverse side of each chain.

Sample 2

Make a length of chain in the same way as sample 1 and then slip stitch back along the length by placing the hook into the single top loop on the front of each chain. The reverse side has been illustrated and this has an attractive knotted effect.

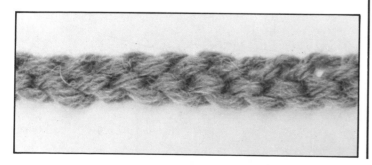

Sample 3

Using No.4.00 (ISR) hook and a double knitting yarn, make a length of chain very loosely. When the chain is the required length, thread four thicknesses of a chenille yarn through the chain stitches.

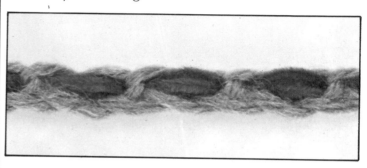

Sample 4

In this sample four thicknesses of chenille yarn are threaded into the cord as you are working it. Using No.4.00 (ISR) hook and a double knitting yarn, make a length of chain, but at the same time pass the chenille to and fro over the incoming yarn behind the hook between every two stitches worked. The reverse side of the chain has been illustrated.

Sample 5

This attractive beaded cord has been worked in a similar way to sample 4. Thread the small wooden beads on to a separate length of yarn. Using a No.4.00 (ISR) hook and a double knitting yarn, make a length of chain and at the same time pass a doubled length of beaded yarn to and fro between every four chain stitches. In the illustrated sample the beads have been positioned in fives followed by threes on either side of the chain.

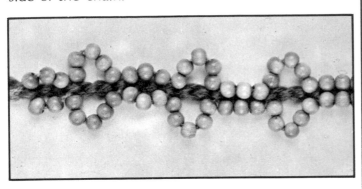

Sample 6

This sample has been worked with a modern interpretation of a lucet which is an old-fashioned tool for making a chain type cord. It is usually in the shape of a lyre and is also known as a chain fork. However, two crochet hooks placed together as in our diagram can be used to make this cord.

Rug wool has been used for this particular cord and you will also need two No.7.00 (ISR) hooks plus a No.2.50 (ISR) hook to work the chain. Place a slip loop on the left hand hook and then hold the two hooks together. Wrap the yarn behind the right hook and in front of the left hook. Hold the yarn behind the hooks and using the smaller hook slip the loop on the left hook over the yarn. *Place yarn behind the right hook in front of both loops, holding it behind the hooks, then slip the under loop over the top loop on both hooks. *. Repeat from * to * for the required length.

Sample 7

Here the same method as sample 6 is illustrated using two No.5.00 (ISR) hooks in place of the lucet, a double

knitting yarn and a No.2.50 (ISR) hook for working the chain.

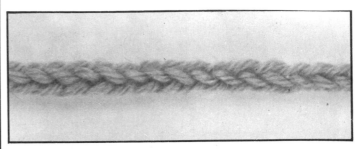

Sample 8

Using two No.6.00 (ISR) hooks in place of the lucet, two thicknesses of double knitting yarn together and a No.2.50 (ISR) hook, place a slip loop on the left hook and then *wrap the yarn round the right hook from behind and then round the left hook from behind as in the diagram. Slip the under loop over the top loop on both hooks. *. Repeat from * to * for the required length. This forms a much firmer cord suitable for a tie belt.

Sample 9

After the completion of a braid made with a lucet, a narrow ribbon has been threaded in and out of the chain, and then it has been drawn up to give a zig-zag effect.

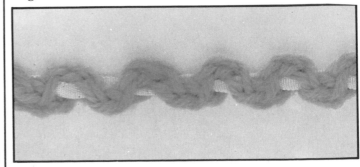

130

INTRICATE BRAIDS

Here are some braids and trimmings more intricate than the simple cords suitable for lacing or ties which were described in the last chapter. The samples in this chapter are worked in a different way and produce slightly wider trimmings which are suitable for clothes, or lampshade braids and roller blind hems. Again, remember that the choice of yarn for working the trimming is very important and should compliment the fabric on which it will be used.

Sample 1

A very attractive braid is formed by a new technique where the work is turned after each individual stitch has been worked. Using a No.4.50 (ISR) hook and a double knitting yarn, make a slip loop on the hook. Yrh and draw through loop, insert hook into first loop made, yrh and draw through loop, yrh and draw through both loops on hook. Turn work. Insert hook from right to left into the small loop on the left hand side, yrh and draw through a loop, yrh and draw through both loops on hook. Turn work. *Insert hook from right to left into the two loops on the left hand side, yrh and draw through a loop, yrh and draw through both loops on hook. Turn work. *. Repeat from * to * for required length of braid.

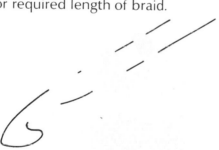

Sample 2

Both sides of this unusual braid are illustrated here as each has a completely different appearance. Using two thicknesses of a double knitting yarn and a No.5.00 (ISR) hook, make a slip loop on the hook. Yrh and draw through loop, insert hook into first loop made, yrh and draw through loop, yrh and draw through both loops on hook. Turn work. Insert hook from right to left into the small loop on the left hand side, yrh and draw through a loop, yrh and draw through both loops on hook. Turn work. *Insert hook from right to left into the two loops on the left hand side as given for sample 1, yrh and draw through a loop, yrh and draw through both loops on hook. *. Turn work from right to left. Repeat from * to *. Turn work from left to right. Continue in this way, turning work alternately from right to left and then from left to right for the required length of the cord. One way of using this braid is for trimming a pocket as in our photograph.

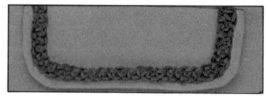

Sample 3

This is worked in the same way as sample 1, but in trebles instead of double crochet. A double length of mohair yarn has then been threaded through the vertical loops on the surface.

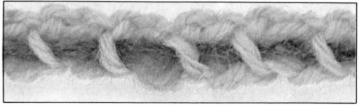

Sample 4

Using a very thick embroidery yarn and a No.5.00 (ISR) hook, work in the same way as sample 1 in half trebles instead of double crochet.

Sample 5

Here is a very pretty shell design which is very easy to make. Using a No.4.50 (ISR) hook and a double knitting yarn, make 8ch. Join with a ss into first ch to form a circle. 3ch to count as first tr, work 7tr into circle, 6ch, work 1dc into circle. Turn work. *3ch to count as first tr, work 7tr into 6ch sp, 6ch, 1dc into 6ch sp. Turn work. *. Repeat from * to * for the required length.

Sample 6

Using two thicknesses of a double knitting yarn and a No.5.00 (ISR) hook, make 4ch. Into 4th ch from hook work 1tr tr and 1dc. Turn work. *3ch, into dc work 1tr tr and 1dc. Turn work. *. Repeat from * to * for the required length. This produces a thick, chunky accordion type braid.

Sample 7

Raffene has been used for this braid to give a shiny and crunchy texture. Using a No.5.00 (ISR) hook work in the same way as sample 1, but instead of double crochet make a 7 loop treble by placing (yrh, insert hook into stitch, yrh and draw through a loop) 3 times, yrh and draw through all 7 loops.

Sample 8

Bobble stitches give an interesting chunky look to this braid. Using No.5.00 (ISR) hook and two thicknesses of a double knitting yarn, make 2ch. (Yrh and insert into first ch worked, yrh and draw through a loop) 3 times, yrh and draw through all loops on hook, 3ch, 1dc into first ch worked. Turn work. *(Yrh and insert into 3ch sp, yrh and draw through a loop) 3 times, yrh and draw through all loops on hook, 3ch, 1dc into 3ch sp. Turn work. *. Continue in this way for the required length.

You will see that the bobbles lie in an alternating pattern with the outer edges forming gently scalloped lines on either side of the braid.

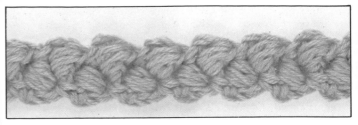

Sample 9

An interesting frieze has been created by working crochet stitches within a border. Using No.4.50 (ISR) hook and a double knitting yarn, make a chain the required length with multiples of 4 stitches.

1st row Into 3rd ch from hook work 1dc, 1dc into each ch to end. Turn.

2nd row 4ch, miss first 2dc, *leaving last loop of each on hook work 2dtr into next dc, yrh and draw through all 3 loops – called a joint dtr –, 3ch, work a joint dtr into same dc as before, miss next 3dc, rep from * finishing with 1dtr into last dc. Turn.

3rd row Work 1dc into each st to end of row. Fasten off.

Sample 10

Two colours of a double knitting yarn, A and B, create an unusual effect in this braid. Using a No.4.50 (ISR) hook and A, make 5ch.

1st row Into 2nd ch from hook work 1dc, 1htr into next ch, 1tr into next ch, leaving the last loop of each on hook work 3dtr into next ch, yrh and draw through all loops on hook. Turn.

2nd row Join in B. *Work 1dc into first st, 1htr into next st, 1tr into next st, leaving the last loop of each on hook work 3dtr into next st, yrh and draw through all loops on hook. Turn. *.

3rd row Join in A. Rep from * to * of 2nd row.

Repeat 2nd and 3rd rows for the required length.

Note Work over the colour not in use to keep the loose ends of yarn behind the work.

BRAIDS USING RIBBON

Braids using ribbons

Most of the braids illustrated can be used for either a trimming added to a garment, or a chosen sample could be incorporated as part of the design of a garment and worked in with the normal crochet stitches. They could be used as trimmings round the hemline of a plain skirt, trousers or jerkins. If the braid is placed on the waistline of a garment, then the ribbon can act as a means of drawing in the waist.

Sample 1

This demonstrates the basic technique used in this chapter and the samples following show developments of this method of work.

Using No.4.00 (ISR) hook and a cotton yarn, make a length of chain with multiples of 2 stitches.

1st row Into 3rd ch from hook work 1htr, 1htr into each ch to end. Turn.

2nd row 4ch to count as first tr and ch sp, miss first 2 sts, 1tr into next st, *1ch, miss next st, 1tr into next st, rep from * to end. Turn.

3rd row 2ch to count as first htr, 1htr into each ch sp and tr, ending with 1htr into 4ch sp, 1htr into 3rd of 4ch. Fasten off.

The ribbon has been threaded through alternate trebles in the 2nd row.

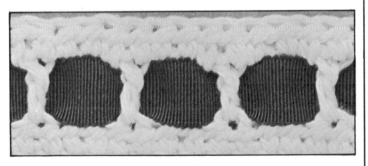

Sample 2

Using No.3.00 (ISR) hook and a cotton yarn, make a chain with multiples of 4+2 stitches.

1st row Into 3rd ch from hook work 1dc, 1dc into each ch to end. Turn.

2nd row 4ch to count as first dtr, 2dtr leaving last loop of each on hook into st at base of ch, yrh and draw through all loops on hook, *3ch, miss next 3 sts, 3dtr leaving last loop of each on hook into next st, yrh and draw through all loops on hook, rep from * to end. Turn.

3rd row 1ch to count as first dc, 1dc into each st to end. Fasten off.

Velvet ribbon has been threaded in and out of alternate double treble groups.

Sample 3

Using No.3.00 (ISR) hook and a cotton yarn, make a length of chain with multiples of 6+3 stitches.

1st row Into 3rd ch from hook work 1dc, 1dc into each ch to end. Turn.

2nd row 1ch to count as first dc, 1dc into each st to end. Turn.

3rd row As 2nd.

4th row 1ch to count as first dc, 1dc into each st working into same sts as for 3rd row – this gives a very firm ridge. Turn.

5th row 6ch to count as first st and ch sp, miss first 2 sts, *yrh 5 times, insert hook into next st, yrh and draw through a loop, (yrh and draw through first 2 loops on hook) 6 times – called 1tr5 –, (1ch, miss next st, 1tr5 into next st) twice, 1ch, yrh twice, take hook in front of last 3 vertical bars worked to the back, yrh and draw through a loop, yrh and draw through one loop, yrh twice, miss next st, insert hook into next st, yrh and draw through a loop, (yrh and draw through first 2 loops on hook) 6 times, rep from * to end, beg each new rep with first 1tr5 into same st as last 1tr5. Turn.

6th row 1ch to count as first dc, 1dc into each st to end. Turn.

7th row 1ch to count as first dc, 1dc into each st working into same sts as for 6th row. Turn.

8th and 9th rows As 2nd. Fasten off.

Ribbon has been threaded through alternate groups of crossed stitches.

Sample 4

Using No.3.00 (ISR) hook and a cotton yarn, make a length of chain with multiples of 6+2 stitches.

1st to 3rd rows As 1st to 3rd rows of sample 3.

4th row 9ch, miss first 6 sts, ss into next st, *9ch, miss next 5 sts, ss into next st, rep from * to end. Turn.

5th row 1ch to count as first dc, 10dc into first 9ch sp, 11dc into each 9ch sp to end. Turn. Fasten off.

6th row Join yarn into 3rd st of first sp between half circles, *9ch, ss into 3rd ch of next sp passing ch length in front of work, rep from * taking the ch length behind and in front of work alternately. Turn.

7th row As 5th.

8th row Make a slip loop on the hook, 2ch, ss into 6th dc of first half circle, *2ch, ss into 6th dc of next half circle, rep from * to end, 2ch. Turn.

9th row 1ch to·count as first dc, 1dc into each st to end. Turn.

10th and 11th rows As 9th.

This braid is reversible and petersham ribbon has been threaded through as illustrated.

Sample 5

Using No.3.50 (ISR) hook and a double knitting yarn, make 2ch. (Yrh and insert into first ch worked, yrh and draw through a loop) 3 times, yrh and draw through all loops on hook, 3ch, 1dc into first ch worked. Turn. *(Yrh and insert into ch sp, yrh and draw through a loop) 3 times, yrh and draw through all loops on hook, 3ch, 1dc into same ch sp. Turn. * Rep from * to * for required length.

Double chain has been threaded in and out of the chain spaces.

Sample 6

Using No.3.50 (ISR) hook and a double knitting yarn, make a length of chain with multiples of 4+3 stitches.

1st row Into 5th ch from hook work 1dc, *1ch, miss next ch, 1dc into next ch, rep from * to end. Turn.

2nd row *5ch, 3dtr into 4th ch from hook, miss next ch sp, 1dc into next ch sp, rep from * to end. Break off yarn.

3rd row Rejoin yarn to other side of foundation ch and rep 2nd row, working the dc into the sp missed on that row.

A narrow velvet ribbon has been threaded in a spiral over the centre core, working in and out of the spaces below the double trebles.

Sample 7

This sample is worked with a No.3.50 (ISR) hook and a double knitting yarn.

1st line *6ch, (yrh and insert into first ch, yrh and draw through a loop) 3 times, yrh and draw through all loops on hook, rep from * for required length.

2nd line *3ch, sl working loop off hook and insert into next 6ch sp of first line, pick up working loop and draw through to front of work, 3ch, (yrh and insert into first ch worked, yrh and draw through a loop) 3 times, yrh and draw through all loops on hook, rep from * joining each 6ch length to the next 6ch sp of the 1st line. Fasten off. Narrow velvet ribbon has been threaded in and out between the 6 chain spaces.

Hatband with leather trim

Size
2.5cm (*1in*) wide by 58.5cm (*23in*) long

Tension
12 sts to 10cm (*3.9in*) and 1 row to 2.5cm (*1in*) over tr worked on No.4.00 (ISR) crochet hook

Materials
Approximately 8.25 metres (*9yds*) of garden twine
Approximately 3.65 metres (*4yds*) of leather thonging for trimming
One No.4.00 (ISR) crochet hook

Hatband
Using No.4.00 (ISR) hook and twine, make 72ch.
1st row Into 6th ch from hook work 1tr, *1ch, miss 1ch, 1tr into next ch, rep from * to end.
Fasten off.

To make up
Press under a damp cloth with a warm iron. Darn in ends.
Leather thonging Cut leather thonging into 3 lengths. Thread through holes in hatband, leaving ends to tie at centre back.

EDGINGS FOR LINEN

Crochet trimmings for household linens

The theme of this chapter is household linens. The samples illustrated are worked in white as traditionally these 'laces' would have been used on white linen sheets and pillowcases. As the trend today is for coloured and patterned bed linen, the trimmings could still make attractive decorations on a number of plainer items such as a tailored bedcover or edging on a sheet.

You must first decide where the trim is to be placed, either on the edge of the work or within the main fabric. This will determine whether you have a trim with a definite straight edge (the other edge being curved, scalloped, pointed or fringed) which is required for sewing on to the very edge of an article or a double sided trim (the two edges are exactly the same) which is suitable for the main fabric and is usually placed well within a border or the hem.

All the designs illustrated may be used as an edging, or can be made into a double sided trim by repeating the design on the opposite side of the foundation chain, as in sample 7. Remember to wash and press all trimmings before adding to the linen to prevent any shrinkage during laundering.

Sample 1

Using No.3.50 (ISR) hook and a cotton yarn, make a length of chain with multiples of 4 + 3 stitches.

1st row Into 3rd ch from hook work 1htr, 1htr into each ch to end. Turn.

2nd row 2ch to count as first htr, 1htr into next htr, *6ch, into 4th ch from hook work 1tr, 1tr into each of next 2ch, miss 2htr, 1htr into each of next 2htr, rep from * ending with last htr into top of turning ch. Fasten off.

Sample 2

Using No.3.50 (ISR) hook and a cotton yarn, make a length of chain with multiples of 6 + 8 stitches.

1st row Into 8th ch from hook work 1tr, *2ch, miss next 2ch, 1tr into next ch, rep from * to end. Turn.

2nd row *3ch, 3dtr into next ch sp, 3ch, 3dc into next ch sp, rep from * to last ch sp, 3ch, 3dtr into last ch sp, 3ch, ss into ch sp. Fasten off.

Sample 3

Using No.3.50 (ISR) hook and a cotton yarn, make a length of chain with multiples of 6 + 4 stitches.

1st row Into 6th ch from hook work 1tr, *1ch, miss next ch, 1tr into next ch, rep from * to end. Turn.

2nd row Ss into first ch sp and into next tr, *5ch, miss next ch sp, (ss into each of next tr and ch sp) twice, ss into next tr, rep from * finishing with 3ss instead of 5 at end of last rep. Turn.

3rd row *Into next 5ch sp work 5tr, 5ch, ss into 4th ch from hook, 1ch and 5tr, ss into 3rd of next 5ss, rep from * to end. Fasten off.

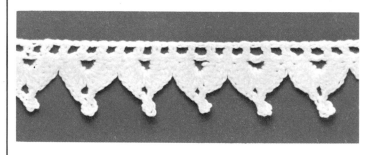

Sample 4

Using No.3.50 (ISR) hook and a cotton yarn, make a length of chain with multiples of 5 + 1 stitches.

1st row Into 3rd ch from hook work 1dc, 1dc into each ch to end. Turn.

2nd row 1ch to count as first dc, miss first st, 1dc into each st to end. Turn.

3rd row As 2nd.

4th row 4ch to count as first dtr, 1dtr into first st, *miss next 3 sts, leaving last loop of each on hook work 2dtr into next st, yrh and draw through all 3 loops on hook – called a joint dtr –, 3 ch, a joint dtr into next st, rep from * to last 4 sts, miss next 3 sts, a joint dtr into last st. Turn.

5th row 4 ch to count as first dtr, 1dtr into first st, *3ch, a joint dtr into top of next joint dtr in previous row, miss next 3 sts, a joint dtr into top of next joint dtr in previous row, rep from * to last 2dtr, 3 ch, a joint dtr into last 2dtr. Turn.

6th-8th rows 1ch to count as first dc, 1dc into each st to end. Turn.

9th row 6ch, miss first 4 sts, ss into each of next 2 sts, *6ch, miss next 3 sts, ss into each of next 2 sts, rep from * finishing with a ss into last st. Turn.

10th row Into each 6ch sp work 3dc, 3ch, 1tr, 3ch and 3dc. Fasten off.

Sample 5

Using No.3.50 (ISR) hook and a cotton yarn, make 13ch.

1st row Into 4th ch from hook work 1tr, 1tr into each of next 3ch, 2ch, miss next 2ch, 1tr into each of next 4ch, 2ch, 1tr into last ch. Turn.

2nd row 3ch, miss ch sp, 1tr into each of next 4tr, 2ch, 1tr into each of next 4tr. Turn.

3rd row 3ch to count as first tr, 1tr into each of next 3tr, 2tr into next 2ch sp, 1tr into each of next 4tr, 5tr into next ch sp at beg of 2nd row, 5tr into next ch sp at end of 1st row. Do not turn.

4th row 1 ch to count as first dc, work 1dc into front loop only of each st to end of row working from left to right instead of right to left. Do not turn.

5th row 3ch to count as first tr, 1tr into each of next 3 sts placing hook into back loop only of each st, 2ch, miss next 2 sts, 1tr into back loop only of next 4 sts, 2ch, 1tr into next st. Turn.

Repeat 2nd to 5th rows inclusive for required length.

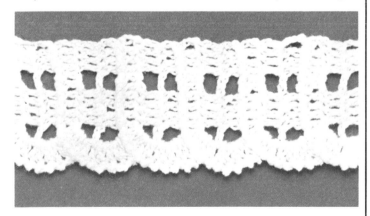

Sample 6

Using No.3.50 (ISR) hook and a cotton yarn, make a length of chain with multiples of 10 + 9 stitches.

1st row Into 5th ch from hook work 1tr, *1ch, miss next ch, 1tr into next ch, rep from * to end. Turn.

2nd row 3ch to count as first tr, 1tr into first ch sp, 3ch, miss next ch sp, *2tr into next ch sp, 3ch, miss next ch sp, rep from * ending with 1tr into last ch sp, 1tr into 4th of 5ch. Turn.

3rd row 4ch, 1tr into first ch sp, *1ch, 1tr into next ch sp, 1ch, 1tr into same ch sp, rep from * to last ch sp, 1ch, 1tr into last ch sp, 1ch, 1tr into 3rd of 3ch. Turn.

4th row 1ch to count as first dc, 2dc into first ch sp, 8ch, *3dc into each of next 3 ch sp, 8ch, rep from * to last ch sp, 2dc into last ch sp, 1dc into 3rd of 4ch. Turn.

5th row Ss into each dc worked and into each 8ch loop work 2dc, 2htr, 9tr, 2htr and 2dc. Fasten off.

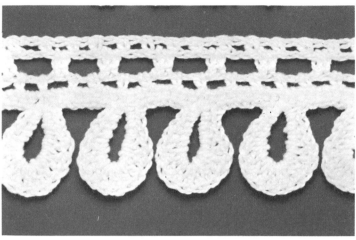

Sample 7

Using No.3.50 (ISR) hook and a cotton yarn, make a length of chain with multiples of 8 stitches.

1st row Into 6th ch from hook work 1tr, *1ch, miss next ch, 1tr into next ch, rep from * to end. Turn.

2nd row 4ch, 1tr into first sp, 1ch, 1tr into next sp, *6ch, miss next sp, 1tr into next sp, 1ch, 1tr into next sp, 1ch, 1tr into next sp, rep from * to end. Turn.

3rd row Ss into each of next sp, tr and foll sp, * into 6ch sp work 2dc, 2htr, 5tr, 2htr and 2dc, ss into each of next 3 sts, rep from * to end. Turn.

4th row *3ch, 1tr into first tr of 5tr gr, 3ch, 1dtr into centre tr of gr, 3ch, 1dtr into same tr, 3ch, 1tr into last tr of gr, 3ch, 1tr into centre ss, rep from * to end. Turn.

5th row *3dc into each of next 2 sp, into next sp work 3dc, 4ch, ss into first ch worked so forming a picot and 3dc, 3dc into each of next 2 sp, rep from * to end. Fasten off. This forms an edging with one straight edge, but the crochet design may be worked on the other side of the foundation chain to give a double sided trim as in our illustration.

EDGINGS FOR SOFT FURNISHINGS

Trimmings for soft furnishings

In the last chapter we showed samples of edgings and double sided braids suitable for household articles. Here we extend the theme to include more decorative and deeper trimmings such as deep shaped edgings and crochet braids with long tassels and pompons. This work is ideal for lampshades, both hanging from the ceiling and table lamps, roller blinds, curtains and pelmets.

Our samples have been worked in cotton yarns, but of course other colours and types of yarn are quite suitable for most of the designs. One word of warning – if you are making tassels the yarn must not fray when cut so leave the tassel in uncut loops to avoid this happening with yarn which unravels.

Sample 1

Using No.3.50 (ISR) hook and a cotton yarn, make a length of chain with multiples of 2 stitches.

1st row Into 3rd ch from hook work 1dc, 1dc into each ch to end. Turn.

2nd row 1ch to count as first dc, miss 1dc, 1dc into each dc to end. Turn.

3rd row 4ch to count as first tr and sp, miss first 2dc, 1tr into next dc, *1ch, miss next dc, 1tr into next dc, rep from * to end. Turn.

4th row 3ch to count as first tr, *(yrh and insert into next ch sp, yrh and draw through a loop) 4 times, yrh and draw through all loops on hook, 1ch, rep from * omitting 1ch at end of last rep and ending with 1tr into 3rd of 4ch. Turn.

5th row 4ch to count as first tr and sp, *miss next bobble, 1tr into next ch, 1ch, rep from * omitting 1ch at end of last rep and ending with last tr into 3rd of 3ch. Fasten off.

Fringe Cut 5 lengths of yarn each 12.5cm (5in) long and fold in half lengthwise. Insert folded end through ch sp in the 5th row, then pull the cut ends through the loop. Pull up tightly. Repeat into each ch sp along the row. Trim ends to an equal length.

Sample 2

Using No.3.50 (ISR) hook and a cotton yarn, make a length of chain with multiples of 4 + 1 stitches.

1st–2nd rows As 1st–2nd rows of sample 1.

3rd row (crossed triple trebles) Ss into each of first 4 sts, 5ch to count as first tr tr, yrh 3 times, insert hook behind ch length into next st at right of ch just worked, yrh and draw through a loop, (yrh and draw through first 2 loops on hook) 4 times – called 1tr tr –, work 1tr tr into each of next 2 sts to the right of last tr tr, *miss 3 sts to left of first tr tr, 1tr tr into next st, 1tr tr into each of next 3 sts to the right of last tr tr always placing hook behind the last st worked, rep from * to end. Turn.

4th row 1ch to count as first dc, 1dc into each st to end. Turn.

5th row As 4th.

6th row 6ch, miss first 2 sts, ss into next st, *3ch, miss next st, ss into next st, 6ch, miss next st, ss into next st, rep from * to end. Fasten off.

Fringe Work as given for sample 1, and thread through each 6ch loop in 6th row.

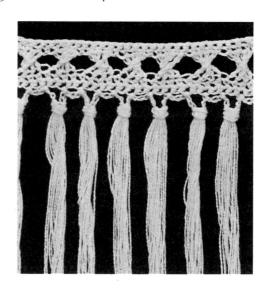

Sample 3

Using No.3.50 (ISR) hook and a cotton yarn, make 20ch.

1st row Into 8th ch from hook work 1tr, *2ch, miss 2ch, 1tr into next ch, rep from * to end. Turn.

2nd row 1ch to count as first dc, miss first st, 1dc into each st to last ch sp, 2dc into ch sp, 1dc into 5th of 7ch. Turn.

3rd row 3ch to count as first tr, miss first st, 1tr into each st to end of row. Turn.

4th row As 2nd row working last dc into 3rd of 3ch, but do not turn, 5ch, ss into base of first dc in 2nd row, 7ch, ss into top of last dc worked. Turn.

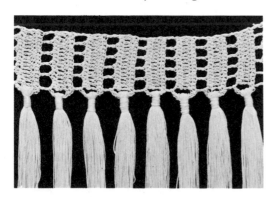

5th row 5ch, miss first 3 sts, 1tr into next st, *2ch, miss next 2 sts, 1 tr into next st, rep from * to end. Fasten off. The 2nd to 5th rows inclusive form the pattern and are repeated for the required length.

Fringe Cut yarn into 30.5cm (12in) lengths and using 34 of these lengths together, place over a length of double chain. Tie very securely in place below the chain. Repeat into each length of double chain along the row, and then trim the ends.

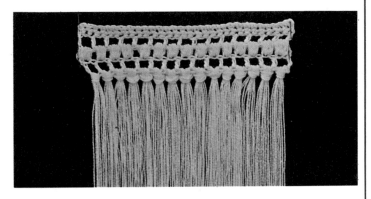

Sample 4

Using No.4.00 (ISR) hook and a thick cotton yarn, make a chain the required length with multiples of 4 + 3 stitches.

1st row Into 3rd ch from hook work 1dc, 1dc into each ch to end. Turn.

2nd row (crossed trebles) Ss into each of first 2 sts, 3ch to count as first tr, placing the hook behind the length of chain work 1tr into next st to the right of the chain, *miss next st to left of first tr, 1tr into next st, placing the hook in front of the last tr worked 1tr into next st to the right, miss next st, 1tr into next st, placing the hook behind the last tr worked 1tr into next st to the right, rep from * to end. Turn.

3rd row 1ch to count as first dc, 1dc into each st to end. Turn.

4th row 6ch, miss first 4 sts, 1dc into next st, *5ch, miss 3 sts, 1dc into next st, rep from * to end. Fasten off.

Pompons Cut two circular pieces of card both 5cm (2in) in diameter and each having a central hole, 2.5cm (1in) in diameter. Use the circles to make a pompon in the usual manner.

Work a length of chain for attaching on to the 5ch loops in the 4th rows.

Sample 5

This is a variation on the traditional filet crochet known as filet guipure. The techniques of working filet crochet are described in detail in the chapters on Filet Crochet given earlier. Here we give a chart which comprises blocks and spaces for you to follow. As usual the spaces are formed by one treble at either side of two chain, and blocks are spaces filled in with two trebles. Also in this design a double space has been worked in an unusual way by making three chain, then working one double crochet where the normal treble would be, three more chain and working the next tr in its usual position. On the following row five chain will be worked above this particular group. This variation is denoted in the chart by the symbols in the following diagram.

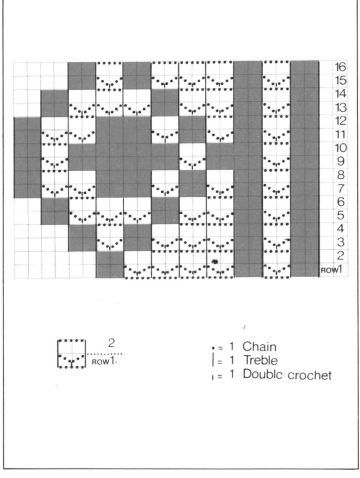

• = 1 Chain
| = 1 Treble
ı = 1 Double crochet

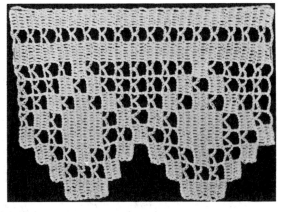

FRINGES

Continuing our chapters on trimmings and braids, we now give you instructions for making some more using fringes as the focal point. These are formed during the working of the crochet by an unusual technique of twisting the yarn to form the fringe. It is a method which requires some practise in order to achieve a good standard of work. Depending on the yarn chosen, the fringes are suitable for both household and dress trimmings.

Sample 1

Using No.4.00 (ISR) hook and a rayon yarn, make a chain the required length.

1st row Into 3rd ch from hook work 1htr, 1htr into each ch to end. Turn.

2nd row (loop row) 1ch to count as first st, miss first st, *insert hook into next st, yrh and draw through a loop, yrh and draw through both loops on hook extending loop on hook for 15cm (6in), hold work over st with thumb and first finger of left hand and with the hook in the extended loop, twist in a clockwise direction approx 24 times, halve the twisted yarn placing the hook into the last st worked, the extended

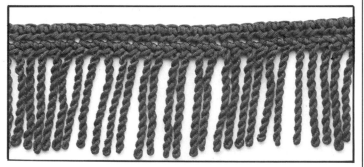

st will twist firmly in an anti-clockwise direction, yrh and draw through both loops on hook, rep from * to end of row. Fasten off. This completes the fringe.

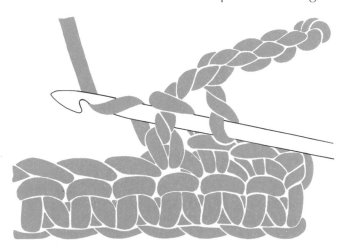

Note The depth of the fringe will depend on the length of the extended stitch and the number of times that it is twisted. You must practise this stitch to obtain perfect results.

Sample 2

Using No.4.00 (ISR) hook and a rayon yarn, make a chain the required length.

1st row Into 4th ch from hook work 1tr, 1tr into each ch to end. Turn.

2nd row Work loop row as given for sample 1. Fasten off.

Velvet ribbon, 1.5cm (½in) wide, is threaded between alternate trebles in the 1st row.

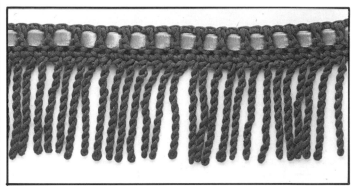

Sample 3

Using No.4.00 (ISR) hook and a double knitting yarn, make a chain the required length.

1st row Work a length of braid as given for sample 1 on page 131. Fasten off.

Join in a different colour of rayon yarn and work the loop row as foll:

2nd row Insert the hook into the loop at the top right hand edge of the braid and work a twisted loop as given for sample 1 extending the loop for 12.5cm (5in), insert the hook into the next loop but at the lower edge of the braid and make a twisted loop so forming a stitch over the braid, continue in this way working twisted loops into alternate stitches at top and lower edges for the complete length of the braid. Fasten off.

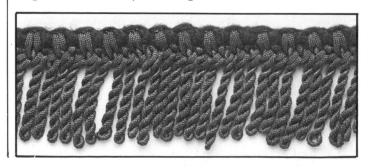

Sample 4

Using a No.4.00 (ISR) hook and a double knitting yarn, make a length of chain with multiples of 4 + 2 stitches.

1st row Into 3rd ch from hook work 1dc, 1dc into each st to end. Turn.

2nd row 1ch to count as first dc, miss first st, 1dc into next st, *1tr tr into next st, 1dc into each of next 3 sts, rep from * to last 3 sts, 1tr tr into next st, 1dc into each of next 2 sts. Turn.

3rd row 1ch to count as first dc, miss first st, 1dc into each st to end. Turn. Fasten off.

Join in a different colour of rayon yarn and work the loop row as foll:

4th row Work as given for loop row of sample 1, placing hook first into (a) next st of last row, then (b) into next st of row below, then (c) into next st of row below that, rep in the order of (b), (a), (b), (c), (b) and (a) for the required length. Fasten off.

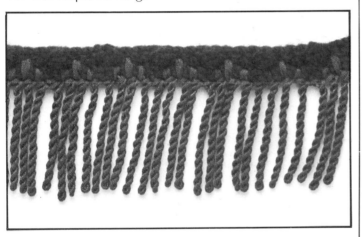

Sample 5

Using No.4.00 (ISR) hook and a rayon yarn, make a chain the required length.

1st row Into 4th ch from hook work 1tr, 1tr into each ch to end. Turn.

2nd row 1ch to count as first dc, miss first st, work 1dc into each st to end placing hook from back to front into sp between normal chain st and horizontal loop below it – this gives a raised chain effect on the right side of the work. Turn.

3rd row (loop row) This is slightly different from the loop row of sample 1. Work 4ch to count as first tr

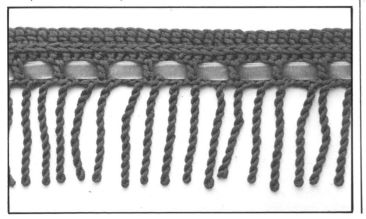

and sp, miss first 2 sts, *yrh and insert into next st, yrh and draw through a loop, (yrh and draw through first 2 loops on hook) twice, extend loop on hook twisting it as before, insert hook into last st worked, yrh and draw through both loops on hook, 1ch, miss next st, rep from * ending with last tr into turning chain. Fasten off. Velvet ribbon has been threaded between alternate trebles of the loop row.

Sample 6

Using No.3.00 (ISR) hook and a cotton yarn, make a chain the required length.

1st row Into 4th ch from hook work 1tr, 1tr into each ch to end. Turn.

2nd row 1ch to count as first dc, 1dc into each st to end. Turn.

3rd row 1ch to count as first dc, 1dc into back loop only of each st to end. Turn.

4th row 2ch to count as first tr, 1tr into each single loop rem from last row – now to the back of the work – to end of row. Turn.

5th row (loop row) Work as given for loop row of sample 1. Fasten off.

6th row (loop row) Rejoin yarn to sts of row 3 on front of braid and work as given for loop row of sample 1. Velvet ribbon has been threaded between alternate trebles in the 1st row.

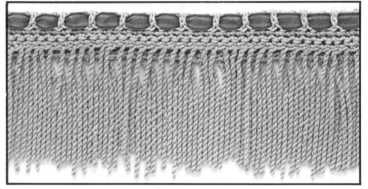

DECORATIVE FRINGES

Decorative fringes

Exciting fringes may be worked in many ways and in this chapter we cover a variety of very decorative ones which would be suitable for fashion garments. The fringes illustrated could be used on jerkins, long scarves, stoles and dresses. Master the techniques described here and when you feel competent, try experimenting with different yarns, beads and threads.

Sample 1

This has been worked in two yarns, a gold ribbon – A, and a tubular rayon – B. Using No.4.00 (ISR) hook and B, make 6ch.

1st row Place yarn A between the incoming yarn B and the hook, placing the cut end to the right hand side of the work, 1ch with B, *take yarn A from left to right placing it between incoming yarn B and the hook leaving a 7.5cm (3in) folded loop, 1ch with B, take yarn A now on the right and place between the incoming yarn B and the hook leaving no loop, 1ch with B, rep from * for the required length of fringe, work 12ch with B. Break off A and reverse work.

2nd row Fold the 12ch length just worked in half and hold in the left hand with the loops to the right, the incoming yarn should be under or behind the work and the hook on top or towards you, *place hook over single thickness of next loop, yrh and draw through st on hook, place hook over next single thickness of same loop, yrh and draw through st on hook, rep from * to end of loops, work 12ch and reverse work.

3rd row Fold the 12ch length just worked in half and hold in the right hand with the loops to the left, rep as given from * of 2nd row to end.

The 2nd and 3rd rows are repeated to give the required proportion of heading to the looped fringe.

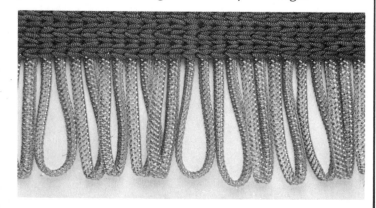

Sample 2

Two types of yarn have been used for this sample,

A for the working yarn and 4 thicknesses of B together for the fringe. Using No.3.50 (ISR) hook and A, make 6ch.

1st row Place yarn B (all 4 thicknesses) between the incoming yarn A and the hook, placing the cut ends to the right hand side of the work, 1ch with A, * take yarn B from left to right placing it between incoming yarn A and the hook leaving a 7.5cm (3in) folded loop, 1ch with A, take yarn B now on the right and place between the incoming yarn A and the hook leaving no loop, 1ch with A, rep from * for the required length of fringe, work 12ch with A. Break off B and reverse work.

2nd row Fold the 12ch length just worked in half and hold in the left hand with the loops to the right, the incoming yarn should be under or behind the work and the hook on top or towards you, *place hook over 4 thicknesses of next loop, yrh and draw through st on hook, place hook over next 4 thicknesses of same loop, yrh and draw through st on hook, rep from * to end of loops, work 12ch and reverse work.

3rd row Fold the 12ch length just worked in half and hold in the right hand with the loops to the left, rep as given from * of 2nd row to end.

The 2nd and 3rd rows are repeated to give the required proportion of heading to the fringe. The loops can either be cut as in our sample or left uncut .

Sample 3

Here is an attractive method of making a beaded fringe. A lurex yarn has been used for the crochet, whilst the beads have been threaded on to a separate length of yarn. The number of beads will of course depend on the amount of fringing required. Using No.3.50 (ISR) hook and lurex yarn, make 6ch.

1st row With cut end to the right, place yarn with beads between incoming yarn and the hook, 1ch with lurex yarn, *place yarn with beads from left to right, placing 21 beads on a loop plus 2.5cm (1in) of free yarn, between incoming yarn and hook, 2ch with lurex yarn, place yarn with beads from right to left, leaving no loop between incoming yarn and hook, work 1ch with lurex yarn, rep from * to give required length of fringe, work 12ch with lurex yarn. Break off yarn with beads and reverse work.

2nd row Hold the work with the chain heading to the left and beaded loops to the right, work 1ch over next length of yarn with beads having one bead on the left, *1ch, 1ch over next length of yarn with beads having one bead on the left, rep from * to end of fringe, work 12ch. Reverse work.

3rd row Hold the work with the chain heading to the right and beaded loops to the left, work as given for 2nd row. Fasten off.

Note The yarn with beads will require tightening in order to give an all beaded loop with no yarn showing between the beads.

Sample 4

Using No.4.00 (ISR) hook and a double knitting yarn, make 6ch.

1st row Into 3rd ch from hook work 1dc, 1dc into each ch to end. Turn. 4 sts.

2nd row 1ch to count as first dc, miss first st, 1dc into each of next 3 sts. Turn.

3rd row As 2nd.

4th row As 2nd, but do not turn, work 24ch. Turn.

5th row Into 4th ch from hook work 3tr, 4tr into each of the next 20ch, 1tr into each of next 4 sts. Turn.

The 2nd to 5th rows inclusive are repeated for the length of trimming required.

Sample 5

To work the braid Using No.4.00 (ISR) hook and a double knitting yarn, make a chain with multiples of 4 + 2 stitches.

1st row Into 3rd ch from hook work 1dc, 1dc into each ch to end. Turn.

2nd row 1ch to count as first dc, miss first st, 1dc into each st to end. Turn.

3rd row 4ch to count as first tr and sp, miss first 2 sts, *(yrh and insert into next st, yrh and draw through a loop, yrh and draw through first 2 loops on hook) 9 times always inserting hook into same st, yrh and draw through all 10 loops on hook, work 1ch very tightly to hold bobble, 1ch, miss next st, 1tr into next st, 1ch, miss next st, rep from * ending with 1tr into last st. Turn.

4th row 1ch to count as first dc, *1dc into next ch sp, 1dc into top of next bobble, 1dc into next ch sp, 1dc into next tr, rep from * to end. Turn.

5th row As 2nd. Fasten off.

To work the crochet balls Using same yarn and hook, place the cut end of yarn in the palm of left hand and wrap yarn once round first finger, insert hook into loop round finger from underneath, yrh and draw through a loop, slip loop off finger and hold between finger and thumb of left hand, *insert hook into ring, yrh and draw through a loop, yrh and draw through both loops on hook, rep from * 7 times more. Tighten ring by pulling cut end of yarn. Mark beg of each round with a coloured thread.

Next round Work 2dc into each of 8 sts. Do not join.

Next 2 rounds Work 1dc into each of 16 sts. Do not join. Place cotton wool stuffing into ball.

Next round (Work 2dc tog) 8 times. Do not join.

Next round Work 1dc into each of 8 sts. Draw sts tog by threading working st through each free st to make a neat end, do not break off yarn, 9ch, ss to braid below bobble, ss back along chain to ball, 9ch, miss next bobble on braid, ss to braid below next bobble, ss back along chain and fasten to ball. Continue in this way, first fastening each new ball below the bobble omitted in the previous joining and so forming a cross-over design.

FRILLS

Crochet frills are easy to work and make effective trimmings for a variety of garments. When working a frill, choose a yarn which is appropriate to the purpose and fabric of the main garment such as a lurex yarn for evening wear or a fine cotton yarn for lingerie. Our samples in the photographs are worked with a No.4.50 (ISR) crochet hook and a double knitting yarn.

We also explain two methods of making frills. One way is to work more than one stitch into each stitch of the previous row and this is illustrated in samples 1, 2, 4 and 5. Sample 3 demonstrates the method of gathering crochet to form a frill. It is simple to work and would look very attractive in a white or ecru yarn. If you prefer, you could starch the crochet frill before applying it to the garment.

Sample 1

Make 31ch. This can be made longer by adding multiples of 4 stitches.

1st row Into 3rd ch from hook work 1dc, 1dc into each ch to end. Turn.

2nd row 5ch, miss first 4dc, ss into next dc, *(5ch, miss 3dc, ss into next dc), rep from * 5 times more. Turn. Seven 5ch sp.

3rd row 1ch to count as first dc, 7dc into first 5ch sp, 8dc into each 5ch sp to end.

Rep 2nd and 3rd rows along the opposite side of the foundation chain. Turn.

4th row 4ch to count as first tr and ch, *1tr, 1ch into next dc, rep from * round both sides of foundation chain. Turn.

5th row Using a contrast colour, join yarn into first 1ch sp, ss into same sp, *3ch, ss into next ch sp, rep from * to end. Fasten off.

Use this frill to decorate the centre front of a long evening gown.

Sample 2

This frill is ideal for a decorative cuff. To work the fabric shown in our sample, make 26ch.

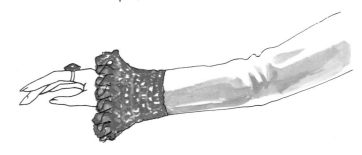

1st row Leaving the last loop of each on hook, work 1tr into each of 4th and 5th ch from hook, yrh and draw through all 3 loops on hook, 1 ch, * leaving the last loop of each on hook, work 1tr into each of next 2ch, yrh and draw through all 3 loops on hook, 1ch, rep from * to last ch, 1tr into last ch. Turn.

2nd row 3ch to count as first tr, *leaving the last loop of each on hook, work 2tr into next 1ch sp, yrh and draw through all 3 loops on hook, 1ch, rep from * ending with 1tr into 3rd of the turning ch. Turn.

The 2nd row is repeated throughout.

To work the frill

1st row 5ch, ss into top of first pair of tr, *5ch, ss into top of next pair of tr, rep from * to end. Turn.

2nd row 3ch to count as first tr, 2tr into first sp, 3ch, 3tr into same sp, *2ch, ss into next sp, 2ch, (3tr, 3ch, 3tr) into next sp, rep from * to end. Turn.

3rd row 1ch to count as first dc, 1dc into each st to end, working 5dc into each 3ch sp. Turn.

4th row 3ch to count as first tr, 1tr into each of next 4 sts, *2tr into each of next 3 sts, 1tr into each of next 13 sts, rep from * ending last rep with 1tr into each of next 3 sts, 1tr into the turning ch. Fasten off.

Sample 3

This sample would also be very effective as a cuff trimming. Using the first colour, make a foundation chain to fit the required measurement, say 30 chain.

1st row Work 1tr by placing the hook under the complete ch so that the st will move freely over the chain when complete, *3ch, work 1tr in the same way, rep from * 8 times more. Turn.

2nd row *3ch, ss into next ch sp, rep from * to end. Turn.

3rd row *5ch, ss into next ch sp, rep from * to end. Turn.

4th row *7ch, ss into next ch sp, rep from * to end. Turn.

5th row *9ch, ss into next ch sp, rep from * to end. Turn.

6th row *11ch, ss into next ch sp, rep from * to end. Turn.

7th row Into each 11ch sp work 12dc. Fasten off.

Next row Using second colour, join yarn into right hand sp at base of first tr worked on the foundation ch, 6ch to count as first tr and 3ch, 1tr into next sp between tr working over foundation ch as before, *3ch, 1tr into next sp between tr, rep from * to end. Turn.

Next 4 rows Rep 2nd to 5th rows as given for first colour.

Next row Into each 9ch sp work 11dc. Fasten off.

Note When using the second colour, if the same side of the dc row is to appear on both frills then the yarn should be cut and rejoined between the 5th and 6th rows in order to work from the correct side. The trebles are arranged along the foundation chain to give the required amount of frilling.

Sample 4

Worked in a fine yarn, this frill will look very good on nightwear or in a thicker yarn, it could be added to a circular hat such as a beret. The basic fabric in our samples is composed of trebles. When working your own sample make sure that you have a repeat of 5 stitches plus one extra. Work until the position for the frill is reached then continue as follows:

Next row *5ch, miss next 4 sts, ss into next st, rep from * to end. Turn.

Next row Into each ch sp work 1dc, 1htr, 1tr, 3ch, 1tr, 1htr, 1dc. Turn.

Continue in trebles until the position for the next frill is reached.

Sample 5

This is a narrow frill which could be used for all kinds of trimming. Make a foundation chain the required length of the frill.

1st row Into 3rd ch from hook work 1dc, 1dc into each ch to end. Turn.

2nd row *5ch, miss next st, ss into next st, rep from * to end. Turn.

3rd row Into each ch sp work 1dc, (3ch, 1dc) 5 times. Fasten off.

FINISHING TOUCHES
BUTTONS

Sample 1   Sample 2   Sample 3

Covered buttons
So often it is difficult to purchase the right button for a garment that you are making. Either the size is wrong or you are unable to match the colour, or maybe you would like an unusual button at a reasonable price as a feature on a plain garment. Crochet covered buttons can be very decorative and add greatly to any simple outfit.

The wooden or metal forms for covering are available from most haberdashery counters in a variety of shapes and sizes. The method of work is simple, but try a sample piece of crochet using your chosen yarn and hook size first. This sample must look correct on the garment for which the buttons are being made and the crochet fabric must be firm enough to entirely cover the form beneath it, so for this reason a smaller hook size than usual is recommended in order to achieve a close stitch.

Sample 1
5.50 metres (6 yards) of Russia braid is required to cover this large round button which is 4.5cm (1¾in) in diameter.

1st round Make a circle with the braid in the left hand, using No.3.00 (ISR) hook, work 8dc into this circle, draw the short end tight to close circle. Join with a ss into first dc.

2nd round 1ch to count as first dc, 1dc into st at base of ch, *2dc into next dc, rep from * to end. Join with a ss into first dc.

3rd round 1ch, 1dc into st at base of ch, 1dc into next dc, *2dc into next dc, 1dc into next dc, rep from * to end. Join with a ss into first dc.

4th round 1ch, 1dc into each dc to end. Join with a ss into first dc.

5th round As 4th.

In this case the back of the crochet work is the most effective and this has been placed on to the button shape as the right side. Lace the edge of the crochet circle on to the wrong side of the shape and secure very firmly in several places all round the edge. Place the metal covering disc over the back or neatly hem a circle of lining fabric to cover the edges. All button shapes should be neatened in this way.

Sample 2
This is a more unusual method of working the crochet covering for a 4.5cm (1¾in) button. Five shades of yarn and a No.3.50 (ISR) crochet hook are used. Using A make 7ch.

1st row Into 3rd ch from hook work 1dc, 1dc into each ch to end. Turn.

2nd row 1ch to count as first dc, 1dc into st at base of ch, 2dc into each st, ending with 2dc into turning ch. Turn. 12dc.

3rd row 1ch, 1dc into st at base of ch, 1dc into next st, *2dc into next st, 1dc into next st, rep from * ending with 1dc into turning ch. Turn. 18dc.

4th row 1ch, 1dc into st at base of ch, 1dc into each of next 2 sts, *2dc into next st, 1dc into each of next 2 sts, rep from * ending with last dc into turning ch. Turn. Break off A.

5th row Using B, 1ch, miss first st, 1dc into each of next 8 sts, using C, 1dc into same st as last dc, 1dc into each of next 4 sts, using D, 1dc into same st as last dc, 1dc into each of next 4 sts, using E, 1dc into same st as last dc, 1dc into each of next 7 sts. Turn.

Note When joining in new colours, follow the instructions given earlier.

6th row As 5th, dec one st at each end of row and omitting increased sts between colours.

7th row As 5th, dec one st at each end of row and inc

146

between colours as before.

Dec one st at each end of every row and omitting increased sts, cont in this colour sequence until there are no sts left. Fasten off.

Sample 3

Eight colours of cotton and a No.3.00 (ISR) hook have been used here to give a subtly shaded look to another 4.5cm (1¾in) diameter button. Using a new colour for each round, follow the instructions given for 1st–3rd rounds of sample 1. Continue in rounds of dc, working 1 more dc between the increased stitches on each round.

Sample 4

This tiny, 1.5cm (½in) diameter, button has been delicately covered in a very fine Lurex embroidery thread. Using No.0.60 (ISR) hook, work as given for sample 3.

Sample 5

Using a Lurex yarn and No.3.00 (ISR) hook, work as given for sample 3.

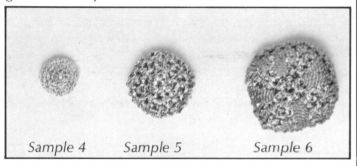

Sample 4   *Sample 5*   *Sample 6*

Sample 6

Lurex and cotton yarns are combined in this design to cover a 2.5cm (1in) diameter button. Using No.3.00 (ISR) hook and the Lurex yarn, work as given for 1st–3rd rounds of sample 1. Break off yarn.

4th round Using cotton yarn, 2ch, *1dc into next st, 1dc into next st inserting hook into 2nd round, 2dc into next st in 1st round, 1dc into next st in 2nd round,

1dc into next st, 1ch, rep from * omitting 1ch at end of last rep. Join with a ss into first ch.

5th round 1ch to count as first dc, 1dc into each st to end. Join with a ss into first ch. Fasten off.

Sample 7

Seven colours of a cotton yarn have been used to cover this square button in varying widths of diagonal stripes. You can vary the colours in any way you want. Using No.3.00 (ISR) hook make 3ch.

1st row Into 3rd ch from hook work 1dc. Turn.

2nd row 1ch to count as first dc, 1dc into st at base of ch, 2dc into next st. Turn.

3rd row 1ch, 1dc into st at base of ch, 1dc into each st to turning ch, 2dc into turning ch. Turn.

Cont inc one st at each end of every row in this way until the crochet is the correct diagonal width for the button shape required. Dec one st at each end of every row until there are no sts left. Fasten off.

Sample 8

This button cover consists of 2 triangular shapes joined together, then decorated with chain stitch. Three colours of cotton yarn, A, B and C and a No.3.00 (ISR) crochet hook are required. Using A, make 15ch.

1st row Into 3rd ch from hook work 1dc, 1dc into each of next 5 sts, join in B as explained in Patchwork Effects, 1dc into each of next 7 sts. Turn.

2nd row Using B, 1ch to count as first dc, 1dc into each of next 6 sts, using A, 1dc into each of next 7 sts. Turn. Working in colours as above, dec one st at each end of every row until there are no sts left. Make another triangle in the same way, then crochet the shapes together and, using C, work a chain st over the colour join.

Sample 9

Work in the same way as sample 8, using 3 colours for each triangle and begin by working 7dc in A, 3dc in B and 4dc in C. When 2 triangles have been completed, place the alternate colour sequence side by side and crochet together.

Sample 7   *Sample 8*   *Sample 9*

FASTENINGS

Crochet fastenings

This chapter illustrates some useful and decorative fastenings all worked by using various crochet techniques. These fastenings are useful when working with fabrics where it is difficult to work the traditional types of fastening such as fabric or machined buttonholes.

The crochet stitches which have been used are all simple and have been explained in previous chapters. It is important to bear in mind the function of the garment and just how decorative you want the fastening to be when you are deciding on the yarn to use.

Sample 1

This toggle fastening is most suitable for a casual garment. Using string make two lengths of cord, one 17.5cm (7in) and the other 30.5cm (12in) long, as

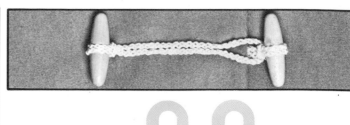

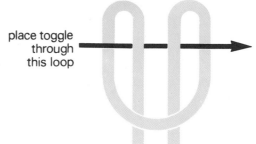

place toggle through this loop

described in sample 10 of chapter 34. The longer piece of cord is fastened into a circle and looped over a traditional wooden toggle. The cord and toggle are then sewn on to the right hand side of a garment, leaving a loop extension over the outer edge. The shorter piece of cord is not joined into a circle, but is looped over another toggle which is then sewn in position on the left hand side of the garment.

Sample 2

The finished effect of these loops and buttons is more decorative, but this will depend on the buttons and yarn which you choose to use. To make the loops in our sample you will need a Lurex yarn, a medium thickness of string and a No.3.00 (ISR) crochet hook. Hold the string in the left hand with the cut end to the right and the incoming string to the left. Holding the yarn in the usual way, place the hook under the string and catch yarn to form a loop on the hook, place hook over string, yrh and draw yarn through loop on hook, *place cut end of string in the right hand and continuing to hold incoming

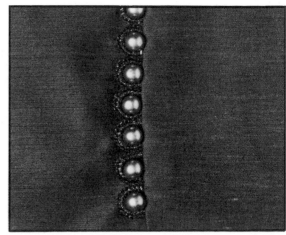

yarn in the left hand, place hook under string, yrh, place hook over string, yrh and draw through both loops on hook, rep from * for the required length. (Our sample took approx 6.5cm (2½in) of string for each loop.) Position the loops one below another so that the chain extends over the outer edge, on the right side of the fabric, making all loops an even size. Tack firmly in place as shown in the diagram. With right sides of the fabric together, tack the facing over the cording and machine firmly along the stitching line. Line up the extended loop with the left hand side of the garment and attach buttons.

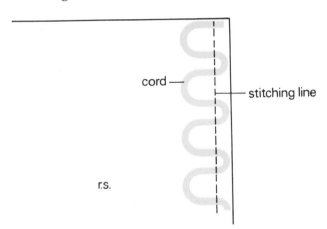

Sample 3

This single frog fastening is more decorative still and would probably be used on its own on an evening cape. Using No.3.00 (ISR) hook and Lurex yarn, work

over piping cord, 38.5cm (15in) to 50.5cm (20in) long as explained in sample 2. Then work the second line by turning the work so that you crochet back along the first line, *(yrh, insert hook into next st, yrh and draw through a loop) 3 times into same st, yrh and draw through all loops on hook, ss into each of next 2 sts, rep from * to end of cord.

Form the cord into the required shape for four loops on the right hand side of the garment with one loop extending over the outer edge and sew neatly, but firmly, in place. Line up the extended loop with the left hand side of the garment and attach button.

Sample 4

For the cord you will require two lengths of No.4 piping cord, one approx 50.5cm (20in) long and the other approx 40cm (17in) long, a No.3.50 (ISR) crochet hook and a chenille yarn. Make 4ch. Join with a ss into first ch to form a circle. Thread No. 6 piping cord through the circle. Tie in an overhand knot about 15cm (6in) from the end of the cord and place the knot behind the circle so that the free cord is coming towards you.

To work the crochet Insert the hook into the back or lower single loop of the first ch, yrh and draw through the loop and st on the hook – one ss has been worked – * insert the hook into the back or lower single loop of the next st and work one ss, rep from * working round and round the cord until the required length has been covered. Position the longer piece of cord on the

right hand side of the garment, forming the desired size of loops with one loop extending over the outer edge. Sew in place. Line up the extended loop with the left hand side of the garment and position the shorter length of cord to give three loops equal in size to those at the opposite side. A covered button has been sewn on to the join of the loops on both the right and left hand side.

To cover the button shape You will need a 2.5cm (1in) ball button, some chenille yarn and a No.3.50 (ISR) crochet hook. Form a circle with the yarn in the left hand, work 8dc into this circle, draw the cut end of yarn tightly to close the circle and ss into the first dc worked.

2nd round 1ch to count as first dc, 1dc into st at base of ch, *2dc into next st, rep from * to end. Join with a ss into first ch.

3rd round 1ch, 1dc into st at base of ch, 1dc into next st, *2dc into next st, 1dc into next st, rep from * to end. Join with a ss into first ch.

4th round 1ch, 1dc into each st to end. Join with a ss into first ch.

5th round As 4th.

6th round 1ch, work 2dc tog over next 2 sts, *1dc into next st, work 2dc tog over next 2 sts, rep from * to end. Join with a ss into first ch.

7th round 1ch, *work 2dc tog over next 2 sts, rep from * to last st, 1dc into last st. Join with a ss into first ch. Fasten off.

FLOWERS

Fluted crochet

Artificial flowers are very much a part of the fashion scene. They are used on day and evening dresses, hats and other accessories. Most commercial flowers are made up in fabric, but here we illustrate how you can make your own by using the technique of fluted crochet.

The type of yarn you choose for making your flower will depend on the sort of outfit you will be wearing it with, perhaps a crisp cotton to trim a hatband or a glitter yarn for an evening outfit. A selection of centres are shown for different flowers.

1st flower

This flower consists of two circles.

1st circle Using No.4.00 (ISR) hook and a 4 ply yarn, make 5ch. Join with a ss into first ch to form a circle.

1st round 1ch to count as first dc, 15dc into circle. Join with a ss into first ch.

2nd round *4ch, ss into next dc, rep from * to end. 16 ch loops.

3rd round Ss into each of first 2ch of next loop, ss into centre of same loop, 5ch, *ss into centre of next ch loop, 5ch, rep from * to end. Join with a ss into ss at centre of first loop.

4th round Ss into each of first 3ch of next loop, ss into centre of same loop, 6ch, *ss into centre of next ch loop, 6ch, rep from * to end. Join with a ss into ss at centre of first loop.

5th round Ss into each of first 3ch of next loop, ss into centre of same loop, 7ch, *ss into centre of next ch loop, 7ch, rep from * to end. Join with a ss into ss at centre of first loop. Fasten off.

2nd circle Using No.4.00 (ISR) hook and a 4 ply yarn, make 5ch. Join with a ss into first ch to form a circle.

1st round 1ch to count as first dc, 20dc into circle. Complete as given for 1st circle.

To make up Place the larger, more fluted circle over the first circle and stitch the centres together. In our sample wooden beads in groups of three, five and seven on a loop have been used as additional decoration.

2nd flower

Using No.4.00 (ISR) hook and a 4 ply yarn, make 6ch. Join with a ss into first ch to form a circle.

1st round 1ch to count as first dc, 20dc into circle. Join with a ss into first ch.

2nd round 3ch to count as first tr, 1tr into st at base of ch, *2tr into next dc, rep from * to end. Join with a ss into 3rd of 3ch. 42 sts.

3rd round 3ch to count as first tr, 1tr into st at base of ch, *2tr into next tr, rep from * to end. Join with a ss into 3rd of 3ch. 84 sts.

4th round As 3rd. 168 sts.

5th round 1ch to count as first dc, 1dc into each of next 9 sts, insert hook from front to back into next st, miss next 9 sts, insert hook from front to back into next st, yrh and draw through first 2 loops on hook, yrh and draw through both loops on hook, *1dc into each of next 10 sts, insert hook from front to back into next st, miss next 9 sts, insert hook from back to front into next st, yrh and draw through first 2 loops on hook, yrh and draw through both loops on hook, rep from * to end. Fasten off.

To make up Make the tufted centre by cutting 40 lengths of yarn, each 7.5cm (3in) long and firmly bind together around the centre with another piece of yarn. Fold the lengths in half and insert the bound section into the centre of the flower.

3rd flower

Using No.3.00 (ISR) hook and a Lurex yarn, make 6ch. Join with a ss into first ch.

1st round 1ch to count as first dc, 17dc into circle.

2nd round 5ch, miss next 2dc, *1dc into next dc, 4ch, miss next 2dc, rep from * to end. Join with a ss into 2nd of first 5ch. 6ch loops.

3rd round *Into next 4ch loop work 1dc, 1htr, 5tr, 1htr and 1dc, rep from * to end. Join with a ss into first dc.

4th round *5ch, pass this ch length behind next gr of sts and work 1dc into next dc of 2nd round inserting the hook from behind, rep from * to end.

5th round *Into next 5ch loop work 1dc, 1htr, 10tr, 1htr and 1dc, rep from * to end. Join with a ss into first dc.

6th round *7ch, pass this ch length behind next gr of sts and work 1dc into next dc of 4th round inserting the hook from behind, rep from * to end.

7th round *Into next 7ch loop work 1dc, 1htr, 15tr, 1htr and 1dc, rep from * to end. Join with a ss into first dc.

8th round *8ch, pass this ch length behind next gr of sts and work 1dc into next dc of 6th round inserting the hook from behind, rep from * to end.

9th round *Into next 8ch loop work 1dc, 1htr, 5tr, 10dtr, 5tr, 1htr and 1dc, rep from * to end. Join with a ss into first dc. Fasten off.

A large pearl bead makes an attractive centre to this silver flower.

4th flower

Here is an unusual method of working a chrysanthemum. Using No.3.00 (ISR) hook and a cotton yarn, make 21ch. Miss first ch, ss into each ch to end, turn. *Miss first st, ss into each of next 2 sts inserting hook into back loop only of each st, work 17ch, miss first ch, ss into loop at back of each ch to end, turn, *, rep from * to * until approximately 60 to 70 petals have been completed. Fasten off.

To make up Beginning at one end of the work, twist the base of the petals round and round, securing with sewing stitches, until all the crochet is in place.

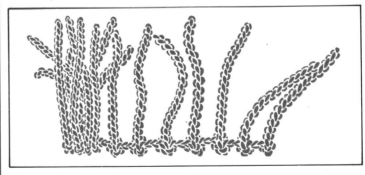

TUNISIAN CROCHET
BASIC STEPS

Tunisian crochet

This is a form of crochet which is similar to both crochet and knitting, and it is also known as Tricot work. The first similarity is in the special tool used for this craft which is a single hooked needle, or Tunisian crochet hook. These hooks are extra long to accommodate the large number of stitches in use and come in an international size range (ISR) with the smallest starting at 2.50 with the numbers 3.00, 3.50, 4.00, 4.50, 5.00, 5.50, 6.00 and 7.00 becoming gradually larger. The fabric produced is very strong and firm and, depending on the stitch used, the finished appearance can resemble crochet or look deceptively like knitting. It is ideal for making furnishing fabrics, for which there are special hooks in three sections that screw together to make an even longer one. Also Tunisian crochet is suitable for heavier outer garments where the intricacies of fine detail would be superfluous.

Several basic points make this form of crochet different to ordinary crochet and they should be referred to throughout all Tunisian crochet instructions.

a) When making an initial length of chain stitches to begin work, you will not require any extra chains for turning, i.e. a chain length of 20 will give you exactly 20 working stitches.

b) The work is not turned at the end of each row so that the right side of the work faces you throughout.

c) Tunisian crochet is worked in pairs of rows, i.e. the first row is worked from right to left and then it requires another row worked from left to right to complete it.

d) Apart from a very small number of exceptions, no turning chains are required at the beginning of each new row.

To work the basic stitch – Tricot stitch Using No.4.50 (ISR) Tunisian crochet hook and a double knitting yarn, make a length of chain.

1st row Working from right to left, miss first ch, insert hook into 2nd ch from hook, yrh and draw through a loop, *insert hook into next ch, yrh and draw through a loop, rep from * to end of ch length so keeping all loops on hook.

2nd row Working from left to right, yrh and draw through first 2 loops on hook, *yrh and draw through next 2 loops on hook, rep from * to end so leaving one loop on hook.

3rd row Working from right to left, miss first vertical loop on the front of the fabric, insert hook from right to left into next vertical loop, yrh and draw through a loop, rep from * to end so keeping all loops on hook.

4th row As 2nd.

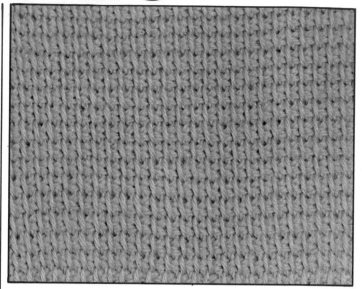

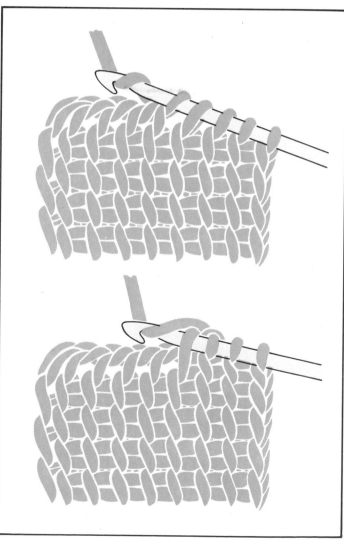

The 3rd and 4th rows are repeated throughout.
Note Care should be taken to check the number of stitches at the end of each row as it is very easy to miss the last stitch when working the 3rd row.

Shaping a Tunisian crochet fabric
When it is necessary to increase or decrease, this is usually done on the first of the pair of rows which you must work.

To increase on the sides of your work The increased stitch is worked by inserting the hook into the single horizontal loop between two vertical loops. To increase one stitch at the beginning of a row, this is usually done between the first and second vertical loops and between the last and last but one vertical loops to increase one stitch at the end of a row.

To increase in the middle of a row One stitch is simply increased in the middle of a row by inserting the hook into the single horizontal loop between vertical loops at the position where the increased stitch is required.

To increase more than one stitch at the beginning or end of a row Remembering that increases are made on the first row of the required pair, to increase several stitches at the beginning of a row, work the extra chain stitches required and go back along these extra chains picking up the working stitches. To increase several stitches at the end of a row complete the row then take a spare length of matching yarn and join this into the last stitch. Work the extra chain stitches required with the spare yarn, then continue working into this extra chain length with the main yarn.

To decrease on the sides of your work One stitch is decreased just inside the beginning of a row by inserting the hook into the 2nd and 3rd vertical loops and working the stitch in the usual way. At the end of a row the last two stitches before the end stitch are worked together in the same way.

To decrease in the middle of a row At the required position, decrease one stitch as given above.

To decrease more than one stitch at the beginning or end of a row At the beginning of a row slip stitch over the required number of decreased stitches and at the end of a row work until the required number of stitches to be decreased are left, then work the second of the pair of rows required.

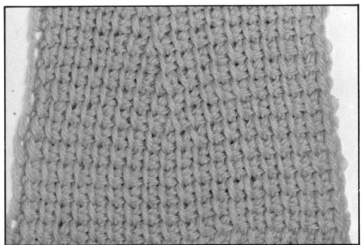

FABRIC STITCHES

An introduction to Tunisian crochet was made in our last chapter. The stitches may be worked in a variety of ways to give very different patterned effects and textures. These are achieved by different positions of the hook insertion on the first row of the pair necessary for Tunisian crochet. For all our samples, it is only the first row which varies and the second is the same throughout.

3rd row *Insert hook into space between vertical loops from front to back, yrh and draw through a loop, rep from * to end.
4th row As 2nd.

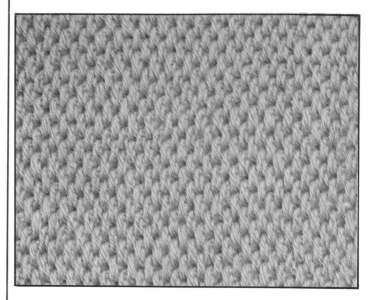

5th row Miss space between first two vertical loops, *insert hook into space between next two vertical loops from front to back, yrh and draw through a loop, rep from * to end, inserting hook into last vertical loop.
6th row As 2nd.
The 3rd-6th rows are repeated throughout.

Sample 2
Using No.4.50 (ISR) Tunisian crochet hook and double knitting yarn, make a length of chain.

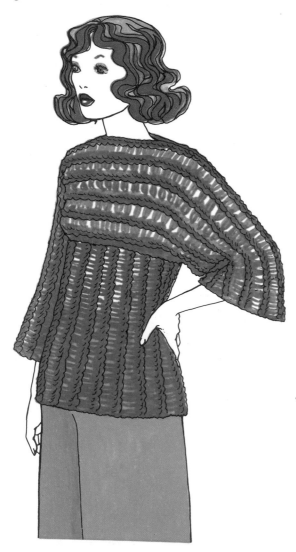

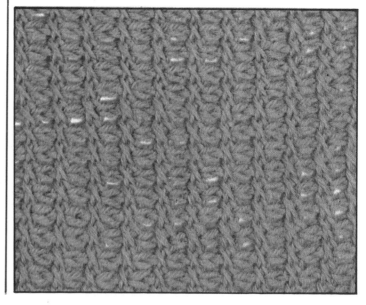

Sample 1
Using No.4.50 (ISR) Tunisian crochet hook and double knitting yarn, make a length of chain.
1st row Insert hook into second ch from hook, yrh and draw through a loop, *insert hook into next ch, yrh and draw through a loop, rep from * to end.
2nd row Yrh and draw through first 2 loops on hook, *yrh and draw through next 2 loops on hook, rep from * to end so leaving one loop on hook.

154

1st-2nd rows As 1st-2nd rows of sample 1.
3rd row Miss first vertical loop, *miss next vertical loop, insert hook from right to left through next vertical loop, yrh and draw through a loop, insert hook from right to left through the missed vertical loop, yrh and draw through a loop, rep from * to end, inserting hook into last vertical loop.
4th row As 2nd.
The 3rd and 4th rows are repeated throughout.

Sample 3
Using No.4.50 (ISR) Tunisian crochet hook and double knitting yarn, make a length of chain with multiples of 3 + 2 stitches.
1st-2nd rows As 1st-2nd rows of sample 1.

3rd row Miss first vertical loop, *yarn over hook from front to back, (insert hook into next vertical loop, yrh and draw through a loop) 3 times, pass 4th loop from hook from right to left over last 3 loops on the hook, rep from * to end, insert hook into last vertical loop, yrh and draw through a loop.
4th row As 2nd.
The 3rd and 4th rows are repeated throughout.

Sample 4
Using No.4.50 (ISR) Tunisian crochet hook and double knitting yarn, make a length of chain.
1st-2nd rows As 1st-2nd rows of sample 1.

3rd row Miss first vertical loop, *insert hook directly through centre of next vertical loop from front to back

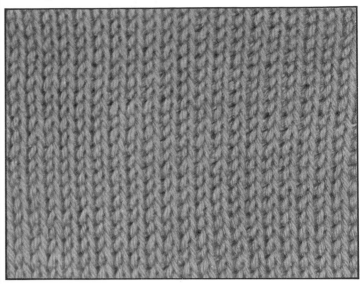

of work, yrh and draw through a loop, rep from * to end.
4th row As 2nd.
The 3rd and 4th rows are repeated throughout.

Sample 5
Using No.4.50 (ISR) Tunisian crochet hook and double knitting yarn, make a length of chain with multiples of 3 + 2 stitches.
1st-2nd rows As 1st-2nd rows of sample 1.

3rd row Miss first vertical loop, *insert hook under next three vertical loops, yrh and draw through a loop, insert hook under middle loop only of this group of three, yrh and draw through a loop, insert hook under first loop only of this group of three, yrh and draw through a loop, rep from * to end, insert hook into last vertical loop, yrh and draw through a loop.
4th row As 2nd.
The 3rd and 4th rows are repeated throughout.

DECORATIVE STITCHES

There are so many different patterns to be achieved when working Tunisian crochet that we are giving the instructions of several more for you to practise.

The tension of your work can be gauged in the same way as for plain crochet and this will need careful checking if you are making a garment. Any tendency for the fabric to curl and twist can be overcome by working the stitches fairly loosely. Always pull the yarn round the hook adequately through the stitch and, when working back along a row from left to right, never pull the first stitch through so tightly that the height of the row is flattened.

Sample 1

This is a variation of the basic Tricot stitch. Using No.4.50 (ISR) Tunisian crochet hook and double knitting yarn, make a length of chain with multiples of 2 stitches.

1st row Insert hook into second ch from hook, yrh and draw through a loop, *insert hook into next ch, yrh and draw through a loop, rep from * to end.

2nd row Yrh and draw through first 2 loops on hook, *yrh and draw through next 2 loops on hook, rep from * to end so leaving one loop on hook.

3rd row Miss first vertical loop, *insert hook from right to left through next 2 vertical loops on RS of work, yrh and draw through a loop, insert hook from right to left into first of these loops, yrh and draw through a loop, rep from * to end, insert hook into last vertical loop, yrh and draw through a loop.

4th row As 2nd.

5th row Miss first vertical loop, insert hook into next vertical loop, yrh and draw through a loop, *insert hook from right to left through next 2 vertical loops on RS of work, yrh and draw through a loop, insert hook from right to left into first of these loops, yrh and draw through a loop, rep from * to end.

6th row As 2nd.

The 3rd to 6th rows are repeated throughout.

Sample 2

Here crossed stitches within the pattern give a vertical ribbed effect. Using No.4.50 (ISR) Tunisian crochet hook and double knitting yarn, make a chain with multiples of 2 stitches.

1st-2nd rows As 1st–2nd rows of sample 1.

3rd row 1ch, miss first 2 vertical loops, insert hook from right to left through next vertical loop on RS of work, yrh and draw through a loop, insert hook into missed vertical loop to the right of the one just worked into, yrh and draw through a loop, cont in this way, working in groups of 2 and crossing the threads, ending by inserting hook into last vertical loop, yrh and draw through a loop.

4th row As 2nd.

The 3rd and 4th rows are repeated throughout.

Note If you are using this pattern for a shaped garment where you are increasing and decreasing, take care to see that the crossed stitches come immediately above those in the previous row so that the ribbed effect will not be broken.

Sample 3

Here bobbles are made on a basic Tricot background by working extra lengths of 4ch before continuing with the next stitch. Using No.4.50 (ISR) Tunisian crochet hook and double knitting yarn, make a length of chain with multiples of 6+1 stitches.

1st–2nd rows As 1st–2nd rows of sample 1.

3rd row 1ch, miss first vertical loop on front of fabric, 1 vertical stitch into next vertical loop, *insert hook into next vertical loop on front of fabric, yrh and draw through a loop, 4ch, insert hook into horizontal loop at base of ch on WS of work, yrh and draw through 2 loops on hook – called B1 –, work 1 vertical stitch into each of next 2 vertical loops, rep from * to last 2 loops, B1 into next vertical loop, 1 vertical stitch into last vertical loop.

4th–6th rows Work in basic Tunisian crochet.

7th row 1ch, miss first vertical loop, *B1 into next vertical loop, 1 vertical stitch into each of next 2 vertical loops, rep from * to end of row.

8th row As 2nd.

The 3rd–8th rows are repeated throughout.

Sample 4

An eyelet stitch gives this sample a simple openwork pattern. Using No.4.50 (ISR) Tunisian crochet hook and double knitting yarn, make a chain with multiples of 2+1 stitches.

1st row Yrh twice, insert hook into 3rd ch from hook, yrh and draw through a loop, yrh and draw through first 2 loops on hook, *miss next ch, yrh twice, insert hook into next ch, yrh and draw through a loop, yrh and draw through first 2 loops on hook, rep from * to end.

2nd row As 2nd row of sample 1.

3rd row 2ch, *yrh twice, insert hook into both next vertical loop and slightly sloping vertical loop to right of it made in previous row, yrh and draw through a loop, yrh and draw through first 2 loops on hook rep from * to end.

4th row As 2nd.

The 3rd and 4th rows are repeated throughout.

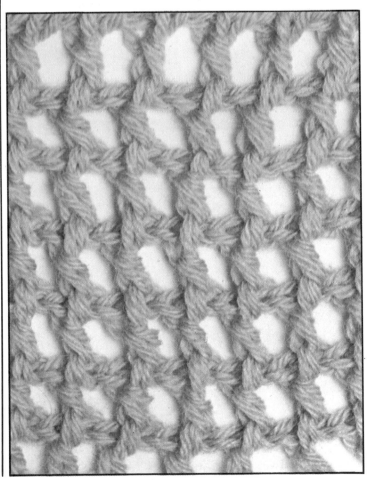

ADVANCED TUNISIAN STITCHES

More advanced designs for Tunisian crochet

Five more interesting Tunisian crochet stitches are illustrated in this chapter, including two which show the technique of using different colours within the work. As all the samples are worked in a chunky knitting yarn they would be ideal for cushions, rugs and blankets. Reference should be made to the first of these chapters on Tunisian crochet, and checks should be made during the working of these samples to keep the number of stitches correct.

Sample 1

Using No.5.00 (ISR) Tunisian crochet hook and chunky yarn, make a length of chain with multiples of 2 stitches.

1st row Insert hook into 2nd ch from hook, yrh and draw through a loop, *insert hook into next ch, yrh and draw through a loop, rep from * to end.

2nd row *Yrh and draw through two loops, rep from * to end. One loop rem on hook.

3rd row Miss first vertical loop, *yrh from front to back, insert hook under next 2 vertical loops, yrh and draw through a loop, rep from * to last vertical loop, insert hook into last vertical loop, yrh and draw through a loop.

4th row As 2nd.

The 3rd and 4th rows are repeated throughout.

Sample 2

Using No.5.00 (ISR) Tunisian crochet hook and chunky yarn, make a length of chain with multiples of 2 stitches.

1st-2nd rows As 1st-2nd rows of sample 1.

3rd row Miss first vertical loop, *insert hook into hole under chain st to right of next vertical loop, yrh and draw through a loop, insert hook under vertical loop to left of last loop made, yrh and draw through a loop, drawing it through one loop on hook, rep from * to last vertical loop, insert hook into last vertical loop, yrh and draw through a loop.

4th row As 2nd

The 3rd and 4th rows are repeated throughout.

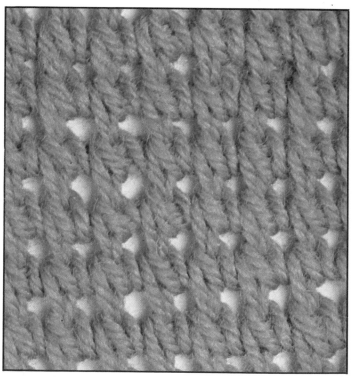

Sample 3

Using No.5.00 (ISR) Tunisian crochet hook and chunky yarn, make a length of chain with multiples of 2+1 stitches.

1st row (Yrh and insert into 3rd ch from hook, yrh and draw through a loop) twice, yrh and draw through 2 loops on hook, yrh and draw through 3 loops on hook, *miss next ch, (yrh and insert into next ch, yrh and draw through a loop) twice, yrh and draw through 2 loops on hook, yrh and draw through 3 loops on hook, rep from * to end.

2nd row Yrh and draw through one loop, *1ch, yrh and draw through 2 loops, rep from * to end. One loop rem on hook.

3rd row 2ch, *yrh from front to back, insert hook from front to back into space on right of next st, yrh and draw through a loop, yrh from front to back and insert into space on left of same st, yrh and draw through a loop, yrh and draw through 2 loops on hook, yrh and draw through 3 loops on hook, rep from * ending with last st worked completely into last space.
4th row As 2nd.
The 3rd and 4th rows are repeated throughout.

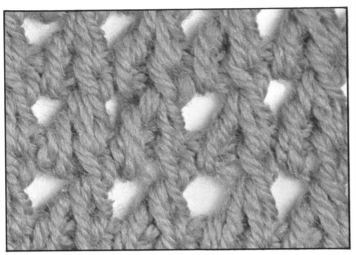

Sample 4
For this sample you will need two colours of chunky yarn, coded as A and B. Using No.5.00 (ISR) Tunisian crochet hook and A, make a length of chain.
1st-2nd rows As 1st-2nd rows of sample 1.
3rd-6th rows Work 4 rows basic Tunisian crochet. Do not break off yarn. Join in B.
7th row Using B, 2ch, *yrh, insert hook from front to back through work under next horizontal st, yrh and draw through a loop extending it to length of 2ch, rep from * ending with last st worked into last horizontal space.

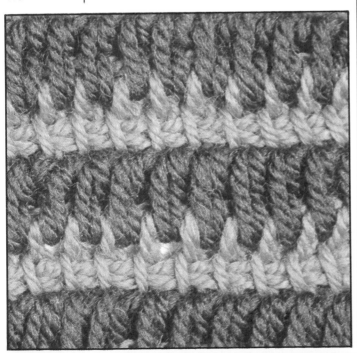

8th row Yrh and draw through 2 loops on hook, *yrh and draw through 3 loops on hook, rep from * to end.
9th row Draw A through loop on hook, *yrh and insert into horizontal loop at back of long st, rep from * to end.
10th-12th rows Work 3 rows basic Tunisian crochet. Repeat 7th-12th rows throughout.

Sample 5
Here we have used two colours of double knitting yarn coded as A and B. Using No.4.00 (ISR) Tunisian crochet hook and A, make a length of chain with multiples of 4 + 7 stitches.
1st-6th rows As 1st-6th rows of sample 4.
7th row Miss first vertical loop, insert hook into next vertical loop, yrh and draw through a loop – called one basic tricot st –, one basic tricot st into next

loop, *using B, (yrh and insert into 3rd vertical loop down from next st, yrh and draw through a loop extending it to meet working st) 4 times, yrh and draw through all loops in B on hook, insert hook into next vertical loop behind bobble, yrh and draw through a loop drawing it through one loop in B on hook – one bobble has been worked –, using A, work one basic tricot st into each of next 3 loops, rep from * to end.
8th-14th rows Using A, work 7 rows basic Tunisian crochet.
15th row Miss first vertical loop, *using B, work one bobble into 3rd vertical loop down from next st, using A, work one basic tricot st into each of next 3 loops, rep from * to last 2 loops, one bobble into next loop, one basic tricot st into last loop.
16th row Work in basic Tunisian crochet.
Continue in this way, working 7 rows of basic Tunisian crochet between each bobble row, for the required depth of pattern.

Clutch bag with woven threads

Size
Width, 35.5cm *(14in)*
Depth, 23cm *(9in)*

Tension
14sts and 14 rows to 10cm *(3.9in)* over basic tricot stitch worked on No. 6.00 (ISR) long blanket Tunisian crochet hook

Materials
2 hanks of Twilley's Health Vest Cotton No. 1
Oddments of contrasting colours for decoration
One No. 6.00 (ISR) long blanket Tunisian crochet hook
Lining material
Heavy-weight interlining
Velcro for fastening

Bag main part
Using No. 6.00 (ISR) long blanket Tunisian crochet hook make 50ch. Work in basic tricot stitch until crochet measures approx 66 cm *(26in)* from beg. Fasten off.

Gusset (make 2)
Using No. 6.00 (ISR) long blanket Tunisian crochet hook make 14ch. Work 8 pairs of rows. Dec one st at each end of next and every foll 4th pair of rows until 6 working sts rem. Work 4 more pairs of rows. Fasten off.

To make up
Cut out a piece of interlining the same size as the main part of the bag. Sew the crochet neatly on to the interlining to hold its shape and steam press. The gussets are not interlined. Cut out lining material to fit the main part and gussets, allowing 1.5cm *(½in)* turnings on all sides. Using the same yarn, a tapestry needle and oversewing stitches, sew in the gussets to the main part as shown in the diagram. Make up the lining as given for the bag, sewing in the gussets. Hem lining on to the crochet. Sew the two pieces of velcro fastening in position, one to the underside of the flap and one

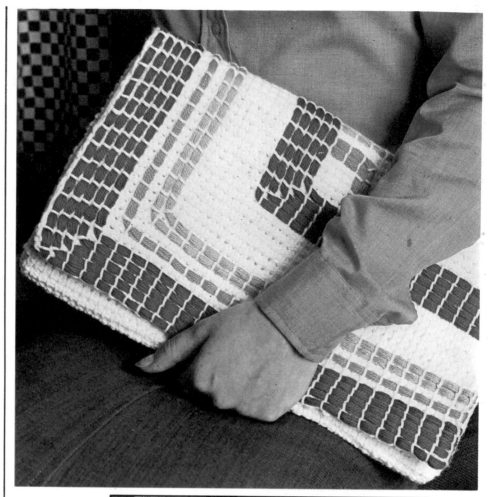

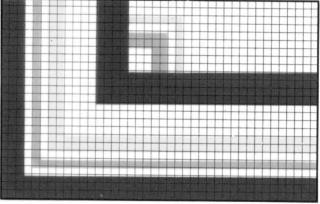

on the corresponding bag section. Follow the diagram and work the required crochet design on the bag flap.

Working the design
You will notice that horizontal and vertical lines of loops are produced on the right side of the crochet fabric. A contrasting coloured or textured yarn is then woven over and under these loops or stitches in straight lines. To achieve a good line, it is necessary to use several thicknesses of the yarn for decoration and a long Tunisian crochet hook in a size smaller than the hook used for the background to pull the threads through the work.

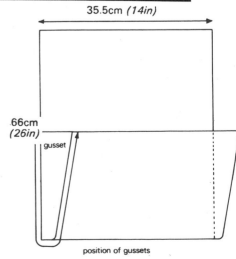

35.5cm *(14in)*

66cm *(26in)*

gusset

position of gussets